Steele Therapi
2014

P9-CQN-394

9112

Sexual
Intimacy
IN MARRIAGE

FOREWORD BY TONY & LOIS EVANS

SEXUAL
Intimacy
IN MARRIAGE
REVISED AND EXPANDED
THIRD EDITION

WILLIAM CUTRER, M.D.
SANDRA GLAHN

Kregel
Publications

Sexual Intimacy in Marriage

© 1998, 2001, 2007 by William Cutrer and Sandra Glahn
Third Edition

Published by Kregel Publications, a division of Kregel, Inc., P.O. Box 2607, Grand Rapids, MI 49501.

All rights reserved. No part of this book may be reproduced, stored in a retrieval system, or transmitted in any form or by any means—electronic, mechanical, photocopy, recording, or otherwise—without written permission of the publisher, except for brief quotations in printed reviews.

The authors gratefully acknowledge the kind permission of Grolier Incorporated to reproduce the diagrams on pages 22, 33, and 269, which are taken from the *Encyclopedia Americana*, 1985 edition. Copyright by Grolier Incorporated. Used by permission.

All Scripture quotations, unless otherwise indicated, are from the NEW AMERICAN STANDARD BIBLE®. Copyright © 1960, 1962, 1963, 1968, 1971, 1972, 1973, 1975, 1977 by The Lockman Foundation. Used by permission. (www.Lockman.org)

Scripture quotations marked NIV are from the *Holy Bible, New International Version*®. Copyright © 1973, 1978, 1984 by International Bible Society. Used by permission of Zondervan. All rights reserved.

Scripture quotations marked NKJV are from the New King James Version. Copyright © 1982 by Thomas Nelson, Inc. Used by permission. All rights reserved.

Due to the sensitive subject matter, names and, at times, other identifying information have been altered to protect the privacy of those whose stories and quotes are included in this book.

Library of Congress Cataloging-in-Publication Data
Cutrer, William.
    Sexual intimacy in marriage / William Cutrer and Sandra Glahn.
      p.   cm.
    Includes bibliographical references.
    1. Sex instruction. 2. Sex in marriage. 3. Sex—Religious
aspects—Christianity. 4. Marriage—Religious aspects—
Christianity. 5. Intimacy (Psychology) I. Glahn, Sandra. II. Title.
HQ31.C985   1998   306.7—dc21   97-34279
                                                CIP

ISBN 978-0-8254-2437-3

Printed in the United States of America

10 11 12 / 5 4 3

To my dear wife, Jane;
my son, Bill, and his wife, Elisabeth;
my daughter, Jennie, and her husband, Casey;
and my youngest son, Bob, and his wife, Meredith—
with deep gratitude to God
for richly blessing my life with each of them.

Bill Cutrer

To Gary, the love of my life,
and our daughter, Alexandra,
through whom God has brought us
many of His sweetest blessings.

Sandra Glahn

The authors and publisher are not engaged in rendering medical or psychological services, and this book is not intended as a guide to diagnose or treat medical or psychological problems. If medical, psychological, or other expert assistance is required by the reader, please seek the services of your own physician or certified counselor.

Contents

Foreword

M ost books on the subject of sex suffer from one of two possible extremes. Some are so overly spiritual that they ignore the human realities of the issue. These works bypass the mental and emotional aspects of sex in favor of esoteric explanations that real people living in a real world can hardly relate to.

On the other extreme are books that address the subject of sex as if it has little or no relationship to the Divine. It is so secularized as to be purely biological and animalistic. With no sense of covenant or of the spiritual uniqueness of sex within the context of marriage, people are left to focus on the physical at the expense of the spiritual.

Sexual Intimacy in Marriage does not suffer from either of these extremes. This easy-to-read book has marvelously blended the glory of sex with the realities of life. It addresses real people in a real world without compromising God's wonderful design and purpose for His gift of sex. The book holds in highest esteem the institution of marriage, and the sexual relationship is given its proper place within the context of marriage.

There is no question that this groundbreaking work by Dr. William Cutrer and Sandi Glahn is the answer for those who wish to take the subject of sex out of the closet while keeping it out of the gutter. It will help readers address their actions and attitudes regarding sex in light of God's unique purpose for humankind. It will also provide hope, encouragement, and direction for those who are open and willing to bring their sexuality under the lordship of Jesus Christ.

The involvement in this project of Dr. Bill Cutrer makes this work all the more special to us. He has served for several years as gynecologist for the women of the Evans' household and also has taught a Christian approach to medical health at our annual Church Development Conference. His medical expertise, combined with his Christian training and commitment, give him a unique blend of skillful hands and a tender heart—a blend that has greatly benefited our own family and marriage relationship.

In *Sexual Intimacy in Marriage* we finally have a book that places the sensitive subject of sex on a low enough shelf for people to reach, yet on a high enough shelf for God to be honored by it. After you read this book, you will understand why marriage is the only context in which authentic sexual intimacy is possible. In addition, you will discover a practical approach to many of the sexual problems and challenges that confront married couples. Most importantly, you will grow in your love for the Creator, who has given us such a wonderful gift to enjoy.

Dr. Tony and Lois Evans

1
In the Secret Place

It happens to every married couple. At some time in their relationship, if not throughout their years together, they'll encounter sexual difficulties or transitional times requiring adaptation, change, and flexibility. One of the most damaging beliefs is, "We're the only ones having trouble. Everyone else has a perfect love life." That's totally false. Consider a few examples, taken from my (Dr. Bill's) years as a physician and sex therapist, of what can go wrong.

- Don and Carrie pledged to stay virgins until they married. While they abstained from sexual intercourse before their wedding night, they had a sexual relationship during their engagement that involved orgasmic pleasuring for both, as well as oral sex. Now they're working through trust issues.
- After their disastrous honeymoon, a couple came for help. "I didn't expect sex to be so painful," the wife told me. "Besides, he wants it every day. I'm afraid he might be some kind of pervert."
- Shanna had a healthy desire for sex during two decades of marriage, but now that she's experiencing perimenopause, sex is uncomfortable, and she has diminished desire.
- Elizabeth was raped repeatedly as a young girl. Now that she's married to a loving Christian man, she has difficulty wanting or enjoying sex.

- When Joe and Rebecca married, she experienced pain during intercourse, for which they never sought medical attention. Three years later, Rebecca has no desire for her husband because she's interested in other women.
- After his wife discovered pornography on their computer, Troy promised Cheryl he would stop. But she recently found new downloads of Internet porn.
- Lorinda has a healthy interest in sex, but her husband's ho-hum attitude about it makes her feel unattractive and unloved.
- Allen has always maintained an enthusiasm for sex that wears out his wife. But lately he's had some prostate problems, and he's worried that he'll become impotent.
- Bart and Shirley engaged in premarital oral sex during which Bart had an oral herpes outbreak (fever blisters); Shirley contracted his herpes genitally. Neither had other partners before marriage. They later married, but the presence of a sexually transmitted disease has caused difficulties in their intimate life.
- Lonnie frequently climaxes too early, leaving his wife unsatisfied and frustrated.
- During Dana's pregnancy, she and Fred experienced the normal challenges in maintaining a strong love life. They tried to make the most of it and find humor in their troubles. Yet after the baby arrived, Dana felt exhausted and remained uninterested in sex for months. Fred felt replaced by the baby and told his wife she'd demoted him from "the king" to "a serf."
- Becky and Brad received premarital counsel that told them the goal of sex should be simultaneous orgasm. The pressure Becky felt over her inability to "time it right" made her unable to reach orgasm at any point in their lovemaking.

Do any of those scenarios sound familiar? They're all common. We may feel isolated in our struggles and consider our own experiences unique, thus hesitating to seek help. Yet what is most personal is often most universal. Yet, help is available.

Whether we believe men and women are basically the same or fundamentally different, we would all agree that male and female anatomies differ and change over the course of a lifetime. The perspective from which we have written this book is that God has created male and female bodies to beautifully complement each other. While this volume functions as a "Christian guide to sexual intimacy," perhaps we need to clarify that there's no such thing as "Christian sex." There is, however, sexual expression in which the participants are Christians, whose activities may or may not reflect a biblical worldview.

For me (Dr. Bill), this book, now in its third edition, comes out of more than a quarter-century of medical practice as an obstetrician/gynecologist. Initially, as I conducted premarital exams and counseling, I was struck by the lack of information among couples preparing to pledge themselves to one another "for better or for worse." Today, as a professor teaching marriage enrichment class (more on that later) and a graduate-level course on Sexuality and Biblical Counseling, I find that now, more than ever, couples wander through a fog of misinformation and partial truths about sex. The questions I get are, in fact, the basis for the Q & A sections of this book.

We've been delighted by the response to earlier editions of this book. In this edition we've left much the same, yet we've updated the medical information, added findings from recent research—especially about women—and added some of the questions and stories readers have submitted to us through our Web site.

After retiring from full-time medical practice (I still practice part-time), I served the Lord as a senior pastor. Only then could I fully appreciate how difficult is the task of guiding couples seeking help for sexual difficulties. The problem, which for many may prove insurmountable, is the limitations on the pastor's accessibility to all necessary, helpful information. Just to help in establishing a physically functional relationship, a counselor needs to be able to draw upon (1) a detailed sexual history, (2) a physical examination, and (3) a thorough understanding of medications either partner may require. These logically precede recommendations and guidance.

Yet a pastoral counselor will probably feel uncomfortable asking "at what age did you become sexually active," or other detailed sexual-history questions. In addition, he or she cannot touch a muscle and say, "This is the one you need to relax when sex is uncomfortable." A physician or trained medical professional will be essential for this. The counselor also may be unaware that the wife's birth control pills have diminished her sexual interest, a piece of information that could save months of counseling that tries to pinpoint sources of suppressed anger or a "sex is wrong" mentality.

Pastoral-staff counselling should ideally incorporate godly physicians to conduct premarital evaluation and education. Following the initial medical evaluation and subsequent "green light," the counselor can then effectively encourage the couple through the theological and marital issues in the ongoing relationship.

Shortly after the wedding and at selected times throughout a couple's marital life—such as pregnancy, nursing, perimenopause, and menopause—medical input may be necessary, as well. Thus, a team ministry approach can help solve some of the devastating real-life situations related in the chapters ahead. Our desire is for this work to bridge that medical/ministry boundary and prove a helpful guide for opening dialogue between ministry personnel and couples seeking the fullest expression of marital love.

Believing that God intends sex to be not only fulfilling and uni-fying but also great fun within the bounds of marriage, we have purposely adopted a rather lighthearted tone. Yet we realize there's nothing funny about sexual difficulties. (In fact, when pastors say that sex is a gift from God, we find that many struggling couples would like to return that gift for a full refund.) We hope that the information presented in this way can both prevent and heal some of the physical and emotional pain that can make sexual intimacy less than the joyful, satisfying experience God intended.

O my dove, in the clefts of the rock,
In the secret place of the steep pathway,
Let me see your form,
Let me hear your voice;
For your voice is sweet,
And your form is lovely.
—Song of Solomon 2:14

2
What Is Sex?

I have come into my garden.
—SONG OF SOLOMON 5:1

What is sex? That might seem like a silly question. Is there anything about sex we haven't already learned from the culture at large via billboards, magazines, radio, television, movies, chat rooms, Web sites—even camera phones? It seems that messages about sex are everywhere. And that information is increasing at an alarming rate. According to a biennial study by the Kaiser Family Foundation, in the seven years between 1998 and 2005, the number of sexual scenes on television nearly doubled. Before the turn of the century, a little over half of all shows had some sexual content. By 2005, that number had risen to 70 percent.[1]

What if we narrow the focus, though, to sex within a biblical framework? We find that, whereas a generation ago only a handful of authors considered sex from a Christian worldview, today when we go to Amazon.com and enter "Christian sex," our search yields us more than nine hundred hits. If we broaden that search to include Web sites, a Google search will bring us twenty-four *million* possibilities.

Our multimedia society saturates us with messages. Yet misinformation abounds. Complicate that with most people's talking a better game than they know. Resources produced by reputable publishers sometimes include unhelpful or downright wrong information. And even a thorough knowledge of the male and female reproductive systems does not guarantee a stellar sex life. The nature of sexual dysfunction even in physician couples (who are trained in anatomy and physiology) is not, in fact, fundamentally different from that of other professionals or laypersons.[2] Still, defining sex is a good place to begin.

Consider the couple whose story begins with a routine appointment in my (Dr. Bill's) office. They had been married for about a year when the wife, realizing her period was several weeks late, came for a pregnancy test. It proved to be positive.

As they answered questions about their medical history, she revealed that she had never had a gynecological exam. They had moved to the United States from another country, where such exams were avoided for modesty's sake. So, to break the ice, I decided to do a sonogram first, since it is less threatening than the physical exam. I would show them the pregnancy sac and then do the examination. The equipment required a full bladder, which she did not have. This rendered the abdominal sonogram useless, so I explained that I could do a vaginal sonogram. They agreed. I prepared the instrument which, although quite slender, was no doubt terrifying to her. I talked about the procedure in an effort to get her to relax, but that didn't help. I saw nothing yet on the screen, so now besides being uncomfortable, they were becoming concerned about the baby because I couldn't image anything. As an experienced gynecologist, I usually could guide the sonogram probe into the vagina in a partially darkened room.

But it wasn't happening. I couldn't find this woman's vagina. I told my nurse that we needed to do a speculum exam to see why. (I can usually do the sonogram without actually touching a nervous patient and so develop some rapport with the "baby pictures," but all the usual techniques were failing.) This patient was now doubly anxious, being for the first time in the "dorsal lithotomy" posture (that very exposed gynecological-exam position).

The nurse handed me a normal marital speculum.

I found no vaginal opening.

I thought, *This lady is pregnant. There must be access somewhere, somehow.* I got the small pediatric speculum and began just below the urethra. I found the vagina completely covered by a thick hymen except for a tiny opening. I could explore the vagina only with a Q-tip; not even my little finger could pass.

In short order I deduced that intercourse had really been outercourse, that no penetration had ever occurred. Some tenacious and goal-oriented sperm had found its way—and a long way it is—from the vaginal opening all the way up the vagina to a fallopian tube. I told the couple I had discovered a minor abnormality and asked the wife to dress and join me in my office.

I tried to frame an opening line more sensitive than "Guess what—you only thought you were having sex." I asked the husband if he'd noticed any difficulty with intercourse, imagining that only Microman would have had any success. He said no. He had found it to be "most pleasurable."

That remark surprised me. So in my kindest and most doctorlike voice, I explained the situation and the surgical remedy, which could wait, if they wished, until the time of delivery. She would need at some point to have a Pap smear, which obviously had never been done, either. But since she hadn't had multiple partners—she'd had no partners, in fact, in the usual sense of the word—she wasn't at a high risk for disease. So I felt comfortable with waiting. The husband, though, whose mind had begun to run full throttle, at last put two and two together (which, of course, he'd been unable to do as yet) and asked if I could do the surgery sooner. I agreed to fix the congenital intact hymen.

I used a laser technique, then told them to wait six weeks. For them this was no hardship since they still didn't know what they were missing. They dutifully waited out the recommended month-and-a-half (unlike most of my patients) and returned to receive the "doctor's clearance to proceed."

On their next visit after that, I saw a glow radiating from their faces. I didn't have to ask if everything was fine. His silly grin screamed it. She shyly smiled and said, "Everything is wonderful. We didn't know it could be like this." The increased elasticity and lubrication of pregnancy prevented any first-time difficulties, and wedded bliss took on a new and more profound meaning.

Another couple came to see me because they were unsatisfied with their sex life due to lots of physical pain. I asked them some questions and learned that she thought he was "in" her vagina during relations. So I asked him how far "in" he got.

He showed me with his thumb and index finger. "About an inch."

I did the exam and found the wife to have a perfectly normal vagina—albeit a perfectly tight one. I gave her some exercises to do, and within two weeks they had "succeeded." She later sent me a lovely e-mail message about the experience of being one with her husband. He was part of her, and they found it exhilarating. They had such joy in the holy experience of being whole.

What is sexual intercourse? From a purely technical viewpoint, it is the insertion of the penis inside the vagina—entirely inside—generally followed by ejaculation. It represents a beautiful example of skillful engineering on the part of the divine Creator. Under normal circumstances, conception occurs when the sperm makes it into the vagina, and sexual intercourse is usually how that happens.

Yet *sex* involves more than the textbook definition of sexual intercourse. The word *sex* can refer to gender or physiology. We might ask, "What is the baby's sex?" meaning, "Is the infant female or male?" In other words, does the tiny human have two X chromosomes or one X and one Y chromosome? In this use, *sex* is the property by which living beings are classified as female or male on the basis of reproductive organs and their functions.

Sex as a physical expression may or may not include intercourse, ejaculation, or orgasm. These are possible options, but not requirements. Sexual activities that do not include intercourse do not affect virginity in its strictest sense. Yet sexually transmitted diseases and complex relational difficulties can result from these other sexual activities.

Even if we know this basic information, we probably have a clouded understanding of our bodies and what physical intimacy involves. We draw many, if not most, of our attitudes and perceptions of sexuality from the erotic images of American culture. Yet developing sexual intimacy involves understanding anatomy, physical response cycles, marriage, communicating with all five senses, and so much more. Intimacy—two becoming one—includes spiritual, relational, *and* physical dimensions. So experiencing sex in its beauty as God designed it requires directed, focused attention in all three aspects of oneness. We will consider each of these in the pages that follow.

Because understanding your own body and your spouse's body is essential to developing sexual intimacy, we'll begin with some foundational common ground—understanding anatomy.

3

The Male Anatomy

His hands are rods of gold
Set with beryl;
His abdomen is carved ivory
Inlaid with sapphires.
His legs are pillars of alabaster
Set on pedestals of pure gold.
—SONG OF SOLOMON 5:14–15

First we'll discuss what's "down there"—the genitalia. Genitalia is not an airline based in Rome. It's the medical usage of "genital," which means "relating to reproduction or generation." It has come to be a general term for the sex organs, both male and female. Once we look at the individual parts, we'll then look at how they work together. The point of this chapter isn't to prepare you to pass a medical school exam but rather to provide accurate information that will make the process of intimacy easier to understand. Also, by using the correct terms, you can be more specific with your spouse in guiding your lovemaking toward greater mutual fulfillment. I've tested graduate students for years on their working knowledge of anatomy, and their knowledge is hardly working. So we begin with some basics.

MALE REPRODUCTIVE SYSTEM

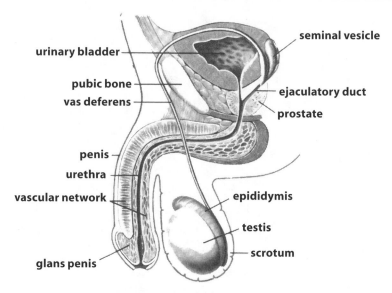

urinary bladder

seminal vesicle

pubic bone

ejaculatory duct

vas deferens

prostate

penis

urethra

vascular network

epididymis

testis

scrotum

glans penis

© by Grolier, Inc. Used by permission.

Gonads

The gonads produce reproductive cells, either sperm or eggs, and thus include the male testicles and female ovaries. The male gonads are enclosed in the scrotum, which is a sac suspended between the thighs. The scrotum in the male corresponds embryologically to the labia majora in the female. (We'll get to that in the next chapter.) God uses remarkable economy in creation, with parts in the male having correspondence in the female. This design is actually helpful in aiding our understanding of the sexual response and location of the nerves designed for sexual pleasure.

The process of producing mature sperm cells begins at approximately age twelve, although the exact time varies from individual to individual. The period of development during which this happens is called puberty, a time when adolescents experience enormous hormonal surges, and their moms and dads may feel like they're living in parental purgatory.

Epididymis

The epididymis is a tiny, twisting segment of the tube that carries the sperm from the testicle to the next portion of the tube called the vas deferens.

Vas Deferens

The vas deferens is the next portion of the sperm-carrying tube connecting the epididymis to the seminal vesicles. When a man has a vasectomy, his physician interrupts a portion of the "vas," thus preventing sperm from passing from the testicle to the ejaculate. Although a high percentage of vasectomies can be reversed by re-opening the vas, antibodies may have developed that have incapacitated the sperm. We'll talk more about vasectomy in the appendix, which deals with contraception.

Seminal Vesicles

The seminal vesicles are the reservoirs where sperm get stored until the time of ejaculation, or release. Most of the fluid contained in the ejaculate is secreted into the vesicles from the prostate (see below). Thus, after vasectomy there is still a release of milky fluid, just no sperm (although vasectomy is not 100 percent foolproof and should not be trusted for contraceptive effect until a sperm count demonstrates zero live sperm).

Penis

The penis is the male sex organ, which—along with the scrotum—is visible and external. At the time of sexual stimulation, blood rushes into its network of blood vessels. At the same time, small valves automatically close, preventing this blood from circulating back into the body. As stimulation continues and blood flows in, the penis fills up, tightens, and stands rigid or "erect." Under normal conditions, when either stimulation ceases or ejaculation takes place, the small valves gradually open, and the excess blood flows back into the circulatory system. The ejaculation of the semen is called orgasm or—in popular language—climax.

Some imaginative folks have theorized that so much blood is collected in the penis during sexual excitation that the man could pass out. This has never actually been reported. The amount of blood normally collected is, in fact, quite small.

In most men the penis responds pleasurably to being stroked. The loose skin around its shaft forms what looks like a seam down the underside of the penis. For some this is the part most responsive to caressing.

It may be helpful here to discuss size. Take note that most women don't receive their most pleasurable sensations from the penis being in the vagina, no matter what size the penis is, although the physical oneness of penetration does bring a sense of emotional satisfaction. Still, a growing number of surgeons now promise to substantially lengthen and widen a man's penis with penile surgery or phalloplasty. Some report satisfactory results; others agree with the patient who concluded after the procedure that "it preys on men with low self-esteem."[1] Men contemplating phalloplasty may need to consider the greater issues of spiritual maturity and relational confidence before going ahead with surgery.

On average, the relaxed penis is about 3½ to 4 inches long. An erect penis is about 5 to 6½ inches long, but size varies from man to man. Sexual difficulties due to male penis diameter and/or length are virtually never a problem except for young, small, or anxious women. Contrary to popular thought, penis size has little to do with sexual pleasure or satisfaction for most women—or men for that matter. The vagina changes to accommodate a rather wide range of penis sizes. As someone has put it, "It's not the length of the wand; it's the magic in the act."

In addition, sexual researchers have found that the size of a penis that is not aroused does not relate proportionately to its size when erect. In other words, "a small, flaccid (limp) penis generally enlarges to a greater extent at the time of arousal than does a larger flaccid penis. In its erect state there is little difference in size between one penis and another, even though they may differ significantly in size when they are unaroused."[2]

Glans Penis

The head of the penis is called the glans penis, and it's a little larger than the shaft of the penis. The glans penis contains a heavy concentration of nerve endings that play a major role in the sexual arousal of the male. The concentration is so heavy that many men would, in fact, prefer very gentle or even indirect stimulation here, as is true of women with the clitoris (the corresponding/counterpart organ in the female).

While the nerve endings that register touch are the same as those in other parts of the body, they form a more dense concentration in the glans penis. Usually, at birth, it is encircled with a thick layer of skin called the prepuce or foreskin. Circumcision is a procedure that removes a portion of this foreskin.

Circumcision is ordinarily a simple operation in which a surgeon cuts the top of the foreskin away, thus freeing the glans penis from its covering. Many couples choose to have their infants circumcised within days of birth for religious, social, or ethnic reasons. Doctors no longer consider circumcision a medical necessity, and many hospitals have moved away from performing it routinely.

Circumcision easily allows effective personal hygiene, although careful attention will normally suffice for both circumcised and uncircumcised men. Two opposing views of circumcision have been suggested—that circumcision either enhances or that it inhibits sexual control and pleasure. Yet neither theory has strong supporting evidence. Some recent work in Australia recognizes that young males don't routinely attend to "penile hygiene," so there may be a move back toward circumcision in the decades to come.

Prostate

Under normal conditions, the prostate is a golf-ball-sized, walnut-shaped gland. It tends to enlarge as men age. Like the appendix, it appears to have little vital function. It secretes fluid into the ejaculate and serves as the counterpart to the same female mucus secreting glands (Skene's glands). As men age, the risk of prostate cancer increases. Prostate removal does not necessarily have to interfere with normal sexual functioning, but some surgical procedures injure or permanently interrupt the nerve supply to the penis, causing impotence in some patients.

Semen

Semen is the thick, white, sperm-containing fluid that the penis ejaculates. Most of the liquid of the ejaculate originates in the seminal vesicles and the prostate gland. The sperm, of course, began the journey in the testicle and moved through the epididymis and the vas deferens into the seminal vesicles.

Testosterone

Testosterone is the primary male hormone responsible for the growth of facial hair, change of voice at puberty, muscular structure and development, sex-drive, and aggressive tendency in males. One man we know, upon learning that men make about fifteen times more testosterone than women, walked around with his arms outstretched as a victor proclaiming, "The man—fifteen, maybe twenty. The woman? Next to nothing." (We noticed he remained silent when he learned that women produce ten times more estrogen than men.)

Females produce testosterone as well, but in far smaller quantities. Administering similar amounts of testosterone into a woman may cause her to grow facial hair, acquire a deepened voice, develop greater muscle tone, and increase her libido (sex drive). Occasionally, small amounts of testosterone are given to postmenopausal women to help with libido, as well as other hormone-related disorders.

So here's the obvious question: Why isn't testosterone prescribed to increase sex drive in women? One husband was so bold as to ask if he could slip some into his wife's drink. Testosterone is actually available and present in some forms of estrogen replacement therapy to restore female testosterone to an age-appropriate level. It's also available for replacement in castrate males. Yet widespread, long-term use is limited primarily because of its side effects. Simply put, most women don't want oily skin, a beard, mustache, and a bass voice.

One of my patients unintentionally took twice the prescribed dosage of testosterone. She came back to report, "Now I finally understand how men feel." She had been chasing her husband around the house for several weeks. At first he felt deeply gratified but, finally in a state of total exhaustion, he sent her back to me for deliverance.

Men have relatively boring, straightforward hormonal dominance compared to women's beautifully complex hormonal cycles. As mentioned, not only do men produce roughly ten to fifteen times the amount of testosterone women do, men also make estrogen in small amounts—only about one tenth the amount that women make.

In addition to the 15:1 ratio of male to female testosterone, males also experience so-called testosterone storms. Actually, they're only surges—but they often feel more like storms. And they apparently have no sexual equivalent in the female. During "storms," men will charge concrete walls if necessary to be with their women. Testosterone can be elevated by sight, scent, exercise, pornography, or any number of factors.

Testosterone production reaches its peak around age twenty, and maintains that level until about forty. After that it slowly drops until it is significantly lower by age eighty. The decrease in testosterone does not need to affect a man's sexual pleasure, although it may affect functioning.

What does all this talk about the hormonal difference between men and women mean in practical terms? I've talked to numerous wives whose husbands' desires fell within normal ranges, yet the wives feared they had married weirdos or perverts. For some it helps to know that a variety of studies confirm that most men think about sex, on average, three to five times daily. And no one should confuse these thoughts of "sex"—as in the sex act or intercourse—with *romance* or *affection*. But to men, such words often translate to sexual intercourse anyway.

Normal, healthy women, on the other hand, think about the sex act (again, not romance or affection) an average of one to two times per month. So it's easy to see how, after marrying, a wife might think her husband is interested only with sex, whereas he often laments her "false advertising." His lamentation may sound something like this: "When we were dating, she couldn't keep her hands off me. I thought, 'This is gonna be so great!' And now that we're married, she always finds other things that are more important than having sex with me. I feel like I'm begging."

I've often needed to assure newlyweds that it's natural and healthy for the husband to have a robust and seemingly endless sexual interest in his beautiful bride.

4

The Female Anatomy

Hurry, my beloved,
And be like a gazelle or a young stag
On the mountains of spices.
—SONG OF SOLOMON 8:14

The week I (Sandi) got married, the mother of a friend told me, "Don't read anything about sex. If you do, it will take away the mystery. Why not just do what comes naturally? My husband taught me everything I know. That's *his* job."

Fortunately, my own mother had a much different view. While attending a seminar on "Talking to Your Kids About Sex," I discovered that I was the only woman present who'd ever engaged in candid discussions about sexual issues with either of my parents. They provided books and explanations and used the appropriate terms for body parts long before I reached puberty, holding to the belief that knowledge is always preferable to ignorance.

True, using euphemisms might make life easier sometimes. I think of a friend who taught her daughter to call private body parts by their accurate names. Fascinated at the differences between girls and boys, the child approached a man sitting on a park bench and asked him, "Do you have a penis?" Just as her mortified mother rushed over to explain, the man answered, "No, I don't have any peanuts, but I do have some candy I'll share."

Still, it helps us articulate our desires if we can call body parts by their accurate names. And we women tend to know less about our anatomies than men know about theirs because more of ours is internal. Yet by learning all she can about herself as God made her, a woman enhances her ability to know her husband—in more ways than one. The word *know* frequently has sexual connotations in biblical writings. Abraham knew Sarah. Joseph did not know Mary before the birth of Jesus.

As the writer of Proverbs tells us, to get wisdom, get understanding. An entire book of the Bible, Song of Solomon, is devoted to helping us appreciate the delicate, God-given gift of our sexuality. This portion of Scripture, coupled with some basic instruction about our anatomies, can reduce a great number of misunderstandings and hurt feelings. (Dr. Bill will take over at this point, describing the female anatomy.)

Breasts

The female breasts are milk-producing glands. They allow most mothers to provide nourishment to their babies and pleasure for themselves and their husbands.

Breast size and tenderness for an individual woman may vary greatly during the various phases of the monthly cycle, and it's also fairly common for one breast to be larger than the other. Some asymmetry is normal. The larger breast is usually on the dominant hand side. Thus, if a woman is right handed, the right breast will often be the larger.

During self-examination, a woman may notice small nodules or lumps. At one time doctors referred to these as the results of *fibrocystic disease,* but because 80 to 85 percent of women have them, they are now referred to as *fibrocystic change.* If a woman with a history of fibrocystic change finds a lump and waits through the menstrual cycle, the lump will often disappear completely. If it does, it's not problematic. If it remains, she should seek medical consultation.

Caffeine, along with certain other medications, can affect glandular tissue and increase breast discomfort.

Almost every woman, if she presses hard enough, may find a tiny bit of secretion from her nipples. Women on birth control pills will often have a slight milky discharge that can result from the hormones in the pill. Vigorous direct stimulation over time can cause a milky secretion, too.

As a rule, women should have any discharge evaluated, especially if it is bloody. In addition, they should pursue aggressive follow-up of lumps. Approximately one in seven women will have a diagnosis of breast cancer during her lifetime. This represents a drastic increase in this generation, for reasons we don't fully understand. Because of the cancer risk, I strongly recommend breast self-exam and mammography, when appropriate. (Organizations differ in their recommendations regarding mammography, based on age and family history, so check with your doctor.) Self-examination may be the most important three or four minutes of a woman's month, although it must be done regularly and thoroughly to be effective. While studies offer conflicting evidence about the effectiveness of breast self-examination, I believe the patient may well be the first to notice a change. And the earlier changes are checked out, the better.

Women should check for any lumps, hard knots, swelling, dimpling of the skin, or thickening. Also look for any abnormal changes of size, shape, color, or discharge. Because hormones can affect the breast, the best time to do the exam is seven to ten days after the start of your menstrual cycle, when swelling is minimal. Postmenopausal women should do their self-examinations on the same day of each month.

The American Cancer Society approves several methods of breast self-exam, but we'll include only one to be done in the shower, as soapy water can heighten the sensitivity of the fingers. The exam is done by raising the right arm behind the neck and using the finger pads (not tips) of the left hand, then rolling and pressing the breast area firmly against the chest wall. The process is then repeated, raising the left arm behind the neck and checking the left breast area with the right hand. The whole breast is covered in circular motion, from the center out, or vertically in strips.

A woman should perform this self-exam thoroughly and consistently, making sure to examine the chest area above each breast and also under the arms. In addition, she should gently squeeze each nipple, checking for any discharge.

For most women, the breasts play an important role in sexual stimulation. We should note here, however, that breast *size* has little to do with responsiveness or sexuality. It's been said that "It's not the size—it's the presentation." Both small-breasted and large-breasted women have an equal capacity for sexual intensity. Usually the only major difference in responsiveness is based on how a woman feels about herself. Many of my patients have confided their dissatisfaction with breast size, yet anything from a double-A cup to double-F can be perfectly functional and appealing. Women with breasts that are large enough to cause back and shoulder pain may wish to consult their physicians about ways to reduce discomfort.

Vulva

The vulva is not to be confused with Volvo, the automobile maker. The two names are sometimes unintentionally confused, resulting in embarrassment for the man who knows cars better than he knows his wife. Vulva is the term for the entire female external (outside) genital area, from the pubic hair down to the anus (see diagram on p. 36).

Labia Majora

The labia majora are the large, outer vaginal "lips." Their size and shape can vary from quite flat to rather full and prominent. The labia majora, which contain hair follicles and sweat glands, do not have an abundant nerve supply. But they provide protection and cushion to the underlying structures.

Labia Minora

The labia minora are the smaller internal vaginal "lips." These are the delicate non-hair-producing tissues that also provide a cover-

FEMALE REPRODUCTIVE SYSTEM

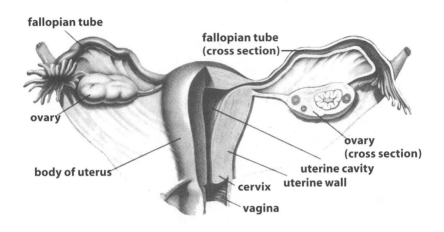

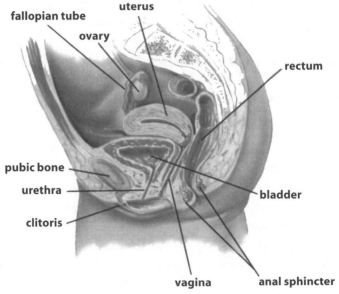

© by Grolier, Inc. Used by permission.

ing or hood for the clitoris. Before childbearing changes them, they meet in the midline to cover the urethra and the vaginal opening. When the legs are spread or sometimes following childbirth, the middle separates, exposing the underlying structures, the urethra and vagina.

Vagina

Many envision the vaginal "tunnel of love" as a tubular (tampon-shaped) organ with the cervix at the far end or tip. In fact, the vagina is more like a flat balloon in which, when deflated, "ceiling and floor" touch with the cervix protruding through the far end of the ceiling (not the tip) before childbearing. Intercourse takes place beneath the cervix—not pointing into it—in the vagina, separating floor and ceiling upon entry of the penis.

The anatomical design of the vagina allows a woman to cough or sneeze without the enormous intra-abdominal pressure that causes the uterus to push out or make the bladder leak. Those who have experienced pregnancy or have recently given birth appreciate what can happen to the bladder (it "leaks") when the growing uterus distorts these normal structural relationships.

The healthy vagina fends off infections through its own acid-base balance. Because of this, douching is unnecessary for the average woman unless her physician directs her to do so for a specific problem or for hygiene (personal preference) during the menstrual flow. Mild vinegar-and-water solutions bought over the counter are safe if used correctly and reasonably.

At mid-cycle, a heavy clear, stretchy discharge indicates the optimal time for conception to occur. This discharge, which signals an increase in estrogen and its accompanying gentle increase in libido, aids in lubrication.

Women on the pill have a light white, sticky discharge that is present throughout the cycle. An abnormal discharge or itch can signal the presence of vaginitis, which has an assortment of causes and may produce pain. Physicians cannot tell accurately without using a microscope whether yeast or abnormal bacteria are present, and the treatment is different for each of these. While we use antibiotics for treating bacteria, yeast is a fungus and antibiotics may well make it worse. Yeast creams don't help some types of vaginitis at all. So see your physician if you have an abnormal discharge or persistent itching.

Another cause of vaginitis is "lost tampon syndrome." Sometimes a string tears off, and part of the tampon becomes detached and left in the vagina. Or a woman may forget that she has used two at a time and only removes one. The diagnosis is quite easy since the discharge produces a strong odor that lingers until the remaining part is removed.

A woman whose husband engages in frequent, vigorous oral sex will sometimes develop a condition termed as vulvovaginitis secondary to saliva. She experiences significant genital inflammation, but when she consults her doctor, the microscope reveals no yeast or infection. We usually recommend abstaining from oral sex for a while in addition to washing and immediately drying off after relations. Sometimes topical steroid creams can hasten recovery.

In my practice, some women came in with what they feared to be a yeast infection, and I was faced with the unpleasant task of telling them they had the herpes virus. Before AIDS, this was one of the most devastating diagnoses our patients could receive, second only to cancer. At present, herpes is a lifetime disease for which there is no cure.

Cervix

The cervix, the so-called door to the womb, is the lowermost portion of the uterus, which opens into the vagina. This organ dilates or stretches during labor to allow the passage of a baby into the birth canal (which, at the end of pregnancy, is another name for the vagina and surrounding structures). The cervix is also the tissue that is sampled during the Pap smear to check for cancer of the cervix. It contains an unusual and unique complement of nerve fibers that register pain when stretched (as in labor) yet can be cut, pierced, burned, and biopsied with relatively little discomfort.

Clitoris

The clitoris is the only organ in human anatomy having the sole purpose of receiving sexual pleasure. A small, approximately pea-size organ, the clitoris contains the high concentration of nerve fibers that transmit pleasurable sensation in most women. It is similar developmentally to the male's glans penis or head of the penis, and it is located in front, just beneath the point where the labia minora join. (The labia minora correspond embryologically to the shaft of the penis.)

When it comes to sexual pleasure, the clitoris is perhaps the most important (yet poorly understood and difficult to find) female structure. When couples arrived at my office reporting difficulties with intercourse or orgasm, I would invite the husband (with his wife's permission) to enter the exam room and be a part of the consultation. More often than not, his understanding of anatomy and function proved remarkably confused, and many misunderstandings could be clarified and corrected. Wives likewise had limited knowledge of the location of their body parts and how they were supposed to function. This lack of knowledge is the major reason for including this explanation of anatomic details and why we've included some self-

VULVA

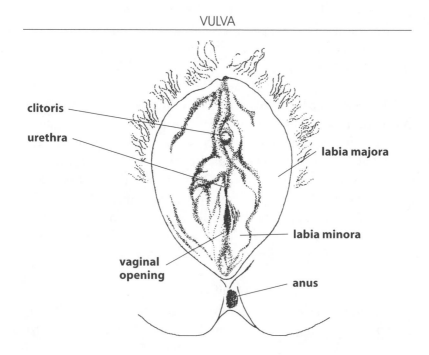

exploration exercises in the workbook (see pp. 265–67). Experience tells me that this topic and the explanation of orgasm may be the only part of this chapter many people will read.

As we stated above, the clitoris has a dense concentration of nerve endings, which God designed to produce sexual arousal when stimulated appropriately. I say "appropriately," because rubbing, squeezing, and/or pinching the clitoris for long periods can be a nuisance or even painful. The clitoris differs from the penis in that it has no opening and it does not directly play a part in the process of reproduction. It is the external trigger that sets off sexual arousal and orgasm for many women.

Some doctors say that clitoral stimulation has to happen for orgasm to occur. For example, one writes: "These nerve endings must be stimulated directly by physical contact for a woman to become sexually aroused high enough to have an orgasm. . . . There must be uninterrupted stimulation of the clitoris and the area close to the clitoris for a wife to have an orgasm."[1] This is false! Some women have orgasms while reading novels or receiving back rubs. Yet for most women, appropriate clitoral stimulation must occur. The nerve endings are so sensitive, however, that many women say they prefer stimulation *around* the clitoris, not directly on it. The flat portion of the palm works better here than fingers for many couples. And some women derive more pleasure through internal stimulation of the "G-spot." More on this in chapter 8.

Hymen

The hymen is ordinarily a thin membrane or portion of tissue that, during the intrauterine development of the baby girl, completely covers the vaginal opening. As a young girl matures and the vaginal opening enlarges, the hymen normally perforates or splits, creating a window of varying size that allows the menstrual fluid to escape at puberty.

The hymen carries potential for difficulty. If it does not perforate at all (which is unusual), a young girl will have "cycles," but no blood will pass, and it will collect in the vagina until detected. Because the vagina is a sterile area before the hymen perforates, this does not pose a medical risk.

More often, though, the hymen will perforate sufficiently to allow menstrual flow but will not comfortably permit tampon insertion or intercourse. Women who develop thick, rigid hymens (although menstrual flow and tampon insertion may present no problem) may find intercourse painful or impossible. This can be readily solved with stretching exercises (included in the workbook section) or surgical removal of the remnant of the hymen. This procedure has proved to be a marriage saver and a boost to a couple's enjoyment of sexual activity. Repetitive, painful intercourse, though, creates negative associations for the wife, which, after correction of the problem, may require many successful encounters to fully erase.

The couple whose story appeared in chapter 2 had difficulty because the hymen made it impossible to permit intercourse. A hymeneal problem cannot always be determined during the premarital exam, although it often can. It may take attempting intercourse to find out if the vaginal opening will comfortably adapt. It's better, of course, to correct any problems "pre-need," but many hymens have been surgically altered after a couple has had less-than-satisfactory attempts at intercourse. If you have difficulty with intercourse, seek medical attention as soon as possible to keep from developing an emotional aversion to sexual intimacy.

It's important to understand that the initial discomfort should, with stretching, go away quickly, within two to four weeks. Once vaginal diameter accommodates penetration, lubrication and elasticity play an even greater role. These generally cannot happen with fear and/or discomfort present. Many women, though, have a sad lack of information about what is normal and have understood that pain is "part of the duty," distasteful as it may be. I've seen cases in which, years down the marital road, the couple has never experienced even minimally pleasurable sex, and the wife considers orgasm a figment of the novelist's imagination.

During the premarital visit, a family doctor or ob-gyn physician should make a thorough examination, particularly of the hymen, checking for thickness and for whether it is completely intact or has an opening sufficient for intercourse. Even an ob-gyn doctor is at a bit of a disadvantage—which is unavoidable—because he or she examines only the female, and a key consideration is comfortable fit.

Urethra

The urethra is the external opening and short tube in the female that leads from the bladder to the exterior of the body. In the male the urethra likewise drains the bladder and is of variable length.

Uterus

Generally known as the womb, the uterus is a smooth, involuntary muscular organ that contains the growing baby in pregnancy. The lining of the uterus under the stimulation of the female hormones prepares each month to receive a pregnancy. When pregnancy does not occur, the thickened lining sloughs off, passes through the cervix, and exits through the vagina as the "menstrual flow." This process occurs slowly so that the blood has time to clot within the uterus, and the clots have time to dissolve before passing out of the uterus. Thus none are visible externally. If the flow is a bit more vigorous, the blood will clot in the uterus and pass as clots into the vagina. This is also completely normal if the clots are the size of a dime or smaller. (Clots as large as a quarter and larger can be problematic.) The passage of clots through the cervix is the main cause of menstrual cramps. Women with heavy flooding, numerous clots, and incapacitating cramps should seek medical attention.

Since the uterus is mostly muscular, it contracts rhythmically with orgasm. Some women feel this sensation is pleasurable; others hardly notice it. Their awareness and enjoyment of such sensations have significance for those considering surgical removal of the uterus (hysterectomy). Knowing in advance that the operation may affect orgasm can help alleviate concern and surprise. It's been suggested that a woman can exercise her uterus for greater sexual enjoyment. For the record, this is a myth. In the workbook, we've provided an exercise that women *can* do to aid in increasing sexual pleasure.

Ovaries

The ovaries are the paired egg-producing organs of the female. (They constitute the female counterpart to the testicles.) They vary in size, depending on the day of a woman's menstrual cycle. At their smallest, the ovaries are about the size of a walnut in its shell, and with normal monthly follicle development, one may reach approximately twice that size. At birth, a little girl has all the eggs she will ever use, stored in approximately 300,000 to 400,000 follicles, tiny cysts in the ovaries that have already substantially decreased in number from more than a million since the ovaries first developed. Only about 300 to 400 of the several hundred thousand will ever mature and release from the ovary during the monthly ovulation cycle, unlike sperm, which a healthy man produces daily.

Each month a number of potential eggs from this vast group will begin the egg maturation process. This process starts at the culmination of puberty, which takes place over several years and usually begins between ages nine and thirteen. It involves the development of cysts, fluid-filled sacs in which the egg develops. The most responsive of these prospects goes on to maturity and is expelled from the small cyst, a process called "ovulation" or egg release. Occasionally several eggs may be released in one cycle, increasing the possibility of fraternal (nonidentical) twins or triplets.

In a normal, functioning ovary, a cyst develops each month on one side or the other and grows until it is approximately two centimeters in length (a bit less than an inch). This normal cyclical enlargement in the ovary can cause discomfort during lifting, exercise, and sexual activity. At ovulation, the cyst "ruptures" to release the egg, sometimes causing sharp pain—known as mittleschmertz—at midcycle. This is a normal process, but it can cause discomfort. Occasionally the follicle will rupture across a blood vessel and leak blood into the abdominal cavity. The resulting pain and sufficient bleeding may, on rare occasions, require hospitalization and/or surgery for pain relief. This occurrence is rare considering the number of "ovulatory events." I've seen fewer than ten in my years of practice. If this happens, it does not alter fertility or affect lovemaking, and for most women it heals on its own.

Fallopian Tubes

The fallopian tubes come in pairs. They are delicate structures connected at one end to the top corners of the uterus and extend to an opening right next to the ovaries. They function by picking up the egg released by an ovary and moving it gently down (not like a drainpipe, but with tiny hairlike structures called cilia) to the portion of the tube where the sperm may fertilize the egg. This structure can be interrupted surgically by cutting, tying, cauterizing with electricity (tubal, tubal ligation, tubes tied), or with other available techniques as a permanent method of contraception.

Pubococcygeus (PC) Muscles

The pubococcygeus or PC muscles are voluntary muscles that extend from the pubic bone in front to the tailbone in back. They surround the vagina, urethra, and anus, and in concert with several other muscles provide support to the floor of the pelvis. This design helps prevent any organs from making their way down the birth canal and "hanging out." Additionally, with a woman's exercise of and skill at controlling these muscles, the vaginal diameter can be managed to generate pleasurable friction during intercourse. We've included instructions for doing so in the workbook section (see pp. 267–68).

Thoughts or touch can trigger the tightening of these muscles. Voluntary tightening can increase sexual pleasure. But the strong, involuntary spasm of these muscles is called vaginismus, or muscular spasms of the vagina. Usually triggered by pain, vaginismus can also be brought about by unwanted penetration, a "bad fit," or painful memories. We generally recommend time, tenderness, and intimacy exercises to remedy this situation. Occasionally, medications are temporarily required to overcome this hurdle, but help is available. If you suffer with vaginismus, don't give up.

Menstrual Cycle

A woman's menstrual cycle is her monthly process triggered by the brain and messenger hormones (FSH/LH—see diagram) from the pituitary, a small gland at the base of the brain. The cycle includes maturation and release of the egg and preparation of the uterine lining for the arrival and implantation of an embryo. In the absence of pregnancy, the cycle concludes with the sloughing and discharge—called menstrual flow or menstruation—of the lining cells of the uterus.

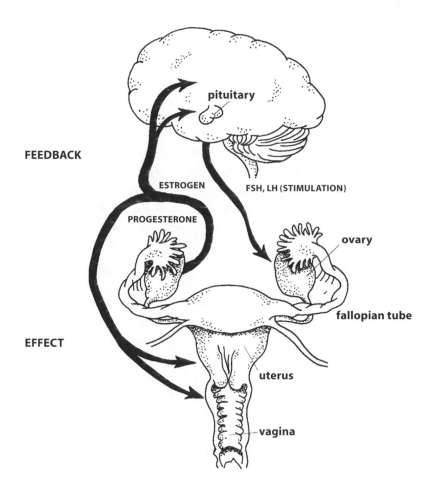

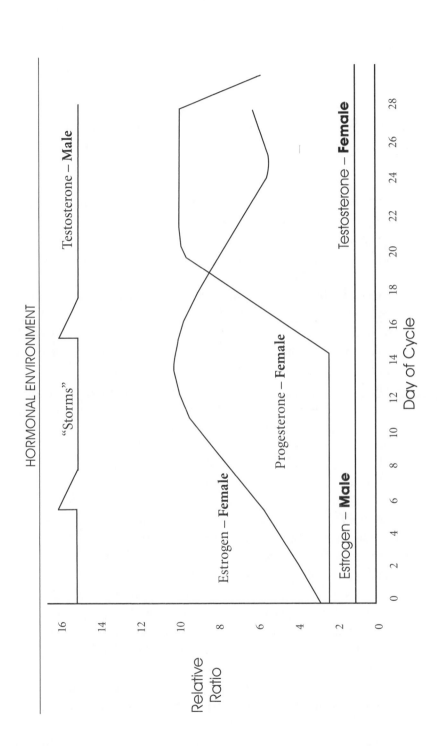

HORMONAL ENVIRONMENT

This entirely normal process is cloudy and mysterious in the minds of many husbands, who prefer to escape to the solitude and darkness of their "caves" during their wives' dreaded "time of the month." For some men, overcoming the embarrassment of buying tampons for their wives may be their idea of sacrificial love, but there's no substitute for comprehending this process and communicating a sense of understanding and support to one's spouse.

Simple education about hormonal events that trigger this normal variation can help alleviate a husband's fear and trepidation. It can also promote a compassionate understanding of emotional peaks and valleys that are quite normal and, to a considerable degree, inescapable. This beautiful cycle of the female is a complex symphony of hormonal crescendo and decrescendo that carries her physically and emotionally through the month.

The average woman cycles between twenty-five and thirty-five days. The twenty-eight-day lunar month is selected as the "norm," but many women experience regular cycles on a different set schedule. The fixed stage of the cycle is that following ovulation, lasting twelve to fourteen days. Thus, the major variable is the number of days prior to ovulation, which can range from ten to twenty-one days and still be entirely normal. This is vital to understanding the fertile period and anticipating those hormonal times when the husband's thoughtfulness may be met with less than warm enthusiasm.

Estrogen, the dominant female hormone, has its major peak around ovulation with a secondary, smaller peak later in the cycle. Estrogen is responsible for the "feminization" of the female adolescent. This includes fatty breast and hip deposits, maturation of the genital organs, and a gentle increase in the libido.

Thus, strictly from the hormonal stimulus, women generally have a stronger sexual desire around the time of ovulation. This "window" of opportunity lasts approximately twenty-four to forty-eight hours. Many husbands have asked how to open this "window" for longer stretches of time. The hormonal environment plays only one small part, however, in creating the romantic atmosphere that supports satisfying marital intimacy. In other words, creating a daily environment of care with kindness can open other "windows" of sexual interest, desire, and passion.

The second, milder elevation of estrogen often gets lost in the strong surge of progesterone, the powerful hormone that follows ovulation. Progesterone, the "pro-gestational" or "pro-pregnancy" hormone, reaches a high level seven to ten days after ovulation. If pregnancy occurs, progesterone will, under normal circumstances, remain high. Besides the positive effect of preparing the uterus for pregnancy, progesterone causes bloating, fullness, and a general crankiness that for some women can be overwhelming each month in the premenstrual phase.

The premenstrual portion of the cycle can be so difficult for some women that the diagnosis of "premenstrual syndrome" or PMS is used. Symptoms go beyond the normal cyclical bloating and moodiness to depression, rage, sleeplessness, and other significant life-disrupting symptoms. In fact, in rare instances a severe form called Premenstrual Dysphoric Disorder—PMDD—can cause a depression so severe that life doesn't seem worth living. For such a woman, effective help is available if she consults with a caring physician.

Numerous theories have been advanced to explain this perplexing collection of symptoms. Only in the past generation has PMS been appreciated as a reality and not as just "all in her head." Multiple therapies with variable success attest that medical science has yet to fully unravel the tangled yarn of this problem. Most physicians will chart the symptoms with a "PMS diary" and then continue to track the significant problems during therapy to see which ones improve. Vitamin therapy with or without minerals, thyroid, progesterone, and antidepressant mood-elevating drugs have been tried. Each regimen has enjoyed some success, but some patients do not respond well to currently available approaches.

We now have evidence that different women metabolize or break down progesterone via different enzyme pathways, producing different end products. The chemicals result in sleepiness for one, rage in another, and depression in yet another. If this theory proves true, it would explain why progesterone therapy makes some women better and some worse. Those with the enzyme that breaks down progesterone into a compound causing drowsiness will do much better than those with the enzyme pathway that produces a compound causing restlessness, anger, or depression. If medical science can develop a compound that will block the harmful pathway, many women may finally find relief from this debilitating condition.

Others suggest that a defect in the production or secretion of serotonin, a chemical in the brain, causes some of the difficulties associated with PMS. Further investigation is currently underway.

There you have it—an overview of the female reproductive system. While it brings a unique set of potential challenges, it's also a marvel of creation. This may have been a review for you rather than all-new information. Today, more than they did in the past, couples read about sexual intimacy, partly because so many more resources are available, often without requiring a trip to the bookstore.

While considering God's design for the female anatomy, we've looked at the individual parts and how they function. But by also recognizing the anatomical counterparts in the male, we see an intelligent and wise Creator who made man and wife to fit like two pieces into one whole. We next look at how He, in His wisdom, created them, male and female, to join together as "two become one."

5

The Sexual Response Cycle

I have come into my garden, my sister, my bride;
I have gathered my myrrh along with my balsam.
I have eaten my honeycomb and my honey;
I have drunk my wine and my milk.
—SONG OF SOLOMON 5:1

Beth gets home from work first, so she makes dinner. Nicholas arrives and gives her a little peck on the cheek. He plays with the kids, then they have supper. Nick helps the oldest child finish her homework, then he and Beth put the children to bed. While she does the dishes, he sits down, hunts for the remote, and reads the paper. They spend the rest of the evening channel surfing. At 10:30, he collects all the garbage for tomorrow's pickup. They watch the 11:00 news, then it's bedtime. He pads off to the bathroom, does his little chores, and changes into his bedtime attire. She does the same, and they climb into bed. Perhaps they read for a while, then he reaches over and turns off his light. She reads awhile longer, then finally reaches over and turns off her light. Everything is still. And then suddenly, in the dark, there it is. A cold hand on her breast. Nick kisses her ear. And seven minutes later, everything is over. Nick snores while Beth stares at the ceiling. Again. When he wakes up the next morning, Nick wonders why Beth always just lies there when they make love.

Gender Differences

Nick probably isn't a clod, and Beth probably isn't unresponsive; they're both uninformed. Neither of them is demonstrating an understanding of the differences in how men and women generally view the sexual process. Their love life reflects how little they genuinely "know" each other. So what do they—and others in the same situation—need to know? Here are some differences in how men and women tend to view the "sex" of sexual expression. Men and women vary in their individual responses, of course, but when they learn about how a husband and wife typically approach sex differently, it helps that couple to know they are "normal."

- *Timing.* Men are primarily quick to respond physically; women are moved along more gently. Some have said, "Men are like light bulbs, women are like electric irons"; or, "Men are like gas stoves, women are like crock pots." One group of researchers found that men and women differ significantly in the time needed between foreplay and orgasm. The average male can go from excitation to climax in three to five minutes. Yet 62 percent of women surveyed need at least fifteen minutes of appropriate stimulation following arousal to reach orgasm. A small percentage need more than forty-five minutes and one percent, an hour or more.[1]
- *Needs.* To a man, sex is primarily about meeting powerful physical needs accompanied by some emotional needs; to a woman, sex is primarily about meeting emotional needs accompanied by some physical needs (although many couples find less of a disparity as they age). Thus, a husband can come home, slam the door, and ask, "Howz about it?" Rarely do we hear of such behavior from wives. "For most men, being sexual is a way of being intimate," write Christian sex therapists Clifford and Joyce Penner. "Women usually see sex as a

precursor to being intimate. It sounds terribly traditional and old-fashioned, but still it is true: when men feel lonely and hurt, they want to be held and make love. When women feel hurt, they want to be understood and talked to."[2] Another sex therapist writes, "According to the men I interviewed, when it comes to sex, a deep emotional bond has definite physical benefits. Some women just can't achieve orgasm unless they know they're in a love relationship. While that's not true for many men, an emotional bond can definitely add to a man's physical pleasure."[3]

Missy, who became a believer after she married, admits, "Before I was a Christian, I was promiscuous. I had multiple sexual encounters, and I faked orgasm every time. Not until I married did I actually experience one. I needed love and security and a patient husband for sex to 'work right' for me." For most women, affection and physical expression are more intertwined. At times a woman longs much more for the closeness and intimacy of the sex act than she does for the thrill of it, while a man more often longs for the thrill, while he enjoys the closeness and intimacy. Yet this may change a bit with age. In one study men under thirty-five reported liking intercourse more than foreplay, but once they reached thirty-five, a higher percentage of men reported liking foreplay more.[4] "Traditionally, 'foreplay' was considered something that a man had to do to get his partner ready for sexual intercourse," writes sex education journalist David Strovny. But "today, foreplay has become an integral part of the whole lovemaking experience."[5] Nevertheless, we still see a disparity in needs being met.

- *Relationship*. Most men and women appear to have some disparity in the degree of emotional involvement necessary to engage in or enjoy sex, although the gap may be narrowing. In 1984, 59 percent of men studied said they found it difficult to have sex without having a love relationship with the woman involved. Ten years later, 71 percent of men ranked the emotional side of sex as "very important"—an increase of 12 percent.

Still, in two separate studies, 86 percent of women said they felt this way.[6] Even Christian men at marriage conferences—a group more likely than average to embrace monogamy—admit they are tempted to have sex with total strangers. Their wives stand aghast, unable to comprehend how it's possible for a man to be so tempted sexually by somebody he doesn't love or even know. In the famous "Attractive Stranger" experiment, good-looking men and women approach members of the opposite sex and suggest a dinner date, offer an invitation to this stranger's apartment, or make a flat-out proposition. The study has been replicated many times, each with the same results: Men overwhelmingly (70 percent or higher) agree to the sexual invitations—even more often than they agree to the dinner date—while women overwhelmingly say *yes* to dinner but *no* to sex.[7] A team of Christian psychologists, the authors of *Secrets of Eve*, released findings from a survey of two thousand Christian wives. Three-fourths of those surveyed ranked physical or emotional closeness as more important than orgasm while only about 40 percent considered the physical release important.[8]

- *Feelings.* Enjoying sex may be harder for a woman if she feels angry or distracted. Some men can stop in the middle of an argument—in which anger permeates the air—and initiate sex; then they can return to a fight. A woman has a harder time shifting gears into sexual mode and resuming the argument afterward. "Most [women] have a difficult time responding sexually when we're angry and upset, particularly if the problem hasn't yet been resolved," writes Vickie Kraft in *The Influential Woman*. "This is true because most women really love with their whole being while most men seem to be more compartmentalized. Your husband may not even like you on a given day but he probably will manage to maintain his interest in the sexual relationship anyway."[9]
- *Process vs. event.* Men tend to be event-oriented. Many husbands can see their wives in anything or nothing, and they want sex. Conversely, women tend to be process-oriented. Sex for them is

not an event but an environment. Thus mood and surroundings may play bigger roles.

- *Stimuli.* Although men become aroused in a variety of ways, visual stimulation is the favorite. In other words they are stimulated *primarily* by the sight of a woman. They like to see women in sexy attire, and they like to see attractive naked women. Many wives readily testify that their husbands enjoy watching them undress and that, upon seeing their wives naked, men become aroused in seconds. A lot of women find this hard to understand because the sight of their naked husbands affects them differently. According to researchers, "Men are usually much more intensely aroused by sexually viewing women than are females viewing men. Females are usually more excited at being seen by men than males are at being viewed by women. Yet, "if a man goes beyond sexual delight and into sexual leering, women will likely feel hurt and resentful."[10] Women respond, although generally more gently, to stimuli from any or all of the senses with the addition of gentleness and affection. An expression of personal care is more likely to light her fire. "You know what gets me turned on?" writes a women's health writer. "The sound of a vacuum cleaner, when I'm *not* operating it. And the sound of a load of clean washing going around and around in the dryer, when I haven't had to put it there. And walking into the bedroom to find the bed made, and towels hanging up in the bathroom, instead of lying in a soggy heap on the floor. That's what gets me hot baby!"[11]

- *Variety.* Men tend to hunger for a variety of sexual practices while women tend to want variety of mood and atmosphere. A man will fantasize about having sex in every room of the house or every seat of the car in every position possible. The woman's perspective is often closer to, "That's not even *comfortable!* But would you like me to light some candles and put on some soft music?" In a study with 16,000 volunteers from fifty countries, when asked how many partners they desired over the next month, men on average said 1.87, while women said 0.78.[12]

With these general emotional and intellectual differences in mind, perhaps it's easy—or at least, easier—to see how men tend to want affirmation without manipulation and women, affection without expectation. That is, he wants lovemaking to happen because she wants him, not as a reward for taking out the trash. She wants him to be able to kiss her lightly on the neck without following up with roving hands.

It's also important to understand how bodies of women and men experience differing physical changes during the act of lovemaking. Masters and Johnson have assigned four labels to describe the textbook outline of what is "supposed to happen" during the phases of the normal sexual response cycle: Excitement, Plateau, Orgasm, and Resolution. We will discuss these with accompanying time frames and intervals.

Yet it's important to note that more recent research into men's and women's sexual responses direct us toward new ways of thinking. The "time honored" work of Freud, Kinsey, and Masters and Johnson may need significant revision.

None of these consider the spiritual dimension or give much credence to marriage and monogamy. The field of Christian sex therapy is relatively new and has drawn from the research previously done. New and important insights, however, are coming from the recognition that gratifying sexual experiences depend on far more than mere anatomy and physiology, important as these are. Even those who advocate sex with numerous partners admit that various techniques—poring over the *Kama Sutra,* trying exotic positions, and dabbling in sex toys and scented oils—are "really the last 10 percent of the experience; the first 90 percent consists of learning how to have basic satisfying sex face-to-face with one partner, factory equipment only."[13]

For years while giving lectures on sexual intimacy in marriage, I (Dr. Bill) have used the Masters and Johnson construct, which sees people's sexual responses as "linear," generally moving through set stages from excitement to orgasm. Yet I've had to qualify so much when discussing their work on the female response that I saw the need for a different approach.

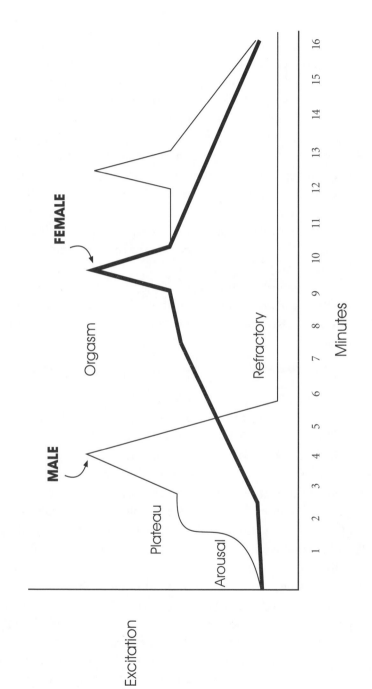

SEXUAL RESPONSE

For this reason I appreciate the newer model developed by Dr. Rosemary Basson (see diagram on p. 60). Her findings on the female sexual response seem to better fit reality. In her description of events, a vast number of women are not "linear" but are in fact more "cyclical," and they don't necessarily even strive for the orgasmic response as the ultimate goal or measure of satisfaction. Basson sees women's sexual desire, particularly for women in long-term relationships, as governed more by thoughts and emotions than by any feelings in the genitals. In a woman's sexual cycle, Basson says, her experience of pleasure triggers arousal, which subsequently triggers desire. And it's all preceded by a decision to "desire" or become aroused. This may help us account for the cliché that "men usually initiate, women respond."

So in describing the stages of the sex act, we'll use the familiar Masters and Johnson descriptions, which do have some merit. But we'll also allude to newer findings as they relate to female response.

The "Normal" Order of Events

Imagine walking into the Louvre in Paris and a guide instructs you to choose the most beautiful painting in the museum. If you spent only thirty seconds looking at each of the Rembrandts, Raphaels, and all the other works of art, you'd need several years to see it all. But the painting you choose would be the best work to *you*; there would be no one *right* answer for everyone. In the same way, imagine sitting in a room with four other people. All of you receive the latest Spiegel catalog and are asked to choose the most attractive model and the nicest outfit. Each person probably would, of course, choose a different "favorite."

The same is true of sex. One's "ultimate" is highly subjective. Yet people often try to classify sex in terms of "normal frequency" and provide the "normal order of events." Everyone is different. Not only is variation enormous from person to person, but variations also occur within an individual during the course of a lifetime—or even in the course of one encounter. What "works" one moment might change in the next. So keep in mind that what works for you as a couple is your own norm.

And now for the first stage:

Excitement

If we equate sex with dining, "excitement" would be the hors d'oeuvres. Others have labeled this stage as "excitation" or "arousal." It's that time of initial interest, the warm, fuzzy glow of attraction. All five senses can serve as channels to arousal. A marathon runner may jog past a home where he or she always smells bacon frying, and it may stir the desire to stop in for breakfast. In the same way, our sexual appetites receive stimuli. Something visual may trigger it—someone or even some*thing* attractive. The moon over the ocean or a light snowfall might "put you in the mood." A sound might start it—a voice, a song, a word. It could be the scent of a favorite perfume. (In some cultures, sweat would make this list.) Sometimes a thought or a memory can set the process in motion. And, of course, touch often arouses—sometimes it's as simple as casually brushing against someone's arm and realizing, "This person is a member of the opposite sex." It might be a passing moment of "connection," or it could become more significant and sustained. God made us such that different body parts and shapes appeal to different appetites, so among various individuals, there is no universal standard of beauty.

Advertisers, of course, attempt to connect their products with that positive sense of arousal. There's the good-looking couple walking down the street, engrossed in each other. She laughs and pats his behind. Buy her brand of perfume. Or there's the woman who peels off her robe revealing a dream-filtered shot of her curvaceous form. She slips into the hot tub and closes her eyes. Ahhh. Then her man does a cannon ball into the water, jarring her out of her reverie and splashing her in the face. He takes a swig of beer. Buy his brand.

Research suggests that many women can "choose" to be excited because they sense a need for intimacy. As we've discussed, intimacy in the mind of most women is often far deeper, far more relational than simply a physical sexual experience. It involves the passion of loving intensely, being deeply known, and being loved completely without fear of rejection.

For her, love at its best involves a longing, a drive to delight because she loves. The intense emotion starts as a spark inside and grows into a body-permeating fire that fills her entire being. It's as if she loves with every cell and must find a means of expressing it.

Do you know the cologne she likes? Use it. Do you know the color he likes? Wear it (or if he likes nudity, don't wear it and think of the money you'll save). Consider lighting and location. Do the ocean or the mountains "do it for you"? These are all matters of taste. Men tend to be more adventuresome, experimental, even territorial. Women tend to be more attuned to atmosphere for the stirring of desire. Do you know, and do, those things that entice each other's imaginations? Expand those thoughts to incorporate all the senses.

In Song of Solomon 1:13, the bride says this to her groom:

> My beloved is to me a pouch of myrrh
> Which lies all night between my breasts.

In the ancient Near East a woman often wore a small pouch of myrrh around her neck at night. The presence of a fragrant aroma between her breasts reminded her of those moments when his body lay next to hers. She connected the aroma of myrrh with their love. In the same book of the Bible, we read about the lover's palate tasting honey, about the sound of her voice, and the touch of his fingers. He is excited by her feet in sandals and a strand of pearls on her long neck. Smell, taste, touch, sight, sound—emphasis was placed on bringing all five senses to bear in lovemaking.

Gender differences may play a role in arousal, too. We are not suggesting men and women have *innate* differences—necessarily. But if a woman has been home with toddlers all day, she may especially need "all-day foreplay"—not physical fondling, but a kiss in the morning, a call at noon, then the sight of her hubby cleaning house, shopping, or doing chores unexpectedly. As alluded to earlier, these actions sometimes serve as better turn-ons than seeing him emerge from the bathroom in a pair of silk boxers. Add romantic dinners, flowers, poetry, and active listening; these provide the affectionate, nongenital contact a woman may desire—or even need—to fill her mind and imagination with thoughts of her man.

During the excitement stage, physical changes in addition to mental stirring or stimulation take place. In males, penile erection is the dominant symptom. The penis becomes erect and hard, and muscles under the skin around the testicles contract, causing them to draw up against his body more tightly. The erection may persist and escalate or diminish as he "deals with" the stimuli—he pursues contact, or perhaps a stop light changes and he must leave the beautiful girl, his fantasy evaporating with the exhaust fumes.

Usually when a woman is stimulated, she experiences lubrication of the vaginal opening (tiny beads like perspiration form). She may lubricate in response to an attractive man and remain unaware of it. One or both of her nipples may also become erect. And she may have clitoral swelling or "congestion" caused by blood and fluid collecting in the sexual organs. The labia majora and minora swell, and heart and breathing rates generally increase.

God designed our genitals to become aroused. What we *do* with that arousal is our responsibility. It's one thing to appreciate beauty when we see it. It's another to drive around the block to get a better look. "We can learn to enjoy the eyes, the hair, the smile, the strength of shoulders and arms, the curve of hips and legs, without leering and lusting," explains author Richard Foster. "They are lovely gifts from the Creator's hand. How dare we despise them!"[14]

The enjoyment of sexual beauty does not need to be wicked; it simply needs to be controlled—and it can be. We can appreciate the lovely form of bicep or breast without falling headlong into uncontrolled lust. Arousal whets the sexual appetite in the same way a banquet table covered with food gets the gastric juices flowing. The presence of food does not necessarily require "gorging," but it gently or not-so-gently turns the mind toward fulfillment. When it comes to sex, sometimes sight is enough.

Variety on many levels is important here for excitation. Even if you tend to be unadventurous, it's good, at least once in a while, to try the sexual equivalent of a raw oyster, sushi, Borscht, or even if you're really a roast beef-and-potatoes kind of person, a taco.

A woman at one of my (Dr. Bill's) marriage seminars questioned her husband's spirituality because he requested colorful, revealing lingerie. As it was the holiday season, I said, "Nobody wants all his or her Christmas presents wrapped in brown paper." We're guessing that neither the "thong" nor the string bikini was invented by women, certainly not by those who wanted to hide extra weight. But couples may feel the liberty to seek plenty of creativity and variety within their own one-flesh relationship.

The need for interesting attire is important for men to consider, too. While males generally find themselves attracted to bikinis on women, many women say "gross" when they see men wearing string-sized bathing suits. Although there appears to be no exact parallel for "what works," women do have *some* visual orientation—so find out what she considers fun or interesting and wear it.

In Song of Solomon 4:9, the groom writes,

> You have made my heart beat faster
> with a single glance of your eyes,
> With a single strand of your necklace.

If "fed," arousal leads to foreplay. Excitement is sustained and increased with gentle physical stimulation of sensitive areas— kissing, hugging, fondling, and caressing. It involves an increasing level of arousal, intensity of feelings, and a desire for further physical pleasuring. Kissing is, in fact, a good indicator of a couple's level of ongoing passion. In the beginning of Song of Solomon 1:2, we read this:

> May he kiss me with the kisses of his mouth!
> For your love is better than wine.

True, wine works as an "uninhibitor." But once intimate touch begins, if both partners are willing, their expression of physical love makes them share more vulnerably than a glass of wine could. The Hebrew word for "love" used here often refers to physical expressions of romantic, sexual love. Sustaining excitation usually requires physical contact—effective, pleasurable stimulation.

Plateau

Many label the next stage the "plateau." The key problem with the "plateau" label is that it gives the impression that things go flat. They stay the same. Yet geographically, it's more like driving up and down some hills than cruising along the rim of the Grand Canyon. This stage varies considerably in length and degree. During this part of the sexual process, the same physical changes continue, but with greater intensity. Seismic tremors escalate, and for some they build in intensity until the whole world rocks.

If we use the food analogy, this is the dining itself. Some days you like home cooking; other times you want a Big Mac and fries. On special occasions you might require beef Wellington. But all can be satisfying and pleasurable, and each "dinner" can last variable lengths of time. Like a menu, lovemaking may include a variety of options—differing positions, locations, and ambiance. You don't want the same steak cooked the same way every night. You have your favorites, but when you have them three times a week, you long for some variety.

In the woman, the cycle of increasing arousal and desire may be short, intermediate, or long. The length of this period doesn't matter. Duration is a matter of an individual's unique design and preference. It may be variable, unpredictable, or prolonged even beyond "normal" experience, assuming the spouse can maintain the endeavor for the desired length of time. She may not even be desirous of orgasm on some occasions and be quite content to remain for long periods of time in this pleasurable "zone," experiencing a sense of well-being and satisfaction without orgasm.

FEMALE SEXUAL RESPONSE (BASSON MODEL)

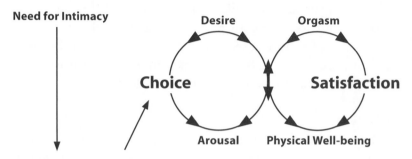

You will note from the diagram that Dr. Basson's model doesn't even include a "plateau" stage. Instead, we see a nonlinear, cyclical picture. Most women enter into arousal by choice, unlike men who can be aroused by sight or touch without a conscious decision. The fulfilling of a woman's inherent need for intimate connection with her husband is what results in ultimate satisfaction. According to this model, each phase of sexual response affects both the next phase and the previous one as well. Women are fascinatingly complex.

Of particular significance here is that the Basson model recognizes women can reach satisfaction without progressing through each phase sequentially, as men ordinarily do. Some phases may be skipped entirely and still result in satisfaction.

The Basson model recognizes human beings as relational with a need for intimacy. A woman's nonsexual awareness of this need may generate feelings of sexuality. She then may choose to move toward desire and arousal. The mental and emotional sense of desire will stimulate the physical response described as arousal by the older Masters and Johnson model. A woman may sense the increased blood supply to the genitals, the increasing sensation of wetness, engorgement of the clitoris, perhaps even nipple erection. And this response can, in turn, create greater desire, stimulating greater arousal. This cycle can continue for many minutes.

Basson would then suggest that a sexual woman, moved with desire and fully aroused may progress to orgasm. Or she may not. Yet she may still experience a deep sense of physical well-being, safety, and security. She feels truly loved. This sense of well-being may move to orgasm, or it may leave her fully satisfied without achieving an orgasmic release.

This model also describes the phenomenon following orgasm in which women can cycle through satisfaction and return to orgasm again. This cyclical process allows great fluidity between desire, arousal, orgasm, and complete satisfaction.

As you can see, the linear excitement-plateau-orgasm-resolution model, which accurately depicts the male sexual response, falls short in describing the complex female response, which may include multiple orgasms or complete satisfaction without orgasm at all. Because the former model has been considered the norm, many women have felt pressure to "achieve" a particular type of orgasmic response within a certain time framework. Basson's work defines satisfaction using words such as emotional closeness, commitment, bonding, affection, and acceptance. This fits nicely with our working definition of intimacy—being fully known, fully loved, without fear of rejection.

For a man in the "plateau" stage, the erection is most firm and achieves its greatest size. Men release small amounts of seminal fluid during this phase preceding ejaculation. As mentioned, men can go from arousal to orgasm in as little as three to five minutes. But it's important to understand that this is not a race; no one wins any ribbons for "doing it" quickly. It's not like steer roping where you try to be the fastest to "get the job done." Nor is it like bull riding where an eight-second ride is okay. Control is the key.

Some studies would indicate that the number-one sexual difficulty among married couples is premature ejaculation (PE). We must clarify that many couples complaining of this difficulty define PE not as a "formal, medical sexual dysfunction," but as times when "he ejaculates before she is ready for him to." This being the case, it is nearly universal that a man will experience PE sometimes, perhaps even often.

Women who experience orgasm arrive there at very different rates. Some cycle through desire and arousal to orgasm in minutes if the relational environment has been particularly warm and close. For others, when they do achieve orgasm, the cycle normally takes ten, twenty, or more minutes. The Basson model fits this nicely, but many husbands complain that it takes their wives too long to get there. Many wives, too, complain, "It takes me forever." At one conference when the men were asked how long it took their wives to go from excitation to orgasm, they answered "hours!" Perhaps some of the pressure comes from not understanding how women are "wired." Most women need an average of ten to fifteen minutes of uninter-rupted stimulation, which includes contact with the clitoris, to reach orgasm. And many women need even more time than this. One woman reported, "It takes thirty to forty minutes, sometimes more. I get self-conscious because I'm taking so long. Then that slows me down because I'm distracted." The ten- to fifteen-minute figure is an average range; it's merely a scientific observation based on intervals that women have reported. (Of course, it's also true that humans compulsively alter the facts in relation to sexual performance and prowess.) What Masters and Johnson may have described as a "long plateau" or an abnormality, Basson's model sees as a normal varia-tion, and a common one at that.

Making love is an art. In the same way that a person who com-pletes a "paint-by-number" picture has made a picture without any personal technique, so the person who understands all the statistics about sex does not necessarily become a good lover. Nor do the sta-tistics indicate couples are "bad" lovers because they have sex less frequently or it takes longer for them. Sex is very personal. More important than knowing what is "usual" and "average" is knowing what works for you as a couple. Mature love seeks the joy of one's spouse, while immature love is all about self. Statistics are about "greatest frequency" and "newest technique." Yet God designed us to have art and mystery. We're each unique, so enjoy the experience and grow *together.*

Orgasm

Some describe orgasm, climax, or in the world of *bon appetit*, "dessert" as explosive, rhythmic pelvic muscle contractions. Others describe a more gradual elevation of variable intensity and duration. It's extremely pleasurable by design, although the range of individual experiences may include a range from "so what" to "I've died and gone to heaven."

During orgasm, men ejaculate, releasing about a teaspoonful of semen that normally contains millions of sperm. The heart rate elevates, breathing quickens, and the end of the world as he knows it approaches. He experiences multiple rhythmic contractions of the vesicles within the prostate gland, ejaculatory ducts, and muscles in the pelvis and penis. His sensations feel more localized than hers, with intense feelings directed toward the pelvis and penis.

A woman experiences the involuntary contraction of her muscles surrounding the outer portion of the vagina, which for most includes thrusting of the pelvis. Contractions of other body muscles may also occur. This whole-body event generally brings intense pleasure and relief. Most women do not technically ejaculate, although the rhythmic contractions of the pelvis, the heart rate, and breathing are similar to what men experience as ejaculation. Unlike men, women return to "normal" gradually, and they can stay stimulated, perhaps desiring further attention sexually.

"Do women really have orgasms?" This question comes up frequently in the premarital counselor's office. The answer is yes. It's unfortunate, though, that some wives don't even realize they've had them. If you are relaxed and satisfied after sexual relations, you may have had one, or you may have progressed to the stage of satisfaction without one. A sex expert tells of men calling in to her talk show asking, "How can I make sure she had an orgasm?" The answer is that she herself may not know. Or the real possibility is this: she was completely satisfied this time without one. Or perhaps she was quite satisfied having had three.

The point is not to count and calculate, but to experience mutual satisfaction in the context of committed, covenant love. Some women (and a few men) think orgasm is overrated and not worth the effort. Like desserts with varying calorie counts, orgasms come in many varieties, some "better than others." You don't always have to have dessert. But if you do, it can be as plain as applesauce with cookies or as exotic as flaming bananas Foster.

Resolution

The resolution, or refractory, period follows an orgasmic response. It may be a pleasurable mellow sensation or, as some have described, a "near death," or at least nearly comatose, experience. "The mythical connection between sex and death in European culture gave rise to the term *le petit mort*, or 'the little death' . . . Read *The Canonization*, by the 17th-century poet, John Donne, and you'll find reference to the superstition that each orgasm subtracts a day from one's life."[15]

At the time of orgasm, the body experiences the release of endorphins, a potent narcoticlike substance within the brain. Endorphins are delightful, creating a desire for more. They also relieve minor aches and pains. Thus, as has often been said, "Sex is good for what ails you." For most, the endorphins produce a contented afterglow, as the satisfied lovers enjoy the pleasurable sensation of intimacy—relaxed, refreshed, and renewed.

If endorphin levels are high, however, they can make a person quite drowsy, so that post-fiesta becomes a siesta. The sensation of drowsiness peaks one to two minutes after orgasm and subsides over the next quarter of an hour. This is "near death" in that endorphins can cause a comalike syndrome, especially in men. (Okay, we've exaggerated. They do remain conscious.) During this time, lasting minutes to months—so it may seem—the husband becomes physically incapable of achieving a second functional erection. Wives, don't dial 911—just make sure he's breathing (some men may not be brought around by anything but an ensuing football kickoff). Or better still, knowing his partner may as yet feel unsatisfied, he will focus his time and attention on her need.

Most women have a deep desire for emotional closeness following their sexual experience, and some desire multiple orgasms. But men usually become totally uninterested in sex within a minute or two of climax. Some men will jump up and take a shower. Others roll over and fall asleep while their wives lie there still aroused and unsatisfied. Men, be sensitive here. Wives, understand that your husband's drowsiness isn't an indication of his rejection, but is perhaps a reflection of the power of your passion.

For a woman, engorgement returns to normal more gradually than for her husband. The process happens still more slowly if she has not experienced orgasm. Sometimes the husband can bring his wife to orgasm for the first or multiple times by non-penile stimulation after he has ejaculated.

Not everyone falls asleep after sex. As one man noted, "Some nights after sex I immediately fall asleep, and other nights, as with any other athletic activity, I'm energized and ready to get some work done." Women report similar experiences.

One female patient claimed to pass out, but if she truly did, I don't think it was due to an endorphin rush. I learned about it when I overheard my secretary handling a call: "Do you want me to call an ambulance? . . . Unconscious? . . . What happened?"

The man on the phone told her, "We were making love—vigorously. And now she's unconscious."

"Is she breathing?"

"Yes, I think so."

"Good. I'll get the doctor."

When I took the phone to handle this "medical crisis," the patient was awakening. I tried to provide some reassuring words to her partner until she could speak to me. When she did, I asked her questions such as "Do you know your name?" "What's the date?" and "Who is the president of the U.S. today?" Then in the solemn tone of a trained medical professional, I asked if she often passed out during romantic activities. She replied (with her partner obviously nearby),

"Oh, no. No one has ever excited me like that." This was their first time together, and apparently the combination of hyperventilation, breath holding, and a tight torso squeeze from her partner had made her lose consciousness.

After that, every time this patient called or stopped in at the office, comments about her partner's incredible technique surfaced. He shattered the mystery one day when he arrived with her, and to everyone's disappointment, he turned out to be a rather average-looking guy. But clearly, in her heart and mind, he was Superman. I'm guessing, though, that yet another myth is being propagated by this couple who believe that passing out is an indication of great sex rather than an indication that the brain needs oxygen.

So there we have it, the marvel of human sexual response, from interest and arousal to afterglow. Husband and wife together form a physical picture of a mystery—that two become one. One flesh. One heart.

It's unfortunate, though, that all too often the man experiences all of the "stages" from arousal to afterglow, while the woman receives little pleasure. An understanding of how we think and experience sex can greatly enhance enjoyment for both partners. Researchers have documented much more technical information than we have provided, but in all my years as a doctor, nobody seemed particularly interested in which muscles contracted, why the testicles elevate at orgasm, or which veins congest permitting erection. The questions people asked were generally more practical: Do we need to make simultaneous orgasms our goal? Are "quickies" okay? How can we increase the percentage of times we both experience orgasm? These practical matters, covered in the next chapter, are indeed the issues that can make or break truly satisfying sexual intimacy.

6

The Wedding Night
and Beyond

Your lips, my bride, drip honey;
Honey and milk are under your tongue,
And the fragrance of your garments is like
the fragrance of Lebanon.
—SONG OF SOLOMON 4:11

Bonnie and Steve are pretty good at caring and communicating, and they have what they describe as a "decent" love life, which involves having sex about twice a week. Bonnie, however, is rarely interested at the onset, and she almost never initiates. Steve's parameters for what he's comfortable doing during lovemaking are wider than hers. She sometimes feels self-conscious that she's not the lover he wants her to be. She feels uncomfortable with some of what he wants her to do, and when she does reach orgasm, it takes her longer than she would like. Steve, on the other hand, gets there rapidly and often finishes just as she's "getting warmed up." They frequently resort to "quickies" rather than endure the frustration of "it happened again."

If it's any consolation, Bonnie and Steve are in good company. The research highlighted in the last chapter, in fact, suggests that their differences fall well into the norm. When they better understand each other's unique makeup, they can lovingly meet both his and her needs. That Bonnie is rarely initially interested reflects the fact that many women don't often focus on the sex act itself, but are stirred by a relational environment of warmth, closeness, and security. They may then choose, either before sexual intimacy begins or soon after, to allow sexual desire to grow by focusing on thoughts and sensations that arouse. Steve should learn to appreciate his wife's response, and to move tenderly and slowly to allow time for arousal and to learn the unique ways in which Bonnie most enjoys stimulation. Bonnie should work to communicate to Steve what she enjoys. While an occasional "quickie" fits most marriages at times, a steady diet of "fast food" is bad for the physical health and destructive of true intimacy.

Attitudes About Sex

As we said earlier, every married couple has sexual difficulties. Why? Because we live in a fallen world. Others take advantage of our nature—our baser desires—appealing to our greed, lust, and self-indulgence; and we cooperate! Thus we have distorted views of physical intimacy.

Type *sex* into an Internet search engine such as Google and you'll get about 180 million hits. A growing percentage of the Internet is devoted to pornography, including chat rooms where people can write their fantasies to strangers. Americans spend about $10 billion a year on pornography, with porn moviemakers churning out about 11,000 titles per year.[1] Also piped into our homes are endless scenes of illicit sex paraded before our eyes through our TV screens. Even if we choose not to watch such shows, intimacy-cheapening commercials flash unwanted images before our eyes.

Another indication of our distortion of sex is the high incidence of sexually transmitted diseases (STDs). More than half of all people will have an STD at some point in their lifetimes.[2] It's estimated that more than 65 million people living in the U.S. have a viral STD, and every year at least 15 million new cases of STDs are reported, only some of which are curable.[3] Like we said, we all bring to marriage distorted perceptions of sexuality.

Most of us do not, after all, initially learn about sex from our parents. Most people who read this book, in fact, probably assume your own parents never actually had sex, right? Even thinking of imagining such a scene can be deeply disturbing. Some will allow that their parents probably had sex, once for each child, and only out of "duty to procreate" with a mentality of no fun, no enjoyment—just "get it done."

So where do we learn about sex? Most guys learn about sex from less-than-accurate sources such as locker rooms, "adult" reading material, and Internet chat rooms. "Studs" bombard each other with information having a 98 percent margin for error, then mix in the "Hollywood Factor," that is, buying in to the belief that movies accurately depict reality, so they believe most people are having sex on the floor of the office copy room, in elevators, or hanging from chandeliers.

One young bride-to-be shared that her parents expected her to figure things out on her own. "I looked up *sex* in the encyclopedia when I hit sixth grade," she said. Younger generations, though, are better educated than their predecessors. They've done some reading, many have had some premarital counseling, and their churches and youth groups stress the importance of purity with programs such as "True Love Waits." Abstinence programs, however, have produced mixed results.

Some learn about sex through unwanted sexual touch. A former student related that, at age twelve, she was told by her brother, "I want to show you something." He manually stimulated her genitals, which she found pleasurable and didn't resist because she loved and trusted him. But she suffered crushing guilt afterward. They never discussed it or acted on it again, but years later when she was involved in a romantic relationship, she had some "flashbacks." So she told her boyfriend, who nearly broke up with her over her "wanton" behavior.

Eventually, she had a healing conversation with her brother, and her boyfriend mended the relationship. But she's still working through her feelings about sexuality.

Another woman related that, as an eight-year-old, she leafed through a pornographic magazine left in sight. Later a frightening experience with a boy in junior high further etched itself on her memory associated with sex. She writes, "Although I wasn't actually raped, he forced me into a dark bathroom and sexually abused me. In the early years of our marriage, I found it difficult to reconcile these memories with my role as a wife. My desires to please my husband and enjoy sexual intimacy were in conflict with my feelings of anger and guilt. I asked God to renew my mind with his perspective on sex."[4]

At another point on the spectrum are those who have learned from their parents or in church that sex is "dirty." The whole process is shrouded in shame. One of my nurses said, "My mom still insists on undressing in the dark. My dad has never seen her undress in their decades of marriage." There's a sense that "good girls" don't have sex, even after marriage, unless it's for procreation. Sex for enjoyment is "carnal." The church father, Augustine, saw sex for enjoyment as a forgivable fault, rather than an act designed by God for good. The mentality is that real Christians should order keep-me-warm-at-thirty-below nightwear from Mammoth's Tusk, Siberia—nightwear so thick that even Superman with x-ray vision couldn't see anything resembling a human form.

The daughter of Russian author Leo Tolstoy wrote in her journal of her mother's attitude about sex: "I am very happy to think that I am a virgin and have not had to undergo that fearful humiliation all married women suffer, as Mother's remarks have made so clear to me; she was so ashamed the morning after her wedding that she did not want to leave her room. She hid her face in the pillow and cried. I am proud not to have known that and I wish I may never know it!"[5]

Even if we are taught healthy attitudes about sex, most of us have had powerful sexual fantasies, have masturbated, or have looked at something pornographic. In addressing a Baptist youth group, a youth leader learned that only one member had never viewed an X-rated or NC-17 movie—the pastor's son. Consider some statistics that reveal how sex-saturated our society is:

- Approximately one in five adolescents has had sexual intercourse before his or her fifteenth birthday.[6]
- More than half of American teenagers ages fifteen to nineteen have engaged in oral sex, with females and males reporting similar levels of experience, according to the most comprehensive national survey of sexual behaviors ever released by the federal government.[7]
- Of never-married females fifteen to seventeen years of age, 30 percent had experienced sexual intercourse in 2002. By age eighteen to nineteen, 69 percent had experienced intercourse. For male teens, the percent of those who were sexually experienced was 64 percent at age eighteen to nineteen.[8]
- A survey of nearly six hundred students by Northern Kentucky University revealed that 61 percent of students who made abstinence promises broke them. And of those who said they kept their pledges, 55 percent indicated they participated in oral sex. Only 16 percent abstained from sex until marriage, although pledge-breakers did delay sex for a year longer than nonpledging teens, until an average of 17.6 years old.[9]

This means most newlyweds are not virgins. Furthermore, before they graduate from high school, one-fifth of all students will have had at least four partners. And if current trends continue, most of today's high school students will live with a sex partner prior to getting married. In a large portion of those situations, the cohabitants will never marry each other, although they will have sexual relations with each other many times before dissolving the relationship.

Yet the situation is not hopeless. Christians are called to live countercultural lives, and many do, by the grace of God, uphold standards of purity in dating and engagement.

For those who have experienced moral failure, however, the human mind has an amazing ability to remember well the very details we most need to forget. Fantasies, magazine photos, graphic movie scenes, and personal experiences follow a couple into their intimate life together, usually to their detriment.

Our minds are in need of repair. We need confession and cleansing, understanding, and a reworking of our thoughts and attitudes. Having worked with couples for years as a physician, a pastor, and now as a seminary professor, I've noticed that many problems and questions adhere to fairly consistent patterns. What follows is a representative sampling gleaned from the office and from twenty-five years of conducting marriage seminars. If a question has been asked repeatedly by women and generally not by men, or vice versa, I've indicated this by wording the question from a gender-specific point of view.

Before You Say "I Do"

Let's examine some commonly asked questions that should be settled in each person's mind prior to marrying. Some of these questions need to be answered definitively early on in a relationship or even before dating begins.

How far is it okay to go before marriage?

Petting, which is the fondling of breasts or genitals to arouse sexual passion, is out. Extensive and intensive "necking" or "major neck action," which includes impassioned kissing—including neck, ears, and any erotic areas around the head and neck—can stimulate couples to desire intensely that which is reserved for marriage. This may also include French-kissing, which has been around longer than France, and which some have variously described as tongue lashing, giving a tonsillectomy, and tongue wrestling.

So what is not okay? Anything that stirs desire to sin. (That would include just about anything accompanied by moaning.) The standard is spelled out for us in 1 Thessalonians 4:3–8, which tells us not to defraud each other sexually. "Defrauding" is intentionally creating or sustaining a desire that cannot rightfully and righteously be met. In 2 Corinthians 10:5, the apostle Paul calls his readers to take every thought captive to Christ. In his letter to the Philippians, he describes what should be our meditation—that which is true, honorable, right . . ." (Phil. 4:8).

Many have defined vaginal intercourse as the only premarital no-no. Thus, many unmarried Christian couples practice oral sex, anal sex, cybersex, phone sex, and "outercourse" (during which there is intentional prolonged genital contact without penetration). They engage in these practices, rationalizing that they have adhered to God's standard. Yet God's standard draws the line at lustful thoughts and defrauding—requiring moment-by-moment dependence on God's power and commitment to His Word and making some difficult decisions about being isolated with someone to whom you have a strong physical attraction.

Rationalizing couples find themselves caught up in a cycle of obtaining sexual satisfaction in illegitimate practices, followed by conviction, guilt, and a hardening of heart against the guilt so it becomes easier to lower the standard the next time. This is a dangerous pattern. It keeps them sliding down a slippery slope as they go further each time, continually pushing the limits. It also helps them link sexual pleasure with guilt, which can create difficulties for them later. One couple remained in this pattern of "crossing the line," feeling guilt, then vowing to do better until their marriage. They came to me (Dr. Bill) after a number of years of marriage to report that their sexual desire for each other was gone. They had tried but could not recapture the excitement of the "forbidden acts." So they both regularly engage in fantasies about other partners.

Staying within boundaries is especially difficult in our culture, which promotes individual dating as opposed to group dating. Young couples who feel strongly attracted to each other are placed in settings that increase the likelihood of violating their own and God's standards. Group settings help take some of the pressure off of couples seeking to control their urges, while helping them develop healthy social skills. Yet ultimately, the battle gets fought in the mind.

In Song of Solomon 8:8–9, we read what the bride's brothers, or perhaps what the bride herself says,[10] about a younger sister:

> We have a little sister,
> And she has no breasts;
> What shall we do for our sister
> On the day when she is spoken for?
> If she is a wall,
> We shall build on her a battlement of silver;
> But if she is a door,
> We shall barricade her with planks of cedar.

It's possible that the little sister is undeveloped and her family members wish to adorn her. Yet Craig Glickman, author of *A Song for Lovers*, sees this as a reference to the girl's morality:

> [The brothers] devise a simple but effective formula for success. If she is a wall, they will "build on her a battlement of silver." That means that if she is virtuous and firm against boys' advances, they'll reward her, trying to improve on what is already good. . . . Yet if she is a door, they would enclose her with planks of cedar. In other words, if she is as open as a door to advances, they would have to be stricter with her to prevent her hurting herself for marriage. If she could handle responsibility, they would give it to her; but if not, she would be restricted.[11]

Apparently, between her youth and the time leading to her engagement, she grew and developed as a woman of moral purity. Here in 8:10 is what Glickman sees as her later response:

> I was a wall, and my breasts were like towers;
> Then I became in his eyes as one who finds peace.

As Jody Dillow wrote in *Solomon on Sex*, her breasts, though "ready for love, were inaccessible."[12] The word *then* in this verse is emphatic in the original language. That is, it implies that her purity played a factor in his attraction to her.

Is the desire to marry a virgin legitimate?

Certainly. Excluding the issues of divorce and death of a spouse, shouldn't we all want to marry virgins? Men and women both should want that. So often we have a double standard that says men should "play around" before marriage but then marry "nice girls" who didn't. Even some "nice girls" want experienced men because these women grew up hearing that men should know all about sex but women should be naive. The nuances of the very terms we use to describe each other reflect this mentality: men are manly, macho, studly (positive); women are easy, loose, sluts (negative).

"I grieved when I found out my fiancé had already had sex," Terri said. "It's really disappointing, because I've saved myself for marriage. But he has a spirit of repentance about it. So I decided that if God has forgiven him, I can, too. I realize we may have to deal with some related difficulties in the future, but I'm willing to face that because I want him in my life."

How much importance a person places on this is an individual matter. For some, marrying a person with a "past" may not be a livable option; for others, it may be workable. When deciding on a future mate, we have to ask ourselves, "What problems am I willing to live with if my future spouse does not live up to my ideal?" (recognizing that none of us meets God's standard).

In the past I was sexually abused, and that makes it difficult for me to enjoy lovemaking. What should I do?

A study published in *Contemporary Family Therapy* estimates that 56 percent of women who were sexually abused as children feel discomfort during sex, and 36 percent seek some sort of sexual therapy.[13] It's been said many times that the mind is the most important sexual organ, and it's perfectly normal for significant problems to stem from past abuses. Yet it's possible to rid one's self of mental images from the past such that they don't interfere. Doing so may require individual counseling, but victims of sexual abuse can find help and hope. When victims get help, the images do tend to lose power over time.

If your partner has suffered abuse, be extremely tender. Try to discover—gently and patiently—what works best for you as a couple.

If you have been abused, you may need to make love in interesting surroundings that differ significantly from those of the negative experience. Try leaving on dim lights to help you stay visually in touch with where you are. Look into your partner's face and associate. Decide to fill your mind with the truth. If the negative distraction happens frequently enough, it might benefit you to find a Christian counselor who specializes in sexual abuse. As a rule, most pastors receive too little specialized training to handle these issues. Pastors are often both uncomfortable with the subject and unqualified to address the issues related to it. Also, going to a pastor can evoke more feelings of pain if the abuser was a person in a position of spiritual authority.

How do I retrain myself to realize "sex is good" and start talking openly about sex?

The church through the centuries has often been of little help here. Jerome, a great Bible translator, disallowed couples from receiving communion after the "bestial" act of intercourse, and he claimed that "he who too ardently loves his wife is an adulterer." Pope Gregory I claimed that "sexual pleasure can never be without sin."

One confused young pastor confessed he avoided sex with his own beautiful wife because doing so filled his mind with images that made preaching about holiness impossible. Another husband explained, "I thought that if I gave my life fully to the Lord, it meant I would have to stop having a good time with my wife. It was a pleasant surprise to find out God gave sex as a gift and that it's supposed to get even better."

If you struggle with the mentality that God frowns on sex, try reading to each other from Song of Solomon and talk about what its poetry means. Fill your mind with what the Bible says about sex as a gift from God. If you're married, begin with the workbook section of this text and work through answers with your spouse so that you begin to become comfortable with the topic. Talk about what you agree with and disagree with, and discuss your personal preferences. If you continue to have difficulty, seek help.

How do we handle going from "Stop! Stop!" before marriage to the mentality that we must be sex gods and goddesses once we're married?

"My fiancée and I have worked hard to keep limits on ourselves during our engagement," one man told me. "How do we go from 'sex is bad' to 'sex is great' in one day after a wedding ceremony?" His fiancée added, "How am I supposed to go from 'good girl' to 'sex kitten' overnight?"

You can begin by changing "Stop, stop" to "Not yet, not yet." The best lovemaking follows covenantal commitment between partners. The classic "Sex in America" study, generally considered the most accurate and complete study ever done, indicated that "intimate, exclusive relationships between spouses or committed partners provide, by far, the greatest degree of sexual satisfaction."[14] It's interesting that evangelical women topped the list of those who were most sexually satisfied. So understand that God designed marriage to provide the right context for sex.

Rid your mind of messages that say sex is bad and replace them with "sex is good—in context." In his book, *A Celebration of Sex*, Doug Rosenau writes, "The Bible describes the beauty and complexity of the marital companionship that creates the context for lovemaking. The loving, intimate relationship of you and your spouse is modeled after the relationship of God and His chosen people."[15]

So the "biblical" view is that sex is good—but not in every setting. We should teach that the sex act is sinful outside of marriage. Yet feelings of physical passion focused on one's spouse are good. God put them there. Sex simply has some boundaries. What we do with our passions has some limits. And both man and woman must take responsibility for avoiding sex outside of a committed one-flesh God-blessed relationship. It's neither "her job" nor "his job" to apply the brakes; they're both responsible for holding the line. Note that after the wedding in Song of Solomon, the lovers are encouraged to "drink and imbibe deeply." The poet seems to indicate that this is the point-of-view of God Himself—as the silent observer, designer, and blesser of their physical love. God pronounces His full approval on everything that has taken place, encouraging the lovers to drink deeply of His gift. He created us—designed us—as sexual creatures. And He has revealed the "rules" for our benefit and in our best interest.

Your first encounters do not have to be your best; you'll probably find yourselves fumbling and groping a bit. Yet these experiences are precious, and they're where you begin. Marriage involves the developing of sexual intimacy. Developing implies a process, a progression. Through understanding, practice, applying knowledge, growing in unity, maturing in love, and abounding in tenderness and kindness, your unique physical love language will develop over time.

Song of Solomon appears to indicate that, over time, lovers gain more boldness and deeper intimacy. Early in Song of Solomon the bride says this about herself (1:6):

> Do not stare at me because I am swarthy,
> For the sun has burned me.

The highest measure of beauty on a Middle Eastern woman was her skin. Women wore head coverings in the sun to keep their skin light. So the bride views herself as "deficient" compared to the standard of beauty in her culture. A little later, she says this (2:1):

> I am the rose of Sharon,
> The lily of the valleys.

The lover has told his beloved that she's beautiful, and she replies with a statement about how self-conscious she is. The "rose of Sharon" probably refers to the equivalent of a narcissus, which abounds in Sharon, a region in the neighborhood of Nazareth. The flower is a flesh-colored meadow bloom with a leafless stem. In effect she's saying "I'm (just) a meadow flower." Likewise, the "lily of the valley" is not the equivalent to our flower by the same name, but probably a crocus. Her two statements are parallel: "I'm just a meadow flower—a mere valley lily."

Her man's love has made her lose her inhibitions to the point that she admits the very things about which she is most self-conscious. This is a deep level of "knowing," and evidences what a safe place this relationship is for her. And notice his response: "Like a lily among the thorns, so is my darling among the maidens." Seizing the opportunity, he has taken the very thing that makes her feel less than beautiful and turns it into high praise: "You surpass the other young women to the degree that a valley lily surpasses a thorn."

Like this couple's, your intimacy can grow. You can grow in vulnerability, and in giving and receiving pleasure and affirmation. One wife explained how she was able to grow in responsiveness:

"One day on our honeymoon, I [Pam] had just stepped from the shower and, looking into the mirror, I began to criticize my body. [My husband] Bill was sitting on the bed, admiring his new wife. As I would comment on an area I thought needed improving, he would counter with how beautiful it was. This went on for a few minutes until he could stand it no longer. . . . He stood up, wrapped his arms around me, and told me to look straight into his eyes.

"I complied, intrigued by the mystery of what my new husband was up to. He very seriously and lovingly said, 'I will be your mirror. My eyes will reflect your beauty. You are beautiful, Pamela. You are perfect, and if you ever doubt it, come stand before me. The mirror of my eyes will tell you the true story. You are perfect for me.'

"Over the last fourteen years, whenever self-doubt was looming on the horizon, through three pregnancies and baby blues, my mirror has never stopped telling me how perfect I am for him. Because of his continual confidence-building, I have grown more sexually adventurous. In Bill's eyes I am beautiful, and in his arms I am safe."[16]

Does sex hurt the first time?

It might. In general, a woman's first time is more difficult than a man's, and sex for her may involve both discomfort and even a little bleeding if she has an intact hymen. This simply means she will require an extra measure of gentleness, and she needs to wait until she is extremely aroused before welcoming penetration so that her sensations of pleasure overpower any discomfort. Some birth control pills can reduce "wetness," so keep a lubricant handy.

While first-sex is often somewhat uncomfortable for women, it isn't always. Discomfort certainly is not unusual or abnormal in either gender. The man's pain is generally emotional and derives from not being nearly as "studly" or in control as he expected or hoped.

Know that cuddling afterward is of particular importance with virgins, both men and women, as those few moments of kindness and reassurance help to shape long-term attitudes about sex. For both partners, premarital evaluation and a discussion with a physician or nurse beforehand can help prevent surprises and decrease or even eliminate the possibility of pain. A woman can do exercises to stretch the hymen, which can significantly decrease the discomfort that she might experience as well as teach control of these important muscles.

Nervousness and anxiety can make muscles tense. The exercises in the workbook can teach a woman to relax, which will enable the muscles to reach the appropriate diameter. The "female on top" or on the side, where she can control entry of the penis and its rate and depth of penetration, can give her more control of what is comfortable as they physically adapt to one another.

Nevertheless, many women continue to have physical discomfort associated with penetration. The cause may be from the absence of one's own lubrication and elasticity, or from her husband's poor quality erections or too-quick ejaculations. If your pain continues throughout the honeymoon, seek medical advice sooner rather than later. Some honeymoons last three days to a week, which is too little time for the hymen to fully adjust. But if discomfort continues beyond several weeks, do seek help.

What should I expect the first time?

Anxiety, curiosity, and anticipation. Pain and pleasure. Possible disappointment. It's highly likely you'll have less of a life-changing, ecstatic experience than you may have anticipated. But you have a lifetime to perfect it. Remember, too, that the occasion truly is perfect in that the two of you are together. Avoid putting too much pressure on the "first time"; it could range from beef Wellington to McDonald's, from a magnificent love feast to an all-too-brief snack followed by a little confusion and some laughter.

You bring both history and experience to the occasion. Even if you're both virgins with a biblical view of sex, you probably won't have the best love life in the world right from the beginning. Keep a sense of humor and a heart of compassion, and you'll get off to a good start.

If you're having trouble with sex, should you go to a doctor, try new things, or go to a therapist?

When a couple has a less-than-ideal love life, it's often difficult to discern whether the problem is founded in skill, technique, lack of communication, or a physical problem. As mentioned, if sex is physically painful, seek immediate medical attention.

If your difficulty relates more to skill or communication, experiment in your lovemaking. Ask each other, "What appeals to you?" What do you wish he or she would do? What are some of your mate's unfulfilled fantasies? Set a time to try those things. Don't keep a score card, but have a goal of *gradual* progress. A sense of humor and a tender heart will go a long way toward developing a satisfying love life.

Later, be verbal about your experiences. That is, hold difficult evaluative conversations at times other than during the act of lovemaking itself. It's always appropriate, of course, to speak up in the moment if something hurts or if a practice or position is uncomfortable. But for more general matters—such as "here's what I'd like us to change"—hug, kiss, and say good night, then deal with it later, when you are not surrounded by the ambiance of nudity and a sense of failure.

Often couples find themselves in a downward spiral of frustration that leads to a conversation that includes crying or other release of emotions. Once relief comes, they feel better, but the sense of urgency is gone. With the urgency gone, though, the motivation to work out possible solutions to the problem sometimes disappears.

So determine to keep your motivation level high. Remember those things that you said you'd do. Next time, try to "knock his socks off" or "rock her world." Rather than acting like you're having a good time when you're only pretending, communicate what you want. Without honesty, it's extremely difficult for a couple's love life to improve. Habitual deception, in fact, keeps beneath the surface many problems that couples could otherwise resolve.

If you find you continue to need additional help, by all means seek medical attention. If tests reveal no medical problems, physicians can refer couples to other trained sources.

As you mature as a person and as a couple, your ability to give and receive physical love will grow. As Doug Rosenau so aptly puts it, "A mature companionship fashions itself after *redemption* in that you die to yourself and let go of any defensiveness. You create a bonded partnership in which you submit your will for the good of your mate. Your union is based on love and trust."[17]

Partnership. Union. Love. Trust. These are not the code words of a sex-saturated culture. Rather, they are the fruits of marital intimacy as God intended it in His perfect design. Knowing this, "know and be known." "Imbibe deeply, O lovers."

7

Questions About Varying Levels of Interest

On my bed night after night I sought him
Whom my soul loves;
I sought him but did not find him.
—SONG OF SOLOMON 3:1

- A forty-six-year-old, married for twenty years, complains she has no libido. She is told to find a new partner to rev her up.
- A thirty-four-year-old has an emergency hysterectomy and her sexual desire is scuttled by her ordeal. The advice to her? "Be grateful you're alive."
- A fifty-year-old on hormone replacement therapy with a declining sex drive is told that it's a normal part of getting older. "Get used to it."

Although sex is usually a source of pleasure, it can also be a cause for stress—and bad advice, as seen in these examples. For most couples, levels of interest and timing are often out of synch.

"The most romantic line I've ever heard came after a night of—how should we put this?—it was after a passionate interlude with my wife, a wife I had to convince to participate in the passionate interlude," actor Ray Romano said. "Afterward she turned to me and said with a very loving tone, 'That wasn't as bad as I thought it was gonna be.'"[1]

One husband approached his wife and handed her some aspirin for her headache. "I don't have a headache," she told him with a puzzled look. He said, "I've been waiting all week to hear you say that!"

The woman's "I've got a headache" syndrome is a sad reality for several reasons. First, as we've already mentioned, men's and women's bodies have different "timing" sexually. Also, some medications, including some birth control pills, may decrease libido.

But it's not just wives who always have lower desires than their husbands. Scantily clad in captivating attire, Debbie met her mate at the door. In her most seductive voice she told him she wanted to make his Monday night memorable. Yet he walked past her, turned on the television, and after quickly looking her over said, "Bring me a Coke and some pretzels, and I'll meet you at halftime."

According to a Journal of the American Medical Association survey of people ages eighteen to fifty-nine, about 43 percent of women and 31 percent of men suffer sexual difficulties for one reason or another. "For more than one-fifth of women the problem was low desire, while only one in twenty men had the same complaint."[2]

What should be done when he's in the mood for lovemaking and she isn't?

Why isn't she "in the mood"? Is it physical or psychological? Where is she in her menstrual cycle? Is there an underlying marital problem? Is there pain during intercourse? Is she annoyed with her man? Captivated by someone else?

After I spoke on marital intimacy, a couple told me they had been married for three years. The wife was postmenopausal, and she tore and bled every time they tried to have sex. Nothing can kill libido quite like pain. And because her husband loved her and didn't want her to hurt, he was trying not to think about sex.

Cases like this stem from physical causes and, of course, require medical attention. But in other cases, mood can often be generated through listening, affection, and sacrificial love. A woman's lack of excitement about the prospect of making love is understandable when you consider the amount of energy most women expend on work, housework, and kids. Wives often have little energy left for this "great experience" we've been describing.

Men, too, complain of fatigue from stress over juggling many demands and opportunities. Yet for them, sex often represents the "therapy," the escape. For women, sex generally requires considerably more concentration and energy. Consider the three to five minutes average for men to climax versus twenty to thirty minutes for women—perhaps the difference between grabbing a piece of apple pie from the fridge and having to take it from freezer to the oven before enjoying a bite.

A huge factor in having a robust love life boils down to priorities. What takes precedence? The immaculately clean house? Gourmet meals? Or erotic sex? What is most important to your spouse? Most men report that sex is number one. Most women report that their own primary needs are more closely related to having a partner who listens and converses intently. *Thus, many a loving spouse spends the most energy trying to demonstrate love with stuff that isn't a real priority for his or her mate. She wants soul communion; he wants physical consummation.*

For the typical woman, getting aroused sometimes is more a decision than a product of stimulation by her husband. So if she's decided she's uninterested, caressing her body will probably annoy her. If she's decided "yes," the same stimulation will usually arouse her.

First Corinthians tells us, though, that when we marry, husbands and wives relinquish solitary rights to their own bodies. (We explore this matter in detail in the chapter titled "A Call to Purity.") Thus, the spouse has a responsibility to meet his or her partner's ongoing sexual needs. It's important, then, for the spouse with the lower sex drive to recognize there are other reasons to initiate sex—closeness, comfort, and love, for example—besides the body's desire for it. Remember, too, while spontaneous episodes are great, most people have more fun and more active sex lives if they actually plan ahead for sex.

What if he has no interest?

The first question to ask is this: *Why* is he not in the mood? Medication? Low androgen levels? Other physical problems? His needs are being met elsewhere (internet or other relationships)? Psychological reasons? Is the lack of interest an ongoing problem or a momentary blip?

If he's tired or distracted, the situation calls for love and grace. If he's *always* distracted, if he's always tired, that's another matter entirely. One observation here: while women are generally unresponsive to tactile stimulation if they have not yet decided "yes" to sex, a man can more often be moved by an alluring wife who begins to caress him. But not always. One attractive patient of mine did all she could to get the attention of her husband, a colleague. Yet he was oblivious and uninterested. She was his "trophy," not his partner. Although he showered her with gifts and baubles, he wouldn't share what she desperately desired—himself.

As Paul wrote in 1 Corinthians 7, both partners have sexual needs that must be met. When those needs go unmet, temptation can gain a foothold. A husband who nurtures and cherishes his wife, as instructed in Ephesians 5, must find a way to meet that ongoing need. Lovemaking is not an optional activity for a growing believer in Christ, whether a husband or wife. But the frequency and degree of involvement must be a matter of mutual consent and satisfaction. And true intimacy, genuine lovemaking, to many wives is much more than the few moments of physical intercourse. Rather, lovemaking involves conversation, caring, compassion, and affectionate attention.

Does he really need sex as often as he asks for it?

Maybe you've heard the urban myth—the one that says men think about sex every seven seconds. It's not exactly true. Okay, it's actually not even close. But it sounds impressive!

The actual research—the most complete currently available—says "54% of men think about sex every day or several times a day, 43% a few times per month or a few times per week, and 4% less than once a month."[3] The same study found that unlike men, "19% of women think about sex every day or several times a day, 67% a few times per month or a few times per week, and 14% less than once a month."[4] Let's lay this out so it's easier to compare:

	Men	Women
Daily	54%	19%
Weekly/Monthly	43%	67%
Less	4%	14%

That's a pretty big gap. And it suggests that, in general, husbands are going to ask for sex more often than their wives do. Yet there's a difference between need and want. Imagine you're on a long trip. One of you has to use the bathroom and the other wants to stop for a burger. Bladder relief and hunger both qualify as needs. Yet at the moment, one is more pressing, more urgent (as in, "We need to find a rest stop *or else!*"). So it is with sexual appetite. His need can vary in its level of urgency.

Despite claims from lonely men and women, if anyone has ever died from lack of sex, it has never been documented in the medical literature. So it's a need, but not like the need for oxygen, or food, or sleep. (Just as a point of information, if a young man neither masturbates nor has sexual relations, he'll have a nocturnal emission [ejaculation] approximately every three to six weeks.) Still, if you feel hungry and you miss breakfast, you'll scope out the possibilities for food nonstop until lunch. If you get turned down for lunch, you'll keep trying until dinnertime. The same is true of sex.

A patient of mine once whined that her husband was always after her for sex. She said, "He probably asks a hundred times a day."

"How often do you say yes?" I asked.

"Never."

When I let the silence speak for itself, she dropped her head and quickly changed the subject.

In your own marriage, if it's *no* far more often than *yes*, you have a foundational problem you need to explore. This is a symptom of an underlying difficulty. If it's existed for a long time, it may be harder to unravel and rebuild. But don't give up or accept this sad state. Seek help.

Probably the most common sexual problem of this sort is that she thinks he has a one-track mind while he thinks she's insensitive, selfish, and uninterested. She wonders if he's perverted; he asks why she refuses to "give it up," since it doesn't cost her anything. Some spouses put this disparity in desire to unfortunate use as a manipulation issue: "I'll give it to you if you mow the lawn," or ". . . if you stop watching TV sports." She knows if she meets his need at the right time, she can get what she wants in return, so sex becomes a means of gaining leverage.

The wife may ask herself, "How can I use this powerful, even irresistible, weapon to achieve a goal?" Her manipulation can lead to glorified begging on his part, which erodes the fragile framework of oneness and intimacy. The result? You'll have a man who asks one hundred times in the hope of hearing an occasional "yes," married to a wife who complains to her doctor that her husband is always after her for sex.

So commit to each other that you'll never use sex as a bargaining chip. Otherwise, as in many households, it becomes a weapon, a commodity, rather than the pleasurable, unifying gift that God intended.

I overheard one of my nurses counseling a young wife about this. "Every time he asks you and you're not driving down the highway, say *yes!* Take ten minutes to swarm all over him, overwhelm him, *take* him. Leave him a heaving breathless mass of quivering gelatin on the mattress. He'll be blissed out, and you can get back to what you were doing. He may even do anything you ask for a month—after he wakes up! You'll spend longer than that arguing about it."

In a healthy marriage, this is good advice.

To the men who frequently get "turned down," I would say this: in the Old Testament the phrase "live with" often carries the idea of "have sexual intercourse with." (See Gen. 20:3; also Deut. 22:13; 24:1; and 25:5.) Peter borrows this idea when he tells husbands to live with their wives in "an understanding way," which implies acquiring knowledge and insight through a process of personal investigation. With this in mind, consider how we might read 1 Peter 3:7–9: "Husbands, likewise, approach sexual relations with your wives in a way that is based on insight gathered from personal investigation of her needs, not returning evil for evil, or insult for insult, but giving a blessing instead; for you were called for the very purpose that you might inherit a blessing."[5]

How do I "get creative"?

Many of us get into an unfortunate butler/maid sort of mentality. We share a bed, we share a closet, perhaps a kitchen. He has his duties of bringing home a check, taking out the garbage, and keeping the car maintained. She has her duties of all the inside-the-home stuff, possibly in addition to a career outside the home. Sex becomes another chore, another duty, part of being married. It's dull. Boring. Another job, when it's supposed to be exhilarating and intoxicating.

So start with an attitude check. Do you tend to roll your eyeballs when you see couples acting romantic? Do you think, "Ha! Just wait. They'll get over it"? We should feel ashamed if we laughed at that crack. Consider how the lover in Song of Solomon talks to his beloved (7:3–4):

> Your two breasts are like two fawns,
> Twins of a gazelle.
> Your neck is like a tower of ivory,
> Your eyes like the pools in Heshbon
> By the gate of Bath-rabbim.

Can you imagine a tower of ivory? No such thing has ever existed, as far as we know. It would be too expensive. And the lover says no amount of money could replace her. She's so beautiful, she's a tourist attraction!

Heshbon was a busy city. And to that man his partner's eyes sparkled like pools of water in a city teeming with vendors, providing for him a retreat from the life-in-the-fast-lane world. In her he found an oasis. Do you have this attitude too?

Next, ask yourself what you can do to draw the five senses into your lovemaking. Powders, scented sheets, body lotion, incense, bubble bath? *Smell*—although the least studied of the senses, probably because it is most difficult to measure—*is the most memory-sensitive sense*. Research has established that female sensitivity to male pheromones (scented sex hormones) is ten thousand times stronger during ovulation than during menstruation.[6] So, men, especially at her mid-cycle—but really *any* time—don't come to bed smelling like unwashed sweaty socks, three-day-old fish, or two-cycle motor oil.

One husband reported that when he was away from his wife on a business trip, he smelled her perfume on someone in a store. He subtly followed the fragrance for ten minutes, just for a "reminder whiff." A physician who investigated sexual responses and their link to smell did so after realizing that nearly one-quarter of forty-six patients who had lost their sense of smell as a result of head injuries also developed some sexual dysfunction.[7]

Next, consider your surroundings. Where do you most frequently make love? If you're like most people, the place that comes to mind is the bedroom. (If you immediately thought of the living room couch or in a tent in the back yard, you may need less help here.) What can you do to your bedroom to express your love, rather than making it the room where all the spare stuff gets stored? One newlywed couple struggling to pay bills reported that they bought a lovely bedroom suite with their wedding money. Rather than decorating the rest of the house first, they wanted to make their bedroom the most beautiful room in the house. "Our parents thought we were impractical," they shared, laughing. "And they were right!"

"Turning your bedroom into a no-stress zone is simple," writes Karen Scalf Linamen in *Pillow Talk*. She continues:

> The idea is to intentionally design a relaxing environment that is off-limits to many of the stresses and distractions that

define your waking hours. Begin with aesthetics, making an effort to keep your bedroom neat and attractive. In other words, aim for *Southern Living* in your private quarters even if the rest of your house looks like *Mechanics Weekly*. Then begin to work on behaviors, keeping your bedroom off-limits to activities other than sleeping, relaxing, or making love. Nix the stacks of unpaid bills, piles of dirty laundry, collections of unread newspapers, and file folders from the office. By fostering this kind of space, seemingly untouched by the nitty gritty of daily life, you will have created a quiet haven where—by simply stepping inside and closing the door behind you—you can take a mini-vacation from stress. This time can then be used to pray, to relax, or to lavish your undivided romantic attentions on your husband.[8]

Ask yourself what you can do to create atmosphere. Can you change rooms? Add music? Use special sheets? Add candles or special lighting? Go outside? In Song of Solomon 7, the young woman speaks of "getting together" out in the vineyard!

What you wear is also important. Not every woman feels comfortable baring her back end in a thong the size of dental floss. And not every man wants to show up in the bedroom wearing a Speedo (nor does his wife necessarily want him to). But showing up in a pair of oversized "buy 'em by the three-pack" undergarments that could substitute as a parachute doesn't exactly communicate, "I want to rock your world."

A woman can accentuate nice legs in a baby-doll or short chemise (a straight gown that clings to her shape). Or she can play up good cleavage with a bustier (elongated bra, often strapless) or halter. Maybe her main asset is toned arms, shown off well in a camisole—a sleeveless top—with matching panties.

Most people look good in black and white (or ivory). Pastels work well for blondes, while brunettes can carry off bolder purples and deep greens. A redhead does better with blues, greens, and earth tones. And as you're buying lingerie, remember the sense of touch.

Satin and silk feel good—on both men and women. Velvet is nice, too. Or if you're going for comfort, look for a cotton tank top or bikini.

Next, consider your words. As one husband has observed, "Making love with words is essential to the continuation of exciting sexual lovemaking." Notice that the couple in Song of Solomon is quite vocal in describing one another's charms and what they desire. Get verbal. If it is difficult for you to express your thoughts and feelings, begin by reading Song of Solomon to each other (4:1):

> How beautiful you are, my darling,
> How beautiful you are!
> Your eyes are like doves behind your veil;
> Your hair is like a flock of goats
> That have descended from Mount Gilead.

On the first reading, these words may seem less than flattering. But think about the shepherd who speaks these words. He looked across the hills and saw a flock of goats coming down in streams. He then saw his beloved's hair coming down in tresses. This is important, because Jewish women wore their hair up. She is showing him something reserved only for him. What pet phrases flatter your spouse? Study him or her and express yourself.

What about time? You have to stop and plan to date. Most couples when they're first going out spend (at least) from 6:30 to midnight on Saturday nights. When they get married, they're fortunate to get fifteen minutes of quality time together every week. Making time for each other is a matter of priority.

Here are some other suggestions:

- Write a love letter and mail it to home or office.
- Prepare your beloved's favorite meal.
- Arrange a special evening out.
- Purchase something frivolous that your spouse wouldn't buy for him- or herself.

- Save up to surprise your spouse with a special trip together.
- Take a walk together. Hold hands.
- Check into a hotel for one night each quarter.
- Meet for a romantic lunch during the workday.
- If you have kids, trade babysitting with another couple, so both can have a romantic night.
- Lay out a blanket in the back yard—or the living room—and have a picnic.
- Create your own list.

Where does oneness come in, or does it?

As one newlywed wife reported, "I want it to feel like 'in the moment' we are emotionally connecting. He tells me that he feels 'connected' *after* he's satisfied."

Orgasm is, after all, a rather self-focused event that does not direct our attention outwardly to the relationship "in the moment." God designed us that way. It's normal, even necessary to focus on one's own pleasurable sensations for much of the time during lovemaking. Think of it this way: when your man brings you Godiva chocolates, you enjoy the wonderful taste for yourself. Part of his pleasure is seeing you enjoy it.

Part of the pleasure during lovemaking involves the desire to satisfy one's spouse. But ultimately, "getting there"—if you choose to pursue orgasm—requires concentrating on your own pleasurable sensations. If you both want to experience orgasm, consider making it your goal to have "two shining moments" rather than one grand simultaneous one. If he feels connected after intercourse, and you want to feel connected "in the moment," take turns. Satisfy him first. Many textbooks on sex emphasize the orgasmic simulcast—or simultaneous orgasms. Yet as one husband shared, "For me to get the 'rhythm' right for her enjoyment, I have to sacrifice some of my own enjoyment. For us it works better to each have two separate moments of intense pleasure—one when we focus on our own sensations and one when we enjoy the fact that we're bringing pleasure to the other."

Everyone is different, and as we've seen, men and women can be very different. Ultimately, each couple has to work out what it looks like for them to love and be loved.

Where does God come into the experience itself?

Having a biblical view of sex is not the same as thinking about the Bible while you're "in the act." Sexual union in marriage can honor God and be a worshipful experience, but that doesn't mean a couple has to be meditating on the Levitical sexuality laws to experience "oneness." Nowhere in the biblical literature do we find that a couple has to be thinking about God or spiritual concepts during lovemaking. In Proverbs 5:18–19 we read this:

> Let your fountain be blessed,
> And rejoice in the wife of your youth.
> As a loving hind and a graceful doe,
> Let her breasts satisfy you at all times;
> Be exhilarated always with her love.

God encourages his children to express physical love, and certainly couples derive at least some benefit in knowing they have God's approval. Sex within marriage glorifies God. He created our sexuality, and when expressed in accordance with His will within marriage, our pleasure is within His plan and purpose. As Colossians instructs us, we should do all for the glory of God. Although sex may be an experience like "the end of the world as we now know it," the time to ponder your theology of the end times (or any other thoughts that take away from focusing on your beloved) is not while engaged in the throes of passion.

Couples experiencing difficulties often find it healing to pray before and after their times together, and we certainly recommend this. One wife shared, "We were having some trouble, and it was painful emotionally for both of us. So beforehand we prayed, asking God to help us. It's wonderful to think that God cares about this area of our lives and we can ask for His help together. It brought peace out of anxiety."

Both our love lives and our prayer lives reveal how we handle intimate relationships; the two are linked. Sexuality is a huge part of the spiritual journey. Many who consider themselves spiritually mature act immature in their approach to lovemaking. They're selfish, impatient, demanding, even manipulative. Or, because they feel little sex drive themselves, they ignore the biblical imperatives to meet the other partner's needs. Considering how much God has to say and how much He cares about our physical bodies, it's vitally important that we demonstrate godly love and seek His help in this as in all other areas.

Childlike playfulness in the bedroom is one thing; childishness is entirely different. It's important to keep the "fun" of the experience as God created it for couples to "delight" in. The idea is for *both* husband and wife to have a pleasurable interlude.

Why can't my husband be physically affectionate without making a sexual move?

Your husband *can* be affectionate without making a move. Really, he can. But God has wired him in such a way that physical affection often brings arousal. And he'll probably assume that if he's interested and aroused, you are, too.

"I feel like we have a third person in our relationship—my husband, me, and sex," Dennae shared. "Sex is this presence that always looms. My man is so easily stimulated that anything remotely sensual makes him 'head down that path.'" Another wife complained, "I can't be 'nice' to my husband without him interpreting my show of kindness as an invitation to the Romper Room, the booty call, the Magic Mountain."

Express to him how important it is to you to be cuddled without its having to "go somewhere." And remind him continually—because in his mind each time may be a "new time," and probably *this* time you want sex. This will surprise, even stun, the average man, but he can learn. Both husband and wife can learn—so be willing to study how each is wired. You might warn him in advance with, "Remember, I need affection without expectation." He may need reminders, not because he's insensitive to your needs, but because what comes naturally for him is so different from what comes naturally for you. He probably has about fifteen times more testosterone running through his veins than you do. Many women do not realize that God made most men in such a way that, under normal circumstances, they desire a sexual release quite frequently. In the same way that you wonder why he can't keep his hands off you even while he's passing you in the kitchen, he probably can't understand why you don't feel the same way—seeing you, as he does, through the fog of testosterone.

Unfortunately, some men show a selfish affection, being tender in words and gestures only when they want sex. Yet the desire for cuddling without sex is legitimate. Relational intimacy is grounded in conversation, and emotional closeness in a marriage is as important as sex. It matters deeply to a wife that her husband loves her mind, heart, and interests as much as he loves her body.

Ordinarily, one partner has a strong need for either physical or relational intimacy, and the spouse has the counterpart. Each, though, should be sacrificially trying to meet the valid, vital need of the other. Both parts of the intimacy equation should be cultivated by every couple interested in developing a deeper, more meaningful relationship.

Every time my husband sets up a special night out, I feel like he's manipulating me to get sex.

One couple recounted this conversation:

HIM: "Let's go out Saturday night."
HER: "Sounds great."
HIM: "What do you want to do?"
HER: "I don't know. I thought you might have something in mind."
HIM: "No, not really. A movie? Dinner? What would you like?"
HER: "How about both?"

HIM: "Okay. And when we get home?"

HER: "We'll see . . ."

HIM: "What do you mean by that?"

HE THINKS: *She never wants to make love. I get my hopes up, and pow. Maybe later, maybe not. Makes me think she doesn't even like sex. Why do I feel guilty for wanting sex with my wife?*

SHE THINKS: *He always thinks of sex first. I feel like a prostitute: How about a movie and dinner in exchange for sex? Does there always have to be a sexual motivation to spend time with me?*

For many, if not most, men, "special night" translates into "manspeak" as "sexual encounter somewhere during the evening." For many, if not most, women, "special night" means affection and emotional connection. Neither is wrong; yet without their mutual understanding, such "specials" may drive them apart rather than drawing them together.

The couple described needs to discuss why one feels manipulated and why they have unequal levels of interest. It may be the way God designed them. But they may also have unresolved issues that need attention.

In one of the places where the apostle Paul gives instructions about sex, he said the decision should be mutual (see 1 Cor. 7:5). He assumes couples will have some differences, but in the spirit of Christian unity they can work it out so both feel loved and both love sacrificially. Marriage is not just to make us as happy as children with cotton candy; it's also designed to mature us.

My husband told me he gets aroused several times during the day when he sees women other than me. Should I be worried?

Probably not. But it depends on how far he allows his mind and actions to go. How aroused does he get? Does he have a fleeting thought, such as, "My, that woman is attractive" or the fixating thought, "That woman is attractive, and I must have her" with an accompanying erection? The first is normal; the second is sinful. He should be trying to rein in such thoughts. He may need the help of a cold shower or an accountability partner, but he *can* control those kinds of musings.

Wives sometimes feel dismayed over their husbands' ability to become sexually aroused by other women. Such arousal is, however, a normal male response. Arousal doesn't mean much to a man. It certainly doesn't have to mean he desires a *relationship* with that woman. Sometimes he experiences arousal when, in fact, he doesn't want to. It's possible to feel the physical sensation of arousal without even engaging in an actual specific sexual thought, although a thought or visual stimulus usually triggers it. Sometimes it occurs spontaneously without a trigger (as it does the *entire year* following puberty for boys!). A woman is often physically aroused by men other than her husband, yet she may remain unaware of her own response.

Is it okay to fantasize?

Here's a little of what we know about fantasies:

- About 96 percent of people fantasize.[9]
- The Romantic Fantasy is women's number one fantasy. This is the fantasy of loving someone and being loved in return. Women's fantasies tend to be more emotional and romantic than men's.[10]
- Men's sexual fantasies tend to be more sexually explicit than women's.[11]

The answer to the question "Is it okay to fantasize?" depends on, as with the last question, what you mean. There's a difference between fantasy and lust. If you mean thinking of an adulterous relationship to help you get or stay excited, no, it's not okay. But if you're thinking about your spouse and allow your imagination to run with some new ideas, it's probably okay. Why do you need to fantasize? Are you unsatisfied in some way? Are you using fantasy as a form of denial or avoidance? Is there something you and your sweetheart need to discuss? Or are you like many who, in the midst of lovemaking, find your vision limited to a small segment of the pillow or the top of your beloved's head? In such a case, if you "imagine" your breathtaking spouse, that's surely an acceptable fantasy.

A fantasy involving someone other than your spouse, though, may be an expression of resentment toward your spouse. If so, talking with your wife or husband and a trained pastor or counselor about the actual source of your resentment is probably the loving thing to do.

Sexual fantasies are designed to meet some need. Often women's magazines run articles on how to "get more interested" with tips such as "watch an X-rated film together," or "read a pornographic novel," or "masturbate," or "imagine an extramarital affair." These are all wrong because they encourage sin in "fantasy worlds." Yet each of these is on-target in starting with the mind as a sexual tool. In Philippians 4, Paul tells us to think about *good* things. So think romantic thoughts. Concentrate on remembering intimate times together, what you love about him, and what is right with her. From there, plot ways to be creative in your lovemaking.

In terms of fantasizing while making love, one man wrote, "I never fantasize that I'm with someone else, but I may fantasize that my wife has a smaller waist. I may fantasize that she has long hair instead of short hair. Those images help me get aroused and make orgasm that much better." Mentally changing your spouse, however, even if only for the purpose of arousal, seems potentially dangerous in that you are expressing your love to that which is not real. In this context, the desire to fantasize may signal a need to talk together.

Most people do fantasize during sex. Some couples report enjoying the process of "going on a fantasy together." If you're comfortable with it, talk to each other during sex: "Imagine we're on a beach in Hawaii . . ."

Who decides when to have sex? The man or the woman?

Some have the idea that the man always has to initiate love-making. Psychiatrists have observed that in a maturing marriage, the wife feels the necessary freedom to initiate more frequently as the marriage relationship grows. Either partner should feel free to initiate when desire develops and "the heat is on." As mentioned, when the apostle Paul spoke of marital sex, he assumed Christ-following couples could make mutual agreements. Unity here is the goal.

The declaration of interest does not always take place verbally. The wife taking a bath at night when she normally showers in the morning could be a "clue." A husband shaving at 10:30 PM (why else would a man shave at 10:30?) or offering, "I'll put the kids to bed if you want to slip into something *less* comfortable" might be his way of communicating desire. You might send a signal with lingerie hung on the door handle, lipstick on the mirror, a lit candle. Be prepared, though—at least occasionally—for such nonverbal clues to be missed, possibly causing feelings of rejection. Only God can read minds. Many men are chromosomally challenged in that they cannot take hints. And when they give hints, they are so obscure as to challenge the most intuitive sleuth.

Also, agree on a gracious way to decline, with a promise to "connect" in the near future. Sometimes there may be reasons to say "not now," and learning to do that in a way that doesn't hurt or offend can take some skill. And it should be the exception, not the rule.

How do I satisfy my husband?

Ask him! Communicate. Find out what his desires are and, as far as you are comfortable, fulfill them. Find out what he likes and doesn't like. What's his favorite environment? What time is best? Is place important? What sort of visual stimulus works best? Get specific about actual activities. This goes for husbands asking wives, too. Don't try to read your partner's mind. Have him or her tell you or perhaps write a wish list, and you do the same.

Communicate, but not necessarily "during the act." As we've said, timing of conversation is important. *How* you do so is also important. Often adults communicate about sex by pouting, mop-ing, withholding, acting petty, and generally behaving like children. Others have discovered that once they stopped resisting adventure, their partners realized that rug burns were less comfortable than mattresses with nice sheets after all.

Realize, though, that it's not your *duty* to satisfy him any more than it is his *duty* to satisfy you. Although part of your marriage com-mitment is to be available to meet sexual needs (see 1 Cor. 7:3), you can't force someone else's *satisfaction*. To some degree your partner's satisfaction is out of your control. While you should *desire* to satisfy your spouse, you cannot control his concentration or participation, nor he yours. If you feel anger, fatigue, or distraction, it may be im-possible for even the most attentive spouse to "satisfy" you and vice versa. Ultimately, you satisfy each other by being satisfied, rather than by merely tolerating the act of regularly lending your bodies to each other. Although marriage partners should desire to satisfy each other, it's the individual spouse who decides when he or she is satisfied. You can't force it. Satisfaction may differ for each of you.

In general, be an active rather than a passive partner. Don't assume a lack of vaginal lubrication means a lack of interest or responsive-ness. Don't tolerate painful sex—get help. And don't feel you must have an orgasm to be satisfied yourself. For a woman, satisfaction may or may not include a desire to experience orgasm—or multiple orgasms.

What are the most common sexual difficulties?

Talking about sex. Sex is the *number one subject* couples have trouble discussing. Some studies reveal that half of all American marriages are troubled by some form of sexual distress ranging from lack of interest and boredom to outright sexual dysfunction. The sexual problems people tell about most frequently have to do with lack of desire, inhibitions and guilt, performance problems, abuse, disease, depression, and anxiety. Probably the most common physi-cal problem for men is premature ejaculation (which we'll discuss in the next chapter). Some of the most common *relational* issues that damage sexual love are selfishness, fear of vulnerability, treating one's spouse as a sex object, anger, and control or dominance.

We often see a wife who is unenthusiastic, content with a rather regimented routine. The husband generally wants more adventure. One wife shared, "I didn't realize my husband thought we were stuck in a rut. But I asked him if he was happy, and he told me nicely that he was rather bored. I was surprised because I was thinking we had a great love life. I asked him to get specific about what he wanted, and then I tried to meet his desires. After many years together, we're both finding renewed passion."

8
Questions About Orgasm

Let his left hand be under my head
And his right hand embrace me.
—SONG OF SOLOMON 2:6

What is an orgasm?

My husband and I (Sandi) were sitting in a church staff meeting listening to the pastor share his thoughts on how the church is not an organization but an organism—a living, growing entity. A college student who had just joined the youth staff raised his hand. "I am little confused," he said. "Can you explain that again—how the church is like an orgasm?"

A young, single girl in my (Dr. Bill's) sexuality class asked, "What is an orgasm?" So while it may be obvious to many of our readers, perhaps an explanation is in order.

In the context of sex, orgasm or "climax" is the "peak of sexual excitement, characterized by strong feelings of pleasure and by a series of involuntary contractions of the muscles of the genitals, usually accompanied by the ejaculation of semen by the male."[1]

What is an orgasm supposed to feel like?

Asking what an orgasm feels like is a little like asking, "What does the color green look like?" or "What does a banana taste like?" The best we can offer is a general description. It's probably safe to say it is supposed to feel good, although sensations of pain and pleasure are so closely related in our bodies that a few people have trouble distinguishing between the two. Judging by your partner's facial expressions and sounds at the height of sexual pleasure, you may, in fact, wonder whether he or she is in agony or ecstasy.

Both men and women report a broad spectrum of sensations, including increased heart and respiration rates, swelling erectile tissues, moistening internal structures, pelvic muscle spasms, "loss of control," and a mellow "glow" afterward brought about by a release of chemical substances called endorphins. But many variables affect the experience. If you ranked every experience from one to ten depending on many factors, most would fall short of absolute perfection, especially if we use for a standard the experiences shown on TV and in movies.

A woman may have an orgasm but wonder, "Is *that* what that was? I'm not sure." A husband may describe his own orgasm in such incredible terms ("Wow, it was the ultimate!") that his wife can't help but think, *That's not exactly my experience.* Dana shared, "I read that on average, a man usually rates his marriage four points higher than his wife does. I'm guessing the same may be true of their sexual experiences."

Several factors can contribute to the degree of intensity experienced from one orgasm to the next. For example, many men who wait more than several days between "encounters" tend to experience a higher degree of physical sensation and relief, in part because the ejaculation spasms may be greater in number and intensity. Also, an extended amount of foreplay can add to the amount of pleasure. In one sense, age can be a negative contributor, as the intensity of sensation and force of ejaculation decreases gradually over time. Yet couples in their fifties, sixties, seventies, and beyond have described quite satisfactory sexual experiences. While some changes occur as we mature, time, patience, tenderness, commitment, and genuine love developed over a lifetime can make intimacy deeper and more delightful with the passing seasons of life.

Ultimately, orgasm is meant to be extremely pleasurable. God created us to enjoy intense physical pleasure. He designed the system, the muscles, the endorphins—the entire sexual response is a gift we can enjoy immensely, in the proper context.

Him: What am I doing wrong? My wife is not experiencing orgasm.
Her: Why am I unable to reach orgasm? What do you suggest?

In the most definitive study yet done with Christians (female Christians report higher levels of satisfaction than women in the population at large), men and women showed significant gaps in their reporting the "absence of orgasm":

Age	Women	Men
18–29	26%	7%
30–39	28%	7%
40–49	22%	9%
50–59	23%	9%

And the priority in intimacy for most women turns out to be something other than physical release:

- 80%   rather have physical closeness than orgasm
- 70%   rather have emotional closeness than orgasm
- 53%   want time together
- 40%   desire physical release

The research also tells us this about women and orgasm:

- 26%   have difficulty reaching orgasm
- 25%   achieve orgasm "always"
- 33%   achieve orgasm 75% of the time
- 15%   achieve orgasm 50% of the time
- 10%   never experienced orgasm[2]

If you're in that last group of about 10 percent of married women—and the statistics on that are the same for both Christians and unbelievers—consider discussing with your husband the choice to manually explore and stimulate your body to learn what sensations you like. You might first learn those sensations yourself while taking a bath. Pour in lots of bubble bath if you feel uncomfortable watching yourself. Once you've learned what you like, teach your husband what, where, and how to touch you. Guide him through the process. We include such a self-exploration exercise in the workbook section.

If the anatomy is normal, the appropriate stimulation over a sufficient amount of time will generally succeed. Some report that spraying warm water on the clitoris helps to relax muscles and can aid in pleasurable sensations.

Vibrators, which are readily available through mail order and on the Internet, may help, too (more on the ethics of this later). It's probably better to use natural stimulation, as the intense, unique sensation of a vibrator cannot be matched by the sensations of manual stimulation or intercourse. And some couples report developing a dependence on vibrators that they regret. Still, if the wife finds she cannot experience orgasm without one, a couple might opt to use it until she becomes familiar with the sensations leading to orgasm.

You might try changing to a position that allows more direct clitoral stimulation. For example, usually the wife receives inadequate stimulation when her husband enters her from behind, although he is then free to caress the clitoral area with his hands. Often she receives more stimulation of her clitoris if she sits astride him during intercourse. If she's on top, she may want him to shift his body slightly toward her feet or toward her head to give sufficient clitoral stimulation for climax.

Many wives, however, find direct stimulation uncomfortable. For such a woman, it may help during the initial stage of lovemaking to straddle her husband's leg apart from intercourse so she can control the level of pressure without direct stimulation. She may later proceed to lie on him with his penis between her legs but not in her vagina, allowing it to stimulate her clitoris rhythmically. Another suggestion is that she try altering her body position by placing a pillow under her buttocks. Couples can try a variety of positions that free their hands, allowing manual stimulation during intercourse.

Be sure that she is getting stimulation for a long enough period. Three to five minutes is generally not enough. As we said earlier, most women need an average of ten to fifteen minutes, or even more, of uninterrupted clitoral stimulation to reach orgasm. If you've been "simmering" in the context of all-day affection, it may take less than ten minutes. But often it takes longer.

One reader wrote this: "If he can't get his hand in a good position, the *wife* can put *her* hand there. I have been doing this since the first year we've been married, and it's the only way I can climax *during* intercourse (which I usually do strive for because *I* enjoy it.)"

This brings us to another concern. The greatest sexual complaint of women is the inability to have orgasms during intercourse. Up to 70 percent of women share this problem. Manual and oral stimulation are also options for many couples. Discover what works best through trial and retrial. Keep trying, but don't force the issue. If you tell yourselves, "This has to be the night," you'll probably set yourselves up for failure.

Not all women even want to achieve orgasm. It involves a degree of "loss of control" or surrender that many would rather not experience, particularly if the relationship is shaky. Yielding can be scary. It also takes more energy and concentration than some women feel like expending. And she may feel sexually satisfied without experiencing climax.

If she's trying but having difficulty, however, she can begin by asking herself if anything is distracting her or is unpleasant to her. Is something breaking the rhythm of physical sensation, such as an abrupt move from manual stimulation to vaginal intercourse at the last moment? (This is where constantly striving for the goal of simultaneous orgasm can take away from an otherwise great sexual experience.) Is her husband ejaculating before she's ready? The two must communicate about the right rhythm and pressure to get to the right places. No guessing!

Anatomical problems, fear, past negative sexual experiences, guilt over illicit relationships, and negative teaching about sex can all contribute to problems in her reaching orgasm. In the absence of these difficulties, however, if given the right stimulation and sufficient time, it will probably happen. Remember, though, that orgasm is an involuntary response. It can't be forced, and the harder you "try," the less likely you may be to "succeed." So with the goal of sexual pleasuring, relax and allow the sensations to grow.

Should I signal my partner that I'm about to climax?

If it enhances the experience for your beloved, certainly you should signal you're gearing up for the big-thunderclap ending. And who wouldn't want to know that his or her partner was gearing up for a grand finale? Anticipation is part of the pleasure. Generally the rhythmic thrusting, heavy breathing, soft moaning, and intensity of the motion will provide the necessary clues, but words can be gratifying and erotic. No need to scream it loudly enough to scandalize the neighbors. Through properly chosen words or uttering your partner's name, you can express an enthusiastic sense of urgency.

How do I communicate, "I don't like that; please try something else"?

Guiding your partner's hand to the right spot is probably better than employing the verbal instructions—"move to the left; no, no down; now up a little"—that we might use when getting a back rub. Be positive, gently directing the activity by moving your own body or your partner's, and with positive vocal reinforcement such as "Wow, that's it. That's great. Oh my . . ." That will permanently etch the activity on your spouse's mind.

For more detailed help, most partners prefer a straightforward discussion after the fact. Conversations about sexual technique are often less threatening outside of the context of the moment. A statement such as, "You're doing it wrong!" made while engaged in the act itself will no doubt abruptly short-circuit any energy and enjoyment present in the encounter. It's better to wait an hour or two, then evaluate what happened: "I liked this. I didn't like that. That was too hard, too soft, too fast." Most couples have difficulty discussing these things openly, but it's important to get the words out. So gently, but clearly, tell it like it is. Assume that if your partner does something you don't like, he or she was trying to please you. Clarify, remind, redirect. Work it out with a sense of anticipation and excitement that the next time will be more fun—and soon.

If you feel too inhibited to talk about sex and you're uncomfortable writing out your thoughts, consider looking up Bible verses about sex and discussing them. (We list some in the workbook.) But somehow find a way to break the ice.

Of course the extreme here is saying, "Honey, you're a lousy lover. Try pretending I'm actually here and alive." Men and women are unanimous in expressing that they want "corrective" information to be delivered kindly. "When he told me I didn't know how to do oral sex, I never did it again," one wife shared. Even oral sex is a skill to be learned for those who are interested.

Know that anything that seems like criticism can destroy confidence to the point that it inhibits the relationship. So be very kind.

What do I need to know about oral sex?

First, make certain you understand both your own and your partner's feelings about even engaging in oral sex. If you both feel comfortable with it, know that the basic disparity between a man's single-orgasm physiology and a woman's ability to have multiples is why a good lead-in to genital sex for many couples is often sustained oral sex. A woman who has had one or several orgasms via oral stimulation—or even if she feels sexually satisfied without orgasm—may be thrilled that her husband doesn't take long to climax during intercourse.

Pay attention to your partner's preferences here. A woman may like it but want extremely light simulation, so the wise husband starts light and slow. He should wait to crank up the intensity until she discovers where she responds best. At the early stages of arousal, or if she's having trouble getting or staying aroused, direct tongue stimulation of the clitoris may feel unbearably intense. It's best to arrive there gradually and stop immediately if it seems to bother her. She can cradle his head with her hands and give guidance as to location and pressure.

The wife who has been satisfied through oral sex should consider returning the favor with some hearty fellatio (wife to husband) just before genital sex—again, assuming both consider that a pleasurable activity. Because he has focused on giving pleasure, he may have lost a bit of his arousal, and both may enjoy a firmer penis if he receives oral pleasure before genital consummation. Then again, if she has been quite responsive to oral sex, he may be highly aroused by her response and ready immediately to "become one." The key, as usual, is gentle communication.

What "technique" your beloved may prefer is quite individual. You might ask your partner to demonstrate what he or she desires with lips on fingers or breasts to show what feels right. It may help to know that for men the "corona," or ridge, forming the head of the penis, is loaded with nerve fibers, whereas the shaft isn't.

My wife doesn't get very lubricated. Does this mean she isn't enjoying lovemaking much?

Not at all. Lubrication is not necessarily an indication of her level of enjoyment. Other factors besides her degree of excitement may play a role here, including individual anatomy, hormones, age, and even medication. If you would like more lubrication, consider using products such as Astroglide, K-Y Jelly, Maxilube, Sensilube, or Replens. Some lubricants are designed to be slathered in the vagina, some on the penis. Most you can use at both locations. Be sure to use enough.

One husband wrote, "If she isn't wet enough, it can be painful for her, and I don't get as much sensation. Then again, too much lubrication cuts down on sensation as well. So I'm careful not to use extra lubricant unless I have to. It's like cooking. You can always add more spices, but once they're in there . . ."

If the amount you use is more than you need, use less the next time. But over the course of even a few minutes, reapplication may be helpful. In fact it will probably be necessary if intercourse is repeated, or if the penis slips out and needs to be reintroduced. It's common for women on birth control pills, women who are nursing, and women in the perimenopausal or menopausal years to need lubrication in addition to what their bodies provide.

Do I have to achieve an orgasm?

No man has ever asked me this. But some women really don't find reaching climax worth the effort required—at least not always, as the statistics above demonstrate. Other women may be unable to reach orgasm because of anatomic reasons, or they may have reached it at times but feel content with sex without orgasm. Some husbands pressure their wives to climax. At this point it's time to reveal an important principle: whether or not she wants to try to achieve an orgasm is her decision. He must let her decide for herself when she's satisfied.

Some have attached the unfortunate label of "preorgasmic" to women who don't have orgasms, implying that they'll get there if they keep trying. That's fine if they want to. But consider the dogmatism of this statement: "The wife who never has experienced orgasm is being cheated out of normal sexual intercourse and needs to ask God for a wise counselor to help find the reason."[3] This attitude simply adds pressure to an already sensitive situation.

Another writes, "The husband is responsible to meet his wife's sexual needs. He must regularly and lovingly arouse her to a complete sexual experience, climax (or orgasm). Likewise, the wife must meet her husband's sexual needs. She must regularly and lovingly arouse him to a sexual experience, climax (or orgasm)."[4]

"Responsible to meet"? "Must . . . arouse"? These are strong words. We need to depressurize this situation, allowing more freedom for partners to express affection the way they want to. While it's important to satisfy your partner, your partner has the privilege and joy of determining when his or her own satisfaction is achieved.

Not every intimate encounter must by necessity end with an orgasm. Remember what the studies cited above told us? Only 25 percent of women experience orgasm whenever they make love. The added pressure to achieve multiple orgasms and/or simultaneous orgasm sets up a standard of success that guarantees frustration and failure for most people most of the time.

Imagine that you've cooked your beloved a nine-course meal. What if he or she is full after the fourth course? Must your partner be forced to "gorge" merely because you've prepared it? For whose pleasure have you prepared it, then?

One counselor has observed that, in his practice, women with an abundance of energy usually choose to climax whenever they make love. Low-energy women or those who feel exhausted at the end of a hard day may choose not to. Yet men almost always choose to, probably because it requires so little additional time and effort—that is, at least, while they're young. But men in their forties and fifties often begin to experience difficulties with erection and ejaculation.

In a giving sexual relationship, both partners will take differences into account. The kind husband will not put pressure on his wife to climax because it may be more enjoyable for her not to have one. Yet if she would like to, he should provide the additional time and effort required.

Again, statistics are only numbers. You are you. Learn what works best for the two of *you* and enjoy the journey of sharing life together.

Where is the G-spot and what is it?

The G-spot is named after gynecologist Ernst Grafenberg (1881–1957), who first put forth a theory concerning this. His theory was that a particularly sexually sensitive area exists within the vagina about halfway between the pubic bone and the cervix at the rear of the urethra. (Others have described its location as being "in the upper interior of the vagina, just beyond the PC muscle." Still another says, "In order to find it, one has to stimulate it; and to do just that, one has to find it!") Sometimes arousal and orgasm triggered in this way are accompanied by ejaculation of fluid through the urethra. This is called a "flooding response," or female ejaculation.

Several years ago at the Masters and Johnson Institute, a physician catheterized women who reported this response so that their urinary bladders were empty. The husbands then stimulated their wives to orgasmic response. When the doctors examined the fluid, it was not urine in chemical composition nor in appearance, even though it came from the urinary bladder.[5]

Some women—it's not clear what percentage, but probably less than 10 percent—do find this general area highly responsive to stimulation, reporting a deep, intense orgasm that occurs when it receives stimulation. Leading scientific papers still do not publish any related research, considering the whole concept "unscientific." So while it may be true that no scientifically verifiable G-spot exists, a particularly sensitive area *may* exist, and the release of fluid in some women is possible.

One husband described the technique that works best for him and his wife: "I insert two fingers into her vagina and rotate them from side to side very fast. Quite tiring, but it has the desired effect." A wife reported that she needed her husband to "tap" the top wall of her vagina. This tapping sensation stimulated the appropriate nerves that, she said, shook her world.

Just as there are a variety of responses to other "standard" erogenous zones, not every woman is particularly sensitive in this area. Yet some people go so far as to claim that "every woman has a G-spot." The proof may not be as important as private perception and preference.

Is it better for my wife to achieve orgasm while my penis is in her vagina or while I'm stimulating her clitoris more directly?

As mentioned, the inability to have orgasm during intercourse is a common complaint of women. Some studies report that as many as 70 percent of women need direct clitoral stimulation to respond with an orgasm. In other words, they find themselves unable to achieve orgasm during sexual intercourse from penetration and thrusting alone. Yet many couples believe that "real" orgasms have to happen during sexual intercourse. This erroneous thinking dates back to Freud, who described clitoral orgasms as "immature" and stated that the "mature" woman would reach a more satisfying release through vaginal penetration. The result of such thinking is that some women who could be at least *experiencing* orgasm are not doing so because they reach a certain point in their excitement level, their husbands enter them in order to pursue the so-called superior means, and the needed direct stimulation ceases. The nerve endings in the clitoris are located such a distance from the vagina that, for many women, intercourse in the "man on top" position won't do much.

So here's the answer to this question: Ask her what's better for her. Then strive to satisfy her the way she wants to be satisfied.

Should we make simultaneous orgasms our goal?

As if the pressure to have vaginal orgasms isn't enough, there's additional pressure to have simultaneous orgasms. What are the chances of simultaneous orgasm? Probably only 3 to 5 percent of couples experience simultaneous orgasm with any sort of regularity. So either something is wrong with our basic physiological design, or more than nine out of ten couples can't do "sex" right, or simultaneous orgasm is an unreasonable goal. Yet we found this information in a Christian sex manual: "[The plateau] phase should last long enough to bring you both to orgasm, usually simultaneously." Others suggested that within a few weeks of "trying hard," a majority of couples could "master this skill." Suggesting that couples should master any skill that requires controlling an involuntary response sets them up for frustration. Try timing your sneezes for the same moment and you get the idea.

As long as both husband and wife enjoy their physical relationship, it's unimportant whether they experience the "simulcast." One couple, who in their fifteen years together have experienced simultaneous climax three times, shared that each time it happened, they said, "Let's write to the people who wrote that sex manual telling us this would be the norm and tell them 'We finally got it.'"

If simultaneous orgasm happens, great; but don't lose energy and enjoyment striving for it. The waiting and waiting to get the timing perfect may produce a less-than-optimal orgasm for one or both because concentration is lost.

Is it always going to be better for him?

While young men rarely struggle with orgasmic response, women may have difficulty. Younger men more often have problems related to the "when" of their response, while their wives struggle with the "if." Men seem to be fairly similar in their orgasmic responses, while women's responses may differ not only from woman to woman but also in the same woman from one experience to the next. Women have the potential for multiple or sequential orgasms, but that actual orgasmic experience can vary from three to five contractions in a mild orgasm to eight to twelve in a more intense one. Also, whereas going a long time without sex will intensify the pleasure for most men, it often has a retarding effect on their wives, for whom an orgasm may happen more easily if she has recently had one. As some sex experts have observed, this tendency to go in opposite directions may be one more indication of the reality that we were created to be together, and to experience sexual release on a regular basis.[6]

The differences have prompted some men to wonder, *If my wife knows how good it feels, why doesn't she crave it again?* Because of hormonal differences, a woman will rarely be as "driven" as her young husband. A man who has been in the post-ejaculatory-bliss stage for about ten minutes is perhaps in the best position to understand what it's often like for his wife. He knows orgasm feels good, but in the absence of a strong hormonal drive to move him in that direction, he probably will not desire sex without some coaxing.

Note how often in this discussion we referred to "young" men. As men age, they often find they have difficulty with sexual functioning. As a result, a woman over forty may find that she's more sexually satisfied than her husband. When viewed over the lifetime of loving each other, sex may have a primary season that happens first for the husband and then for the wife.

It's difficult, though, to compare the intensity of pleasurable sensations. Different does not mean better or worse. Sex can be wonderful for both partners. If it's unsatisfactory for you, don't just accept it. Search for causes and solutions. There are many simple means of evaluating and improving. And your love life is worth trying to improve even when you're eighty or older!

Is it possible to have multiple orgasms?

If you mean more than one in a lifetime, certainly! If you mean in one encounter, probably—if you both desire it and you're patient. Men and women differ in their orgasmic potential.[7] Men generally need time for recharging between encounters—an average of twenty to thirty minutes. Women differ here in that it's possible for them to have more than one orgasm within several minutes (although it usually takes ten to twenty minutes to achieve the first one). A woman can have an extended orgasm with additional contractions (which some have termed "multiple") without the same kind of refractory period a man requires, or she can have a slight "plateau" of several minutes and then achieve orgasm again (called "sequential"). Gearing up for a second or third orgasm, however, may postpone her enjoyment of her endorphin release because of the concentration and focus required. Additional orgasms are not necessary and many do not desire them, but it's helpful for some to know the potential exists.

How do I keep from ejaculating if she's not ready for me to do so?

As one woman shared, "He wants me to be more 'into it' but premature ejaculation is a problem. I know that if I get more 'crazy,' he'll 'lose it' faster. Then I'm left unsatisfied. What should I do?"

Experiencing orgasm before they want to is the most common sexual problem men face. The fear of "Oh, no; it's going to happen again" can become a self-fulfilling prophecy for some. Holding back requires a combination of physical sensation and mental focus. Most men over time can develop reasonable control if they want to. For some, mastery may require professional help or even perhaps medication. Men, the first few times you have sex you'll probably find you have little control, and that can be discouraging if it surprises you. But you can develop a pace, tempo, or position that is less overwhelming in terms of sexual stimulation.

One frustrated wife stated, "The only thing that makes it better is to do it more often, and that makes me feel more pressure."

Here's an option that may help remove some pressure: Consider planning to have sex twice in the same night. Make the first time the faster of the two. During the second encounter, take the slow road. The second erection is not only less firm, it's also less sensitive and will thus help him to gain control. This means, if you are night lovers, starting earlier in the evening (as in 8:30, not the typical 11:30) and allowing about a thirty-minute window for the second erection. Once you've had some positive experiences, the confidence you gain will become self-reinforcing.

The first sexual encounter of the night focuses on his pleasure; the second focuses on hers. Couples can find ways to satisfy both. After the first time, he will have virtually no interest in his own sexual response and should be able to focus fully, devote his full attention to his wife for a little while because of the nature of the refractory period. During this time he may be tempted to say, "Never mind. We've had enough for one night." That's why couples need to allow about thirty minutes before trying again.

Some recommend the "squeeze technique" (included in the workbook section for those who are interested). This technique has been helpful to many because understanding the "point of no return" and learning to control the level of excitation are positive steps to developing good control. Others suggest that the man find a distraction—such as thinking a sad thought or mentally rehearsing multiplication tables to "slow him down." I don't recommend this latter option. Interjecting negative thoughts or sensations right before a man is ready to orgasm creates negative associations with sex.

As one frustrated wife shared in response to these techniques, "The whole thing about premature ejaculation is that it's not that simple to just follow some instructions in a book. It's a very long process of working together at finding a satisfying solution." While this is true, the eventual decrease in frustration and increase in satisfaction is well worth the time and effort.

How do I deal with impotence?

Most males experience occasional times when they lose an erection or cannot even become erect for intercourse. When my wife and I were looking into building a home, a contractor we consulted was apparently suffering from erectile dysfunction. He told me, "Doctor, if you can help me 'raise a stake,' I'll build your house for free." It took a while for me to figure out what he was talking about, but eventually it dawned on me. Erectile dysfunction can be devastating because, generally, a man's feelings about his sexual functioning are rather fragile and ego-defining.

The first step is medical evaluation, which may include urological examination. There is much debate about what percentage of erectile difficulty is psychological and what percentage is biological. The best evidence now is that often erectile dysfunction is more biological than psychological in origin. Alcoholism prevents many men from attaining erections. High stress or illness may drive down testosterone levels, thereby reducing erectile ability. Many medications, especially heart medications, reduce sexual function somewhat. Long-term and uncontrolled diabetes may also cause erectile problems. And aging is a factor. So we often find a medical cause.

One step to take in self-diagnosis is to observe whether you ever wake up with an erection. If you do, that demonstrates you're physically capable of achieving an erection. Physically healthy men have erections for a few minutes every ninety minutes all night long.[8] If you're not having nighttime erections and you're not becoming somewhat sexually aroused by attractive stimuli, it's possible that you have a physical problem. Psychological causes also factor in. For example, feeling intense guilt over an affair can cause erectile dysfunction.[9]

Childbirth can also cause difficulty for both. She may have less sensation or experience pain; he may not feel the same level of "friction" in that "the parts don't fit as snugly as before." There's also a psychological side to childbirth. Some men who have witnessed the delivery room scene find themselves repelled, having seen the blood, stretching, and tearing that happen as a normal part of the birth process. It may take time for husbands to view their wives as sexual creatures after that.

In addition, much of sexual functioning is dependent upon ambiance. Does your wife take care of herself? Does she exercise good hygiene? Has she had a recent vaginal infection? Allow sufficient time to create an inviting atmosphere and incorporate all five senses (through clothing, lighting, music, scents, and oils) into your lovemaking to help focus on positives.

Although diagnosis may sometimes be easy, treatment is always more difficult. For example, if medication is causing the difficulty, you can't always just stop taking it. Often there are appropriate substitutes without the unwanted sexual side effects, but not always. In such cases, find alternative ways to give and receive pleasure together.

Researchers are actively investigating ways to help couples cope with erectile dysfunction. Some therapies involve pellets of medication that, when inserted into the male urethra (this is not painful), will usually produce an erection. This developing method may replace some penile injections, and adds another alternative to surgical implants and prosthetic devices that enable erection and penetration. There are also penile injectables and the prostheses (plastic parts). One is rigid and "locked into place." The other is inflatable.

Erectile dysfunction has become a commonplace TV commercial focus. The development of Viagra, Cialis, and Levitra—medications that enhance blood flow to the pelvis—allow many men suffering from impotence to achieve erection and satisfactory intercourse.

If you suffer from ongoing impotence, explore with your physician the causes and options.

My husband has a sensitive ego when it comes to lovemaking. How should I respond when he has a premature ejaculation or temporary erectile dysfunction?

Be as gentle as possible. Do all you can to keep from turning the temporary embarrassment into a lifelong dysfunction, source of grief, or damaged self-image. For most men sexuality is a central issue of pride or ego. Men in general have the "I could satisfy any woman any time, anywhere" mind-set—not that they would act on this credo! But the ability to function has deep roots. If there's a medical diagnosis, this tends to be less of a problem. He can tell himself, "It's not my fault; it's not really *my* problem." But he still often has a sense that "If I'm unable to satisfy her, then I'm no man." Your husband needs you to take the attitude "This is normal—we can work it out!" And he needs continual reminding that he is, in fact, "The World's Greatest Lover."

The beloved in Song of Solomon told her man, "The maidens love you." A wise woman communicates, "Any woman would give anything to be your wife, but I got you!"

What is a "quickie"?

A "quickie" is generally considered a rapid, intense romantic encounter that skips significant foreplay and goes directly to intercourse. The quickie can take many forms, though, and it may involve only manual or oral sex for some couples. A steady diet of this type of sex is bad for a relationship. It usually does not allow the woman to experience orgasm, and as a rule it satisfies only the man's desire. She might be "attending to" him so she can get back to what she feels she needs to be doing. If she's not that interested (she's not in the mood, has a million things to do, or feels too tired or distracted to focus) a quickie can be a loving response to a genuine marital need as long as he meets her needs when she wants "all the bells and whistles." The quickie is one possible solution for the complaint that "He's always asking, and I'm always saying *no*."

The goal of a quickie is sexual release. Often circumstances are such that the time available makes the nine-course meal impossible, or even unappealing. When you're seeking quick satisfaction, usually for the male, this can be perfectly reasonable. Some nights when the kids have soccer practice, you go to a drive-through restaurant instead of sitting down to dinner together. It's a reasonable option.

It's not great for your health, though, to have a steady diet of only fast food and French fries. So be flexible; ride the ebb and flow of life events, making intimacy a priority.

The idea of "imbibing deeply," as we see in Song of Solomon (5:1) refers to "meals" shared throughout years of developing intimacy, communication, and oneness; it's not a life of quickies. Talk to couples who are still in love after several decades, and they'll often tell you, "It's so much better years later. The embers burn more deeply."

Is it okay for my spouse and me to have manual sex, bringing each other to climax with our hands?

Certainly. This is an option, particularly if the wife is menstruating; the husband feels the need for sexual release, and she's not in the mood; or if one partner has an active herpes lesion or other medical condition preventing intercourse. Couples should find many ways to please each other, and they can use the whole arsenal when the time is right. Some have argued that manual sex does not measure up to the "one flesh" ideal. The one-flesh relationship, however, is a far greater picture than merely that of sexual intercourse. When two are one, they want to satisfy each other and meet each other's needs as well as possible.

Is it okay to use devices such as vibrators to enhance pleasure?

This is a question the Bible nowhere addresses directly, so it would appear that it's up to the couple to decide mutually what works best for them. A potential danger is that vibrators create such intense sensations that it's difficult to match them with normal skin-to-skin activities. Thus, vibrators may become exclusively used, making regular sex unsatisfying. Any "sex toys" used to enhance stimulation or to spice up a couple's love life should be used only by mutual agreement. To my knowledge, there is no such thing as a "Christian sex toy," although at several marriage conferences people have asked me if there is. If you as a couple find delight in pleasuring one another with "extras," I believe you have liberty to try.

9

Other Questions Couples Ask

What kind of beloved is your beloved?
—SONG OF SOLOMON 5:9

My partner wants to do things that make me uncomfortable. Is oral sex even biblical?

Couples frequently ask some variation of this question: "Which behaviors and frequencies are okay for the heterosexual, monogamous Christian?" A wide range of behaviors fall within acceptable parameters. Yet each of us has a feel for what we personally consider normal or weird or sinful. Some people have a strongly negative response to the practice of oral sex. Others draw the line at anal sex. It's important to understand how you and your spouse think and feel about these delicate areas. And physical restrictions may factor into your feelings.

Some religious leaders teach that procreation must always be a possibility in any sexual connection that results in ejaculation. Thus, they rule out oral, anal, and manual sex. The Bible, however, neither outlines nor implies such limitations. Many base their application on an interpretation of a biblical text about a man named Onan. He "wasted his seed on the ground in order not to give offspring to his brother." In Genesis 38 we read about how God condemns Onan for disobeying the clear command to try to give his deceased brother a heritage (offspring) so that the brother's name will be remembered. Onan's action was coitus interruptus (withdrawal), not masturbation, oral sex, or anal sex. Yet Genesis 38 is used as a "proof text" to condemn such practices, as well as contraception.

Lacking specific prohibitions we must ask, "What is loving?" and "What is satisfying between husband and wife?" Within the clear biblical parameter of sexual activity between husband and wife, anything mutually agreeable is probably acceptable. Some individuals and even members of entire cultures reject practices that go beyond "only in bed; only on Saturday night; only with the lights out; only in the 'missionary position.'"

The Bible allows for much more between married couples than such limitations imply. Because something is allowable, however, it does not necessarily follow that it's best. If you or your partner grew up thinking "Yuck! That's the *worst!*" about a particular sexual practice, respect those feelings. Don't pressure your beloved to do anything that feels exploitive.

During one of my premarital talks a woman in the front row blurted out, "Why do all men love oral sex so much?" Actually, not all do. But some who do explain that it's an entirely passive sexual experience—you can focus only on receiving pleasure for a time without also worrying about whether you need to shift your weight, what to do about your arms getting tired, or being out of breath. Ninety percent of couples engage in some sort of oral/genital foreplay on occasion, so it is common.

Also, it's important to communicate what is actually desired here. One wife said she spent years hating oral *foreplay* because she thought her husband wanted oral *sex* (i.e., ejaculation).

To clarify about oral sex with ejaculation—I'm often asked if swallowing the ejaculate is dangerous. In fact one of my colleagues in Texas had a patient who was terrified that she had conceived a life-threatening "abdominal pregnancy" through the practice of oral sex. While such a conclusion may sound outlandish, many people do not understand the intricacies and delicacies of human sexuality.

To answer the question, swallowing the ejaculate is harmless. It has a high salt content like other bodily fluids, so it tastes salty. Sperm die upon contact with stomach acid.

As for a connection with oral sex and abdominal pregnancy—abdominal pregnancies are dangerous, but they result from conceptions that arose from vaginal intercourse. In such cases the embryo, rather than moving down the fallopian tube to implant in the uterus, fell upon some abdominal structure, such as the ovary or intestine, and began to grow there. All that to say, there's absolutely no risk of pregnancy with oral sex.

Legitimate dangers of oral sex include the vast array of sexually transmitted diseases. There are also serious emotional consequences. Even more so since former president Bill Clinton's declaration that oral sex was not really sex, many individuals, Christ-followers and not, have rationalized this very intimate sexual behavior as "acceptable" outside of marriage. In fact, many churched youth practice oral sex with some regularity.

Vaginal, oral, anal, and manual orgasmic activities do not belong outside a committed covenant relationship. For consenting married partners, oral sex may well be part of the sexual landscape. If either partner feels used, degraded, or defrauded by oral sex, however, it should be avoided.

In Song of Solomon 2:3 (italics mine) there may be an implicit reference to the oral pleasures of sexual love:

> Like an apple tree among the trees of the forest,
> So is my beloved among the young men.
> In his shade I took great delight and sat down,
> *And his fruit was sweet to my taste.*

The apple, or possibly "apricot," tree is a frequently used symbol in the ancient Near East for sexual love (perhaps similar to what we think when we hear "mistletoe"). In extrabiblical literature, "fruit" is sometimes equated with the male genitals or with semen, so it's possible that here we have a delicate reference to an oral genital caress, which she initiates. Later she says this in 7:13:

> The mandrakes have given forth fragrance;
> And over our doors are all choice fruits,
> Both new and old,
> Which I have saved up for you, my beloved.

On first reading, this may seem rather unromantic. But the original Jewish audience probably would have said, "O-o-h, I cannot believe you said that!" A mandrake is called a *man*drake because the unusual shape of its large, forked roots is said to resemble the form of a human body. In the ancient Near East the mandrake was known for its narcotic properties and was eaten to create desire and fertility.[1] What do you do with mandrakes and fruit? You put them in your mouth. Is that what she means here? If so, this is very provocative language.

Notice, too, that she says she has *something old and something new* for him. Variety is good. Be inventive. As we said earlier, it's easy to get in a rut. You and your husband or wife will have different views on what's weird, sinful, risqué, fun, or great. Within your comfort zones, explore and discover new avenues of expression rather than the "same old, same old" all the time.

Medically speaking, the practices we've been discussing are not generally harmful, although patients sometimes get infections from having anal sex followed by vaginal sex—or even anal sex followed by close proximity to the vagina—allowing for fluids to mix. Also, I've seen cases in which foreign objects (bottles, in particular) have become caught in the vagina and the suction created has done considerable damage when couples forcibly extracted the object. Here's another principle: *Use common sense.*

A final word here: submitting to one another (Eph. 5:21) means sacrificing our own desires for the good of the other. If your spouse is genuinely uncomfortable, find other ways of expressing your love.

Either partner needs to know he or she can gently say "no" at any time. Both must feel safe to remain in their comfort zones.

Are there any sexual practices that are biblically not okay?

Some sexual practices are clearly forbidden. For starters, God forbids sex with animals and close contact with dead people (most people have little trouble adhering to this standard). From there He also prohibits engaging in premarital, extramarital, or group sex, both actual and mental. (The mental part is what catches most of us.) Oral and anal sex are not mentioned in any list of prohibitions. Some states have laws against anal intercourse, but as far as we know, no married person has ever been prosecuted. When used in the Bible, "sodomy" is condemned, but in that context it was always between consenting males—also prohibited.

The general placement of nerve endings (they are densely concentrated around the anus) would indicate that anal sex could potentially bring a high degree of pleasure. In my years of practicing medicine, however, I've never met a woman who engaged in anal sex because she thought it was the best thing going. Most were doing it because their partners were pressuring them. So it's imperative that the partner wishing to engage in this practice consider and defer to the preferences and/or conscience of the one who has misgivings. The fact that anal sex is not specifically listed among the biblical prohibitions, in addition to what we know about how God placed the nerve endings, causes me to conclude that we should exercise caution in declaring this to be "big time sin" between consenting, married partners. That being said, though, if couples wish to have anal sex, they should know that at first it can be somewhat painful, cleanliness is important, anal contact followed by vaginal contact can cause infection, and anal sex carries with it the potential for damage to the sphincter. Couples should always avoid anal sex during pregnancy, as the risk of contamination and serious infection are too great to make this a safe practice.

Why does he/she have to be reminded 100 times about what I like?

People have short memories, and we're all wired differently. The general placement of nerve endings, hormones, media influences, and wishful thinking combine to create specific desires and expectations. We have to be retold because we cannot read minds. What the other person wants does not come instinctively to us. One bride shared, "I have to remind myself that he's not being thoughtless. One time we were getting into it, and he did something I had just told him I didn't like. I stopped him and asked, 'Don't you remember?' He covered his face and said, 'Oops. Sorry. Let me leave the room and come back in and start over.'"

A husband observed, "I tend to think it will intoxicate her with passion for me to move fast because that's what I find exciting. To me, bold is beautiful. But the opposite is true for her." His wife confided, "Yes, after years of telling him, 'Start subtle, be subtle; that's what works for me,' I still have to remind him sometimes that I want him to slow down."

I miss kissing. Why doesn't my husband kiss me anymore?

Make sure you've used breath freshener and remind him that kissing "lights your fire." Most partners will give what's desired once the desire is expressed. As we stated above, though, you may have to provide gentle reminders. For a marriage-enrichment class my wife and I teach, I assign the husbands the task of kissing their wives each day for approximately one minute without it leading anywhere—affection without expectation. A wife stopped me in the bookstore to thank me because prior to the assignment her husband had fallen into the rut of kissing his young bride only when he wanted sex.

Why do I sometimes sneeze when aroused or after enjoying sex?

Some people do. Along with other areas that become congested, the nasal passages can congest leading up to and/or during intercourse. Fascinating creatures, aren't we? God has created us with such diversity and complexity.

What is the normal sexual frequency for couples?
How often do most people have sex?

One person asked, "How often is okay?" I responded, "How often is it okay to go to the grocery store?" You decide what works for you.

I hesitate to define "normal," as I explained earlier. I had one patient who, after thirty years of marriage, reported that she and her husband had sex every day of their marriage except when she was hospitalized for surgery or giving birth. She thought that was normal and delightful. Another patient shared that in their three years of marriage, she and her husband had sex three times a day. We would certainly hate to discourage couples if this is what they desire. On the opposite end of the spectrum, couples have sex quarterly or get together only on holidays.

To have no sex at all is usually a symptom of significant marital problems. I've had many couples come to talk with me about "problems with frequency." Typically, the wife says, "We're very satisfied sexually, having sex once per month, or every other, or every third month." I turn to him and ask, "Is that satisfactory to you?" He pauses, and sheepishly says, "I'd like it more often." When I ask, "In an ideal situation, how often would you like to have sex with your wife?" he usually says, "Two or three times per week would be great." Note the significant difference of perspective and the unwillingness to ask out of fear of rejection or of having to submit to demands. This is an unhealthy marital portrait.

If you want to know the statistical averages as reported, they might be summed up as progressing from "tri-weekly" to "try weekly" to "try weakly" over a lifetime. Couples aged twenty to twenty-nine generally have sex three to four times a week. Couples aged thirty to thirty-nine have sex an average of two to three times a week. People from forty to fifty average one to two times a week, while couples over fifty make love less than once a week. (We'll talk about the sexual habits of older couples later.) It's important to note, however, that many have admitted to me that they lied (both in saying they got together "more often" and "less often") on all sorts of reports of frequency. Thus, it's hard to know what's true. But at least the statistics give us some general ranges.

When we ask husbands and wives to list what they consider their top marital needs, women nearly always say affection/cuddling and conversation. Men, particularly young men, almost always say sex. And when men hear the question posed, they are usually disappointed to hear their wives exclude sex from the list.

Several newlywed women, in adjusting to marriage with normal, healthy husbands, have told me how surprised they were that their men had such active interest in sex. Perhaps the "normal frequency" figures can help these women to see that their men may not have "issues" with sex after all.

By the way, there's no prize at the end of life for the couple who made love the most times.

Is masturbation okay within marriage?

Masturbation within marriage is not generally okay as the sole means of sexual experience, but perhaps as an occasional adjunct. Mutual masturbation (manually bringing each other to orgasm without sexual intercourse) may be a good option at times, particularly in the late stages of pregnancy. If your spouse has extended illness or fatigue, or you must endure a lengthy separation, this may be an acceptable option. There is no biblical prohibition, but Christians will want to consider broader issues as well.

Solo masturbation, while quite common among Christians according to the best available information, can be obsessive, detracting from the intimacy between husband and wife. The fantasy life and images required for the continual practice of masturbation certainly pose a potential danger. And nowadays masturbation is often associated with viewing pornography, particularly on the Internet. This is *very* unhealthy and causes enormous spiritual problems as well as problems in marriage. Even if you're thinking about your spouse when pleasuring yourself, it's easy to imagine practices that can make the "real thing" rather dull by comparison. Also, with self-gratification you don't have to communicate to someone else what you want. For most people these do not turn into major issues, but for some they can become a problem.

Masturbation is not just a "male thing," either. One husband shared that his wife lay tense and motionless when they had sex, but afterward she would get up and masturbate. She apparently experienced no pleasure when she was with him, but she experienced intense pleasure from self-stimulation. This pattern proved damaging in their relationship, which eventually ended in divorce.

The biblical instruction to husbands and wives is that they are to fulfill their duty to each other (see 1 Cor. 7). Consider the situation of a wife, deprived of sex for weeks, who found her husband masturbating. She felt deeply wounded that he had not allowed her to share his body. In a case such as this, masturbation as a regular means of sexual gratification is damaging when used within marriage in place of intercourse.

As mentioned earlier, when a wife is having difficulty achieving orgasm, she may benefit from exercises that involve self stimulation, either manually or using other techniques. Such exercises are in the context of a loving relationship, and her husband should know and be fully supportive of the treatment plan that will one day, hopefully, result in a more enjoyable sexual relationship together.

Masturbation is a controversial issue. Some have touted it as God's gift to singles, others as a nearly unpardonable sin. I reject both extremes. While masturbation produces no physical side-effects, it can become habit forming, even an obsession, when connected with pornography. What happens in the mind of the person masturbating usually involves sinful, lustful imaginings. Thus, I reject masturbation as a healthy or godly practice outside of marriage. Within marriage, if one fills his or her mind with images of husband or wife and with the spouse's knowledge and permission, while not ideal, it may be permissible. For example if one's spouse is in the military, stationed overseas for six months or a year, masturbating while focusing on that absent spouse may be acceptable if both agree.

Does sex always have to be spontaneous?

No, sex does not always have to be spontaneous. Spontaneous sex may, in fact, be *impossible* with children and certain living arrangements. (It's hard to engage in spontaneous lovemaking on the floor of the den with teenagers around or mom-in-law breezing through for a midnight snack.)

Some couples bristle against the idea of planned sex because they hate to feel regimented. But planned sex is better than no sex! Besides, planning can bring delightful aspects to the experience—creating ambiance with music, rose petals, perfumed sheets—that spontaneous sex cannot. And while spontaneity is wonderful, in a world where schedules are booked solid, spur-of-the-moment encounters are rare to nonexistent. Planning ahead assures that a couple will make time for the intimacy they need. Planning demonstrates interest, and it provides opportunities to create the environments that can fulfill each other's desires.

What does sex mean to him? To her?

What does sex mean to you and your partner? The ideal would be to ask your spouse this question. Is it the ultimate expression of intimacy? Is it the thrill of knowing you have given pleasure to the other? Is it both and more? Is it the expression of intense loving feelings? Is it primarily about pleasure for you? Is it about meeting needs? Is it some of all of these?

In general, men consider sex very important. They certainly find it satisfying and unifying. It is the ultimate expression of *pleasure*. While it has relational implications, the relationship is not the central focus. A wise wife will not underestimate its significance to her husband. It has been suggested that perhaps it's as important to him as "being listened to and sharing your heart" is to her (something that is often unfortunately considered an "extra" by men).

What does it mean to her? In general, at its best it is the deepest expression of loving *feelings*—communicating through the fingertips what the mind cannot articulate because even the best words cannot find utterance for its depth. Good sex for her is the crowning relational moment. When she's in love and the relationship is good, having sex is really about loving with her *whole* being. For her, "full meal" sex (as opposed to the "fast food" quickie) is a deeply loving experience, the most intimate expression of herself. Most wives link how they feel about sex with how they feel about their entire marital relationship and its emotional climate. If a woman feels something lacking when it comes to communication, cuddling, and romance, she'll feel emotionally disconnected from her man. Consequently, she remains rather uninterested in sex until the emotional climate improves. A man may tend to compartmentalize his sexuality more than this. It takes less to arouse him, and his ability to become aroused is often less linked to the emotional temperature of the relationship. In fact, he can be "ready" even if he and his wife just had an argument—and sometimes if they're still having one!

Can marital sex match the "excitement" associated with forbidden relationships?

Marital sex can exceed, as well as fail to measure up to, illicit six. Most surveys show that monogamous people in committed relationships are the most satisfied over the long haul. The very nature of sin, however, is that it entices for a season, before bringing consequences. Fiction writers know that the best way to increase intensity of emotion is to add suspense. And marriage, by its very nature, provides a measure of security.

Some of the attraction in forbidden relationships may have its source in the rationalization that "I can be perfect" or "That person can be ideal for me" because the two people in the illicit relationship don't know each other like married partners do. The fantasy—complete with white knight or fair maiden—becomes reality . . . temporarily. The illusion remains unchallenged by dirty socks on the floor or globs of toothpaste left in the sink.

Make no mistake about it—sin in the short term can be intensely pleasurable. That's why it's so tempting! But over the long term, it fails to deeply satisfy. Often men who selfishly pursue women with whom they have no personal interest have an "It's over; I'm outta here" attitude immediately after sex. For example, someone with a sexual perversion that drives him to seek out a prostitute will often leave immediately after he ejaculates—the moment of "conquest." The thrill is usually followed by guilt and negative feelings. We see this in the Bible story of David's son Amnon, who "fell in love" with his half-sister, Tamar. He longed for her until he raped her. Afterward, "Amnon hated her with a very great hatred; for the hatred with which he hated her was greater than the love with which he had loved her. And Amnon said to her, 'Get up, go away!'" (2 Sam. 13:15).

Proverbs has much to say about sexual purity—both the benefits of sex within marriage and the consequences of immorality. In chapter five we read of a father instructing his son to view his wife as an active source of abundant and exclusive satisfaction. Then in chapter six we read, "Can a man scoop fire into his lap without his clothes being burned? Can a man walk on hot coals without his feet being scorched? So is he who sleeps with another man's wife; no one who touches her will go unpunished" (6:27 NIV). In the chapter of Proverbs that follows, we read of a man who follows a prostitute "like an ox going to the slaughter, like a deer stepping into a noose till an arrow pierces his liver, like a bird darting into a snare, little knowing it will cost him his life" (7:22–23 NIV). These are stern warnings.

Regina learned the pitfalls of a forbidden relationship the hard way:

> God's Word is a map through a mine field, designed to enhance rather than take away fun. I dated a guy named Chad in college. We were both believers who actively participated in the campus outreach for Christians, but we slept together regularly. Amazingly, I never got pregnant. About a year later we broke up. Five years after that, I married my husband. Now more than ever, I have so many

regrets—the greatest being that Chad was a better lover than my husband.

Actually, I wonder if that's true. Stolen cookies taste better. There's a sense in which there's more excitement in sneaking. True, the relationship was less secure and there was guilt, which took away from what we had, in one sense. But in the pure physical pleasure of it all, Chad was more exciting. It's hard to get him out of the bedroom every time my husband and I are together. I have to decide *every time*; it never gets easier. I wonder if my memory presents the past in accurate terms. Have I idealized what actually happened? I wonder if God is punishing me. Sexually speaking, ignorance would have been bliss. The short-term pleasure is definitely not worth the long-term pain.

This sad situation has been echoed by many of my patients when they've told about past lovers who were "better" sexually than their spouses. They remember fondly the bodily attributes of a past lover, especially if married to someone who has become careless about appearance or selfish and self-absorbed about sexual pleasure. It's difficult to keep from thinking of one who listened and loved, and loved, and loved.

It's interesting to note, however, that some credible researchers have discovered that people who engage in extramarital affairs in general report that they are more gratified sexually by a spouse than a lover. Those who "cheat" also have sex less often than those remaining faithful within marriage. It's been suggested that part of the reason for the decreased level of gratification stems from the practical torments that a faithful person generally does not have to think about, but that enter the mind of one engaging in extramarital sex: Will he like it? Will she have an orgasm? Is my body attractive? Can I keep going long enough? Will he *really* like me? Am I better than she has had before? Am I being too rough? Not assertive enough? Too responsive? Not responsive enough? And on and on.[2]

Can't sex become an addiction if I engage in it regularly?

As mentioned, in 1 Corinthians 7 we read that God *intends* for couples to "engage regularly." In fact, he warns against too much abstinence. When discussing addiction, therapists often ask, "What is your favorite defense against emotional pain?" In the context of sex, is it an increasing indulgence in pleasure to the point of ultimately caring only for your own desires and not for your partner's needs?

Some define "addiction" as a preoccupation that interferes with a normal sexual relationship with one's spouse. This can be anything from thoughts, obsessions, and compulsions to addictions in which you don't care who the partner is. The activity does not necessarily require physical involvement; it may be mental. Couples report having phone sex, in which they talk through the act while masturbating. The Internet provides a means of connecting with perfect strangers and having intensely sexual conversations. (More on this in chapter 16.) If you're seeking only self-gratification, you're driving down the wrong road.

What are your suggestions for sex during pregnancy?

Many a husband finds his pregnant wife cute, if not downright sexy, during pregnancy. Her breasts swell, which is often a source of pleasure for both partners (although the breasts can be too tender to touch for a while). But others find pregnancy distracting and distasteful.

Many pregnant women are especially interested in sex because their estrogen climbs to high levels during this time. Yet for most women in the first trimester, nausea makes sex the last thing on their minds. The middle months of pregnancy can be a time of reconnecting sexually, but some creativity is required for finding comfortable positions, and the distraction of the baby moving during relations can present a challenge. During the later stages of pregnancy, sex is difficult, even impossible. So it's important to keep a good sense of humor, a spirit of adventure, and mutual understanding.

Remember, too, that the uterus contracts with orgasm. For this reason, with some pregnancies sex may be a bad idea because it can initiate contractions, making preterm labor a risk. This is unusual though, so check with your own doctor as to any restrictions. But don't give up on intimacy. Even if the best you can do is a back rub or a neck rub, find a way to express love through the sense of touch (more on this subject in a moment).

"Now that I'm pregnant, I'm a lot more tired," a young wife confided. "I need to have hope that just because I'm pregnant, it doesn't mean I'll have to wait another eighteen years to have a love life again." Although many, if not most, pregnant women have these thoughts, experience tells me there is reason to have hope—lots of hope.

What about after delivery? What should I expect?

When a woman is nursing, her hormonal environment is such that she has less estrogen, less lubrication and elasticity, less desire, and more discomfort or even pain. Some normal women have *no* interest for months. The doctor may well give the green light for sexual intimacy, but some of my patients asked for an "extension." Rather than quarrel with their husbands, they wanted a "doctor's excuse" to abstain.

Admittedly, the changes following a pregnancy can be dramatic. After a vaginal birth, the anatomy is different, and muscle tone and control may take time to return. The tissues don't feel the same, so couples need to be patient, recognizing that desire and response are altered. The sleep-deprivation and fatigue that come with having a newborn can tax couples to their limits. It has often been said that husbands recover much more quickly than wives following childbirth. But then, the husband had the easier part.

It may take three to six months or more before a new mom's body begins to return to its pre-pregnancy state. This is generally an unhappy time sexually, and couples should recognize that this is normal. They will need to make the extra effort to express their care and support for each other.

So what about those times in a marriage when sex is impossible for whatever reason?

A single friend told me, "I heard on the radio that the average person needs twelve physical touches a day to feel loved. I'm down by about two hundred and forty." Let's face it, touch is important. Numerous studies confirm that humans need touch. Even newborn babies thrive with touch or die without it.

God has created us with a deep need for touch, and partners must make time to mutually meet these needs. For some, touch is more important than for others: "People have different 'love languages,'" writes Gary Chapman, author of an entire series of books on the subject. "We know that physical touch is a way of communicating love. Holding hands, kissing, and embracing are all ways of communicating emotional love to one's spouse. For some individuals, physical touch is their primary love language. Without it they feel unloved."[3]

"A pat on the shoulder, a warm hug, or a tender kiss on the cheek often generates a strong sense of caring and concern, which is important for a best friendship in marriage," write Robert and Debra Bruce, authors of *Reclaiming Intimacy in Your Marriage*. Especially when your spouse is unable to engage in full intercourse, a tender pat on the shoulder, a warm hug, a gentle caress, an unexpected kiss, sensual words, and sensual strokes generate a strong sense of caring. Touching breaks down barriers and says, "I love and care about you."[4]

Hugging is known to lift depression. And it can empower the immune system—to the point that nurses in burn wards have received training to help them know when and how to hug their touch-starved patients. Touch can energize tired bodies, slow aging, curb appetite, boost feelings of worth, and reduce tension.

It's vitally important for the spouse who is sexually impaired to communicate continuously, "My current inability is not because you are unattractive or unlovable," and for the unimpaired spouse to communicate, "I love you for more than your ability to 'perform.'"

What if one of us has an STD?

If you've been diagnosed with an STD, you know what it feels like to find out that you have one. Many of my patients, on receiving the news that they had an STD, sat in stunned silence and then wept profusely. Emotions are mixed—usually including anger, often guilt, then shame. Protect yourself and others until you find that person with whom you want to share your life in marriage. Then tell that person about the infection before you marry. It need spread no further. Your spouse will certainly be at increased risk of contracting a viral STD, but the other STDs can be successfully treated.

Many Christian husbands and wives do deal with STDs. They can attest that, although it is difficult, STDs can be handled within marriage in a way that both strengthens their relationship and honors their partnership.

What effect does aging have on a couple's sex life?

Sex drives change some with age, as we mentioned earlier, but often couples report an increase in pleasure. Although drives may decrease, with the fear of pregnancy gone couples may find they have less disparity in interest levels. It is hoped that after years of marriage, your love for each other will run deep and strong as you've grown in the ability to listen and bring pleasure to your beloved.

James and Carolyn Childerston and Doug Rosenau, authors of *Celebration of Sex After 50*, outline some *myths* about sex and aging:

- Youth rules and old age stinks. We must maintain our youthfulness at all costs.
- We can define the stages of middle- and older-age maturity using the same ideas and vocabulary with which we define younger stages.
- Sexual desire and a longing for erotic connection are for the young, and fade rapidly in our fifties and sixties.
- Great lovemaking depends on healthy, youthful bodies with stamina, flexibility, and exuberant intercourse and orgasms.

- Pain and mishaps, which totally impede happiness and contentment, must be avoided at all costs.
- Mortality should be feared, and aging bodies are a curse.[5]

One man wrote this observation about his decreased interest in sex: "I'm thankful for my less powerful sex drive. I used to battle with lusting after women I could hardly stand. It bothered me that my sexual urges were so out of line with my feelings. That's different now, and what a relief."

A gradual increase in the time needed to reach orgasm has certain benefits, enabling an older man to prolong the pleasure for himself and his partner. While textbooks might tell us men reach their sexual peak in adolescence with women reaching theirs shortly thereafter, such research is actually focusing only on genital responsiveness. Such tests measure, for example, the quickness with which a man will have an erection, his speed in getting a second erection, and the strength of his ejaculations. Yet speed can actually hinder sexual fulfillment for wives, so the aging process can equalize a couple's timing.

In addition, "If you want intimacy with your sexuality—which has a huge psychophysiological impact—then there isn't a seventeen-year-old alive who can keep up with a healthy fifty-year-old," writes David Schnarch, PhD, in *Psychology Today*. He continues, "As people get older, their capacity for self-validated intimacy—and intimate sex—increase. . . . In terms of sex at profound intensity or emotional depth, most of us are virgins. . . . If we teach teens that they won't reach their sexual potential for another thirty years or so, they can relax (and parents can too)."[6]

A survey conducted by AARP and *My Generation* found that 58 percent of men and 48 percent of women say they secretly dream of having a more satisfying love life. In summarizing the findings, a journalist wrote, "And what do so many mid-lifers think they're missing sex-wise? When men talk about having better sex, they usually mean more frequent lovemaking and especially more oral sex. The more often men have oral sex, research shows, the happier they say they are with their marriage. . . . Being desired is what women need at this age. . . . Women in midlife need to know that their husbands accept their changing physical appearance and think they're aging well, which they get from physical closeness and sexual intimacy."[7] The same survey found that six in ten baby boomers love to make love.

As couples reach their elder years (one in eight of us is now over sixty-five), sex often remains important because it's such an integral part of maintaining self-esteem and expressing love for one other. Many older people maintain active sexual relationships. In fact, two-thirds of husbands and wives over seventy report having sex an average of once a week.

Often, though, senior men have difficulties with erectile dysfunction. They can still enjoy providing pleasure to their wives, however, through manual stimulation. All evidence affirms that clitoral sensation remains throughout life, so older women can retain the capacity for orgasm.

The following information about seniors' love lives, taken from a poll done for *Parade* magazine, reveals some interesting statistics:

- On average, of the last ten times they had sex, men sixty-five and over reported reaching orgasm eight times, women five times. Almost half reached orgasm every time.
- The percentage of sexually active seniors declines with age: 55 percent of those between sixty-five and sixty-nine are sexually active; 48 percent between seventy and seventy-four; 28 percent between seventy-five and seventy-nine; 21 percent between eighty and eighty-four; and 13 percent of those eighty-five and older.
- Seniors reported having orgasms an average of seven of the last ten times they had sex, compared with eight in ten for younger lovers.
- Seniors reach orgasm sooner—in an average of 12.4 minutes, as opposed to 17.3 minutes for the younger sample. (Perhaps years of practice pay off.)
- 4 percent of senior women who are sexually active reported that they had never experienced orgasm.[8]

What about those who become physically disabled? They can often express themselves sexually using a wide range of pleasure-enhancing techniques, from stroking the face to oral-genital sex. Many disabled individuals are still able to provide sexual pleasure for their spouses. Even if a person is unable to experience orgasm, it is tremendously rewarding and stimulating to arouse one's spouse to the point of orgasm.

How will menopause or hysterectomy affect our love life?

Physical intimacy need not end following surgical procedures such as hysterectomy or after the normal "change of life"—menopause. It may require some change and creativity but a satisfying sexual relationship can result for most.

Hysterectomy and other surgical procedures performed on the female reproductive tract (ovaries, tubes) can bring certain freedoms. Pregnancy is essentially impossible following hysterectomy. Only the extremely rare instance of abdominal or ectopic (tubal) pregnancy following hysterectomy clouds perfect results. And with the fear of pregnancy removed, so is one of the major fears inhibiting sexual enjoyment. Surgeons reconstruct the vagina in such a way during surgery that following the normal post-operative recovery period, most find intercourse quite comfortable. In women for whom endometriosis, symptomatic fibroids, or excessive bleeding prompted the surgery, intercourse may become far more enjoyable, with decreased pain and reduced difficulty with flow and cramps.

It's possible, though, for the opposite effect to occur. The ovaries, remember, secrete small amounts of testosterone until a woman is into her eighties. Disease or a family history of ovarian cancer may necessitate ovarian removal separately or at the time of hysterectomy. Since testosterone stimulates sexual desire, her drive may decrease noticeably once the ovaries are removed. If this becomes a problem—that is, if she notices a difference—estrogen tablets that also contain testosterone or testosterone cream can be prescribed. So this matter is easily addressed for some women.

Menopause and the several years preceding the ultimate cessation of menses (*perimenopause*) are particularly critical times in the life of a woman. The regular, predictable release of female hormones eventually decreases in all women, upsetting the emotional environment for many and physically bringing to an end the childbearing years. During the perimenopause, which may last several years, cycles and moods may be irregular, with unpredictable fertility and distressing hot flashes. Many women are candidates for estrogen replacement therapy during this time, but this is a complex decision requiring in-depth consultation with your physician.

About two-thirds of women make the passage into menopause without too much difficulty. The other third have a difficult time, however, especially if they can't take estrogen. The emotional and physical changes can disrupt normal patterns of intimacy. One patient described a hot flash saying it was "like being dipped in hell." She said, "I wanted to tear off my clothes and jump out the window." Others have called it the "private summer," or nuclear-core meltdown.

Perimenopause may take three to five years to complete, and couples can learn to adapt within the change, although the process can be challenging. Most women complete menopause and, with estrogen replacement or lubricants and otherwise healthy lifestyles, continue to enjoy an active and satisfying sex life. Another patient said her sex life and her husband's sex life were better than ever—no bleeding, no worries about pregnancy, and "We've finally figured out what we like!"

10

What Is Marriage?

Look at King Solomon wearing the crown . . .
on the day of his wedding, the day his heart rejoiced.
—SONG OF SOLOMON 3:11 NIV

Imagine exercising only half of the body. Kind of illogical, right? In the same way, when discussing marital intimacy, the "how-to's" about sex constitute a mere fraction of the whole. We've started with the physical description, but what about the spiritual and relational elements? A couple can understand all about anatomy and function, but without a foundation for relating as God desires, their sexual relationship will suffer.

First of all, sex is no surprise to God. He made it. It is not, as some suggest, the product of male lust. At one extreme we get the idea that "spiritual Christians can't have good sex." At the other end of the spectrum, we've seen religious people who have an "anything goes" attitude about sex. Karl Barth observed that human sexuality has been a vacillation between evil eroticism on the one hand and an evil absence of eroticism on the other.

God created us to be sexual beings, and as our Creator, He invites us to fully enjoy sexual pleasure—within the boundaries of marriage. Yet consider some views from what might be called the secular "Revised Standard" version of marriage:

- "I will be devoted to my spouse as long as the love shall last."
- "When you run out of romance, you run out of the marriage."
- "A marriage license is just a piece of paper."
- "Marriage is an outdated, old-fashioned institution."[1]

When my wife and I teach marriage enrichment classes or conduct marriage retreats, we begin at the beginning—in the book of Genesis—as we address three questions: Where did marriage originate? What does it mean? Where does intimacy fit into marriage? When I teach a premarital seminar, I ask engaged couples these questions. Often they stare blankly at me in response. They're about to enter into this relationship, but they can't even say what the goal of marriage is. So let's consider what the Bible has to say about these questions.

Where did marriage originate?

In the first book of the Bible we read that God created humankind—male and female—in His image. Gender differences are no mistake; they originated in the mind of God. The man/woman mystery, the drive that compels them to connect, explains why they would leave father and mother and be "cleaved" to each other. That drive to connect is received passively—it's something God does. Marriage begins at the beginning.

Marriage isn't society's idea; it's God's. It began in the garden of Eden. We read in Genesis 2:18, "The Lord God said, 'It is not good for the man to be alone; I will make him a helper suitable for him.'" Up to that point God had spoken all of creation into being except for humans. Then God formed Adam from the dust. Finally, He fashioned Eve from Adam's rib.

We also read in the second chapter of Genesis that marriage began at God's initiative. Note that God instituted marriage before temptation and sin entered the world. And later, although humanity had fallen into sin, Jesus blessed and validated marriage at the wedding in Cana by performing His first miracle. So sin did not erase God's blessing of and plan for marriage.

What does marriage mean?

Marriage involves making a legal contract. When you stand to-gether, whether before a justice of the peace, a pastor, or a rabbi, if you exclude all the religious trappings, the fancy clothes, and the music, you commit yourselves to each other legally. Anyone who's tried to escape that legal relationship realizes how difficult and costly it can be.

Yet marriage is ultimately much more than a legal contract—it's a covenant, a binding agreement, made before God; and it is *God* who joins husband and wife together. Marriage, then, is unlike a business partnership, although some people think of it that way; if it doesn't work out, they feel they can always sign off as they would with a failed business relationship. But if you enter a business part-nership, you have clearly defined limitations. You have to devote only so much of your life to the business—even if it's seventy hours per week. When you're "off," you're truly off. You have times in your life during which that business deal has no force. Not so in marriage. Every moment—from the repeating of vows until the Lord takes one home—you are connected, committed, one.

God has involved Himself in the covenant made before Him. And He is the one who seals that covenant—which makes marriage different from all other relationships and is why efforts to "undo" marriage create enormous problems and evoke profound pain.

According to God's description, marriage involves two things: (1) leaving father and mother; (2) cleaving to each other. Leaving and cleaving involve decisions to "leave" one's family of origin and be joined to one's spouse for a lifetime, establishing a new family and a new priority. Why is that important?

Going back to the beginning, when God made Adam, He created man alone. Then He declared that it was *not good* for the man to *be* alone. After Genesis records numerous times when God made something and declared it "good," we suddenly have a contrast. He says it is *not* good for man to be alone. As Adam named the animals, exercising his God-given authority, he no doubt quickly realized that male horses have female horses, and male monkeys have female monkeys, yet he himself had no counterpart. God revealed to the man his need. Then He met that need by creating—spectacularly—his wife. We read what the man said when he first viewed the woman: "This is now bone of my bones." In the Hebrew, Adam's "This is now" statement carries considerable enthusiasm, like saying "Yahooooo! Finally!"

Parents whose children marry would be wise to note that God describes "leaving and cleaving" as the natural order of events when couples marry. Their new relationship takes priority over even the parent-child relationship. I hear about parents who tell their children on their wedding days, "If your spouse ever treats you badly, if you're ever unhappy, you can always come home."

They would do better to advise, "When you say 'I do,' keep your commitment in sickness and health. We're renting out your room tomorrow. Drop by sometime—for a visit!"

What does it mean to "leave" your parents? Many marriages first falter right here. Dan and Carla had struggled with in-law problems throughout their entire ten-year marriage. One day Carla and her mother-in-law, Mary, disagreed over how to spend leisure time. Mary felt Carla should cook meals when the family vacationed together; Carla, who worked full-time and rarely got a break, wanted to order pizza. Dan sided with his mother because she was his "blood" relative. Within the year, Dan and Carla divorced. Although your spouse may not always be right, your first loyalty is to him or her.

"Leaving" does not necessarily mean moving physically, although that might be wise. Rather, it means choosing to nurture the new relationship over those with one's blood relatives.

What does it mean to "cleave"? It means to cling together, to be joined together. The marriage relationship *takes priority* over the parent-child relationship. God joins you together.

In Deuteronomy 24:5, we read that God told husbands to stay home from war during the first year of marriage so they could "give happiness" to their wives. It's important to spend extra time in those first, foundational days of being joined, so the two of you can adjust to being married. During this time you'll need to work out who will do what, figure out your unique styles of communicating, and develop sexual intimacy. Couples go off together for a "weekend honeymoon" and expect to return knowing how to live as one!

There is no "leaving and cleaving," however, when it comes to premarital sex or adultery. God says clearly that sexual intimacy outside the marital union is sin, not instant marriage. Michael, a single man, was serving as an associate pastor when he met Pam. They started dating, and he found himself fascinated by her. Even though he saw many indications that she had a half-hearted commitment to the Lord, his attraction to her caused him to ignore them. Before long their physical relationship had progressed further than it should have. Soon after that, they began having sex. Michael would repent, but then a week later, the same thing would happen. In his mind they had become "married in God's eyes," yet this union did not come with God's blessing. Guilt overwhelmed him. So he tried to "make it right" by proposing to her. Within two months they married. And they have been miserable together ever since. Some believe, as Michael did, that if you have a sexual relationship with someone, God considers the two of you married. That is untrue; it's not what Scripture teaches. You are engaging in sin, not marriage. Marriage is a leaving, cleaving, lifelong commitment that involves vows and promises, not merely inappropriate and sinful sexual involvement.

Where does intimacy fit into marriage?

The Creator's design for marriage is spiritual, emotional, and physical oneness. Imagine a pyramid divided into three levels. The first, the foundation, is essential to developing true marital intimacy. It's the sphere of *spiritual* oneness. We'll consider the spiritual implications of marriage in the chapters that follow. Suffice it to say now that when a couple marries, they are spiritually one. That doesn't mean they share a single soul; it means that in a sense they are one, like a head and body connected to each other, because God declares it so. "What God has joined together . . ."

From the moment the "I Do's" are spoken until the death of one or both, the couple is spiritually united, spiritually one. Knowing this, a wise couple will invest the time and energy necessary to develop this spiritual sphere by growing deeply in their devotion to God, even as they are deepening in their love for each other. This is essential!

Picture yourselves as two individuals who are one in a very real, spiritual sphere. So, while you certainly need your own time alone with God, recognize that the two of you also form a united picture of man and wife together devoted to God and worshipping.

This is one reason it's so important that believers marry only other believers. The Bible warns us to avoid becoming "unequally yoked" (2 Cor. 6:14 NKJV). The metaphor springs from the image of two oxen plowing a field together. They can't accomplish anything if they're going in different directions or if one is trained to the yoke and the other too lazy to pull. In context, the passage is talking about a business relationship, but how much more important is the marriage relationship? Believers who marry unbelievers are asking for trouble. They don't live in the same kingdom; they don't worship the same Lord; they're not headed in the same direction. Paul advises the widow that, should she choose to wed, she should marry "in the Lord" (1 Cor. 7:39).

Now, as it turns out, divorce happens, but God allows it by concession. Divorce is an exception because some people have such hardened hearts, hearts so closed to God that they deal treacherously with those they've pledged to love; their spouses cannot live with them in this sinful world.

God makes a couple "one flesh." He's an integral part of each marital union. What about people who don't even believe in God? Marriage is God's institution, and it's meant to operate according to His plan, whether or not those involved acknowledge Him.

Next is the relational level. This is the sum total of all the "together moments of life"—conversations, phone calls, e-mails, even text messaging. While we will consider sexual intimacy as a separate part of marriage, it does overlap into the spiritual and relational levels. Still, most of the hours that God gives to marriage partners are spent building intimacy by "intercourse" of the verbal and nonverbal but nonsexual variety.

It's a sad reality, though, that not all relational interaction is conducive to intimacy. We see it on television and we read about it in the newspaper: spousal verbal abuse is on the rise. Partners commit acts of physical violence against each other that sometimes even lead to death; this is not the intent of the vow, "Till death do us part." Yet even more unsettling than all the lawyers and custody battles are the emotional divorces. If surveys and studies included those, we would find a large, lonely group of "unhappily married people." What are emotional divorces? These are the relationships of couples who live under the same roof but say no more to each other than, "What's for dinner?" "Have a nice day," and "Did we get any mail?"

Finally, the third level, the top of the pyramid, is physical intimacy. Adam and Eve were naked and unashamed. Only sin brought the awareness of shame. The body is beautifully crafted by God in His own image—it is complex, intricate, amazing in its ability to function. We learn in 1 Corinthians 6 that the body of the believer belongs to God, and He indwells this "temple" with His Holy Spirit. We are instructed, therefore, to glorify God in our bodies. Adam and Eve felt comfortable together. They received each other visually and appreciated and enjoyed each other.

Marriage is a serious commitment. It isn't the sappy emotional bond we may connect with the saying, "Sugar is sweet and so are you"; it's a decision of the will: "I take this woman . . ." or "I take this man for better or worse; for richer, for poorer; in sickness, in health, till death do us part." In Matthew 19, we read what Jesus taught about marriage. He said, "What therefore God has joined together, let no [one] separate" (v. 6). God puts husbands and wives together in a unique one-flesh union and no one should tamper with it.

It's been estimated that of a dozen couples, four divorce and six stay together without love or joy for the sake of their children (or for continued access to them) or due to their religious beliefs or careers. It's tragic that only two couples—one in six—enjoy an intimate and happy marriage. So obviously a happy marriage takes a lot of cultivation. Divorce is more the norm than the exception: "The chance of a first marriage ending in divorce over a forty-year period is 67 percent. Half of all divorces will occur in the first seven years. Some studies find the divorce rate for second marriages is as much as 10 percent higher than for first-timers. The chance of getting divorced remains so high that it makes sense for all married couples—including those who are currently satisfied with their relationship—to put extra effort into their marriages to keep them strong."[2]

For the many survivors of divorce, regardless of who was at fault, remember this: divorce is not the unpardonable sin. Earlier in Matthew 5, Jesus said divorce does not automatically reflect sin on the part of the divorced person. Even if you were at fault in a divorce and have since wrongly married again, you did so either out of ignorance or out of rebellion. Confess this decision to the Lord. Find His forgiveness and focus on making your current marriage what He wants it to be.

Does remarriage constitute an ongoing adulterous relationship? No. In Deuteronomy 24 we read about instructions for a woman who has divorced and remarried. Her new spouse is called her "husband," not her "adulterous relationship." When Jesus met the woman at the well, He said she'd had five husbands—not one husband and four adulterous relationships. So apparently, in God's eyes remarriage exists, and the marital relationship in which you currently find yourself is where you should remain and grow.

Is marriage forever? No. Each of us has a spirit that will live eternally—believers will dwell in the presence of God and unbelievers will be separated from God's loving presence. If we were spiritually "married," or united, even death would not end the marriage, and the remaining partner would not be free to marry. But we read that in heaven there will be no marriage (Mark 12:24–25), and the bereaved spouse left on earth is no longer bound to his or her departed spouse (Rom. 7:1–2).

The disciples responded to Jesus' words about divorce, "If this is so, it's better not to marry!" (see Matt. 19:10). Jesus basically replies with, "You're on the right track; it is better not to marry than to marry wrongly." So don't marry unless it is to another believer and you are committed to that one for a lifetime of sacrifice. If you're willing to give yourself to that person by choice of the will—in sickness or in health, for richer or poorer, and until death separates the two of you—knowing there will assuredly be tough times, marriage can be one of life's greatest blessings. Understand that one of God's purposes for marriage is to present, through your relationship, a picture to the world of how Christ and the church relate to each other.

When I teach a premarital conference, I use modeling clay—a lump of blue and a lump of yellow. When you take the man and woman—represented by two colors of clay—and mix them together, signifying life's trials and triumphs, a change takes place; you get green clay. And no matter how hard you try, you can't get the yellow and the blue back. You can split the combined lump up into two lumps again, but some changes are irreversible. The two "colors" have become one new color, one new entity. So it is with marriage. Those who have been through a divorce or the death of a spouse realize how dramatically marriage changes you internally and "in essence." You become part of another person and that person becomes part of you. The combining goes beyond the physical.

As I look at my own marriage, I see that in some mysterious way God has joined me to my wife—through the years of quiet evenings when we've connected; through surgeries, kids' accomplishments, parenting challenges, and loss of family members; through sweet stolen moments, family vacations, and failures; through times we have ministered together, endured serious illness, and through personal accomplishments, hers and mine. The sorrows have been easier to bear, the joys heightened. As life has pounded us, "mixed" us together, our synergy—the "together we are stronger than as two individuals"—has made us resilient because we've had each other.

Maybe we all tend to hold a lower view of marriage than we should because we see the world's standards displayed in TV sitcoms and movies. But marriage is of God's origination, not Hollywood's. He sets the rules and we ought to know them and walk in them. Obviously, starry-eyed nearly-weds need little encouragement here, but physical intimacy cannot develop in the absence of spiritual harmony. I'm not saying folks can't have enjoyable sex for a time; but apart from a relationship with Christ, they just cannot experience the fullness of marital intimacy that God intended.

Love that endures is much more than just erotic attraction. Marriage is not merely something to be endured. Many say, "But we just don't love each other anymore." When questioned about how much effort they had put into restoring their marriages, most say they tried but got tired and frustrated. They have confused the emotion of love with the commitment to love unconditionally. There is still hope. If Christ can be trusted for eternity, surely we can trust Him in day-to-day difficulties.

Someone asked a wife celebrating her fiftieth anniversary, "What is your secret to remaining happily married as long as you have?" She answered, "When we married, I made a list of ten faults—ten flaws—that, for the sake of our marriage, I would overlook in his life." She never actually wrote them down, but whenever a difficulty or argument arose, she would say to him, "You're lucky that was on the list." This wife demonstrated the kind of forgiveness and acceptance necessary to make a marriage work. So often we demand our own rights, and in the process we miss out on the joy God intended. In practice, marriage works when we willingly sacrifice ourselves and our rights for the sake of the beloved:

> My beloved is mine, and I am his.
> —Song of Solomon 2:16

Remember that marriage, as designed and ordained by God, provides a picture of God's heart to a world in darkness, a world in desperate need of reconciliation in its most intimate relationships. During His earthly sojourn, Jesus demonstrated complete submission to the will of His heavenly Father. Jesus walked in humility and compassion, the perfect servant leader. Jesus Christ embodies the faithful "lover" of all who respond in faith to the sacrificial offer of His pure life for theirs. In earthly, God-centered marriages, such faithfulness, gentleness, and steadfast love should reflect the sweet relationship God desires with His people. Thus, marriage not only fulfills us as created beings, it also gives testimony to a needy world of God's marvelous provision and His passionate desire for abiding fellowship with his children, who are created in His image.

Scripture calls this one-flesh picture a "mystery," but not the same sort of mystery as a Sherlock Holmes whodunit. The type of mystery I'm describing is something we would never have guessed had God not chosen to disclose it. Yet he did reveal it. He tells us that the marriage of one man to one woman for a lifetime pictures Jesus Christ and His bride, the church. Throughout Scripture we find that Christ considers His relationship with us to be personal and intimate, as groom and bride. He loves us as individuals, and He wants to relate, to fellowship, and to commune with us. Jesus leads with humility and total sacrifice. He shows this in the deepest, most personal human relationship we as men and women can experience—a godly marriage.

11
A Word to Husbands

Like an apple tree among the trees of the forest,
So is my beloved among the young men.
—SONG OF SOLOMON 2:3

When Ron and Cindy married, Cindy was the picture of perfect health. A fine athlete, she enjoyed a weekly round of tennis and played on the church softball team. But then she started experiencing numbness in her legs. She sought medical diagnosis and the report came back with bad news: Cindy had a debilitating disease. Today she can barely move most of her muscles, and she constantly fights depression because she must rely on her family to serve her day and night. "I have the mind and motivations of an athlete," she shared. "Yet my body will not cooperate. It's so frustrating! I can only cope with each day by God's grace, taking one day at a time. Sometimes I would like to take *two* days at a time!"

This was not what Ron expected to happen when he married a vibrant, healthy young woman. Together they have grieved the loss of Cindy's health, and it's been a constant battle to remain optimistic. Nevertheless, Ron shared, "Our communication is at its deepest level ever." He has taken seriously his vows to love his wife "in sickness and in health." By God's strength he continually—day in and day out—models God's picture of a self-sacrificing, loving husband, and she a godly, supportive wife, to the best of her ability.

After addressing wives in Ephesians 5, Paul shifts gears and instructs husbands. He records detailed guidelines for men, no doubt because we need it! Under the Holy Spirit's guidance, Paul wrote,

> Husbands, love your wives, just as Christ also loved the church and gave Himself up for her; that He might sanctify her, having cleansed her by the washing of water by the word, that He might present to Himself the church in all her glory, having no spot or wrinkle or any such thing; but that she should be holy and blameless.
>
> So husbands ought also to love their own wives as their own bodies. He who loves his own wife loves himself; for no one ever hated his own flesh, but nourishes and cherishes it, just as Christ also does the church, because we are members of His body. For this cause a man shall leave his father and mother, and shall cleave to his wife; and the two shall become one flesh. This mystery is great; but I am speaking with reference to Christ and the church. Nevertheless let each individual among you also love his own wife even as himself; and let the wife see to it that she respect her husband. (Eph. 5:25–33)

Having first addressed the entire church and admonished everyone to be filled with the Spirit, Paul outlines the specifics of what that looks like in the first-century home. He addresses wives, husbands, children, and finally the slaves who would have lived under the same roof with their masters. Notice that the context is Paul's recognition of the necessity of being yielded to the Spirit of God. Without the Spirit's enabling power, wives cannot submit to their husbands as to the Lord; husbands can't truly love sacrificially as Christ loved the church; children cannot honor their parents, and slaves cannot obey their masters. Yet Paul gives us a glimpse of how it will look if family members *are* yielded to the Spirit.

In his word to husbands, Paul admonishes them to model Christ's love, which is *sacrificial, sanctifying,* and *satisfying* for the beloved.

Sacrificial Love

God calls Christian husbands to a life of sacrifice. He sets a high standard for us. The word translated "love" is *agape*, a selfless, sacrificial love. It's what Paul describes in 1 Corinthians 13:5 as love that does not seek its own way. This love is primarily "other-centered." A lot of men like to regard submission as subjection, thinking of the husband as commander-in-chief with his troops. But the reality of the biblical picture reveals that the husband never gives orders. Rather, he acts in *agape* love. Such love is more than a "willingness to lay down your life for your wife" (should she ever need you to take the bullet). Rather, it's an actual sacrifice, a yielding that seeks her best, that lives with her in a way that she grows in godliness as the result of such love. How did Christ love the church? He modeled an exemplary life, but then died that "she," the church, might live eternally. Husbands love well when their pursuit of Christ "leads." The wife follows him while he devotedly follows Christ, sacrificing his personal dreams at times so that God in Christ is glorified. When we insist on having our own way, our expression of love is clearly not of God.

The military picture often used of "subjection/submission" found in Ephesians 5:22 is overused and overemphasized. Even the beautiful word "leadership" is now so loaded with images of authority and "rule" that Christlike maturity is not pictured at all. And, more importantly, the imperative to submit is directed at the wives, not for the husbands to dangle over their wives' heads as the "spiritual way" for *her* to live! It's like reading someone else's mail to demand submission. The Bible nowhere authorizes the husband to require submission. As we'll discuss in the next chapter, submission is an expression of maturity not a "role," and it is a voluntary act of worship before God. The imperative to husbands is to love as Christ loved and gave Himself up for His bride the church. The implications and application of this one imperative will require a lifetime of focus *and* the supernatural enablement of the Holy Spirit. Without God's help, this love is impossible. It's not natural; it is supernatural.

Reject the whole military picture, then. There is to be no marching about, screaming orders, nor should men expect to be saluted like General Patton or *The Sound of Music*'s Baron Von Trapp who used a separate whistle tone to summon each of his children! Instead, picture Christ washing the disciples' dirty feet, allowing Himself to be arrested, bound, flogged, spit upon, and crucified. "Greater love has no man than *this* . . ." That's how a godly husband loves his wife. If you bark commands, if you make demands, if you expect your wife to wait upon you, you violate the imperative to love in the biblical sense. Authentic Christian manhood in the home models sacrificial love, bringing order, not chaos. It involves men giving of themselves—not giving commands, not laying down the law, not expecting maid service. Men are to lay down their own wills, yielding the desire to have things their own way—to the point they would give up their very lives.

Are you willing to pay the price? Are you willing to give yourself up for your wife? No commands or demands, but servanthood by choice, setting an example by following Christ? To make this choice as a husband is to truly act in obedience to Christ.

Sanctifying Love

A husband's love is to sanctify his wife. "Sanctify" means to set apart or to make holy. When a couple marries, God sets them apart, and they forsake all others in the most intimate sense. Saying *yes* to one means saying *no* to everyone else.

When we say the husband must have "sanctifying love," we can give the wrong impression. A lot of people think that this means the husband has to possess more spiritual information than his wife does. But not every husband has the same exposure to spiritual information as his wife, though a husband should passionately pursue such information through having an active devotional life, being involved in local church ministry, meditating on Scripture, and being a man of prayer. A man's wife and family—if he has children—need to know he is striving after God.

A godly husband does not *have* to hold a formal instructional time for his family, as many have suggested. The Bible doesn't say, "Every Tuesday night you will lead family devotions." This is a wonderful model, but not the *only* model. Godliness is first a matter of character over activity and may be expressed differently in different homes.

A godly husband loves the Lord with all his heart, soul, and might. And he teaches God's Word to his children (if he has any). He speaks the Word in his house, when he walks, when he lies down, and when he rises up (see Deut. 6:5–7). He initiates spiritual conversation while he's hanging out at softball practice, taking his wife to dinner, driving on vacation, participating in small group fellowships. He models a godly example, initiates setting a Christ-centered tone, responds sensitively to spiritual truth, and encourages and affirms his family members in their efforts to pursue their individual relationships with God. He genuinely cares about the spiritual growth of his family. He asks spiritual questions. He seeks answers to things he doesn't yet fully understand. He is a lifetime student of God's revelation and of his wife.

Jesus Christ is the ultimate example of sanctifying love. He gave Himself for us in such a way that He purifies His bride, the Church—male and female. So a husband must love his wife in a way that purifies her. His love should challenge and encourage her to grow in holiness.

In turn, Christian marriages reflect this picture of purity and holiness to the world. We must make it our priority to spend time with God personally because we can get going so fast that we fail to recharge spiritually. Then in turn, our marriages suffer. We have to be growing spiritually on an individual basis to be able to create a home environment where spiritual truth is affirmed. We also need God's supernatural power to enable us to "lay down our lives."

With Christ indwelling both husband and wife, each should make it a priority to have individual times of prayer and Bible study. Then together they seek His will, submitting themselves to Him. Husbands should model a life of devotion and submission to God, but that too will vary in appearance. Godly friends and solid church-family relationships contribute significantly to maturing in the Christian faith. Do you as a husband make fellowship with other believers a priority? Does your wife need you to take the kids to the park or vacuum the hall so she can spend a few quiet moments with the Lord? This may be the model for you.

Satisfying Love

Additionally, we husbands must demonstrate satisfying love. Paul says a husband must "nourish" his wife as his own body. This "body" imagery doesn't refer just to personal physical fitness. Neither should we totally ignore our own physical condition, appearance, or hygiene. Rather, the focus is on nourishing the wife as part of the one—head and body—within the context of being filled with the Spirit. In the same way we care for our physical bodies by giving them proper rest and nutrition, we should care for our wives as spiritual "bodies"—because husband and wife are one.

The key imagery of this entire one-flesh passage, then, has to do with the "total body." The husband is the spiritual head, the wife is the spiritual body; together they are one. And in the one-flesh picture, divorce is "decapitation" because God has joined the two individuals together. So, in a very real sense, marriage should picture two becoming one.

When I care for and nourish my wife, Jane, I'm caring for myself at the same time. Not in a selfish, self-serving way, but I'm honoring the woman whom God has entrusted to me, living in a way that enables her to grow in godliness. An investment in your wife is really an investment in yourself, because the two of you have become one. To nourish implies the provision and protection of careful tending. A farmer who nourishes his garden by weeding, watering, and watching over it with care anticipates a bountiful yield, trusting God to provide rain and sun.

Many men feel comfortable that they're taking care of the "nourishes" part. We often say, "I'm working long hours and putting food

on the table and a roof over our heads, so I must be doing all right."
Yet, if during our own childhood we had experienced only this kind
of provision, we would have reached adulthood as emotionally deprived people (which is an unfortunate reality for many of us). God
created us to need so much more than that.

Do you nourish your wife's physical needs? Do you nourish her
intellectual needs? Her spiritual needs? Her emotional needs? Her
conversational needs? Do you encourage her to share her heart freely
with you, and do you confide your deepest thoughts and dreams?

The "cherish" part of how we men are to relate to our wives is
even more challenging. It reminds me of the story of a wife who
had been married twenty years. She asked her husband, "Do you
still love me?" "I said I did when we got married," he answered. "If
that changes, I'll let you know." When was the last time you said "I
love you" with meaning or demonstrated your care with an act of
thoughtfulness, of affection without expectation—perhaps a call,
a note, a surprise lunch or date? God instructs husbands to cherish
their wives. "Cherish" is a tender word, carrying the idea of being
full of compassion and sentiment. The closest description of *cherish* that comes to mind is something like "cuddling" or "lavishing
with tender affection." As Proverbs 19:22 states, "What is desirable
in a man is his kindness." God paints a picture of a hopelessly head-
over-heels-in-love romantic wooing his bride of however many years
(unlike many men today who think romantic foreplay is shouting,
"Ready or not, here I come . . ." or "Brace yourself"). Do you cherish
your wife? Does she receive from you the comfort, compassion, and
tenderness that God made her to need? Not sure? Ask her!

We all have different needs—intellectual, emotional, physical, and
spiritual. You cannot begin to meet your spouse's every need. Yet
you can play an integral role in fulfilling those needs, particularly if
she spends all day with toddlers or is dealing with moody teenagers.
Can you put down the paper so you can talk together? Do the dishes
so she can talk with a friend on the phone? Feed and bathe the kids
while she takes a night class? Or even change the dreaded diaper?

Think of her intellectual needs. She may have watched sixteen straight hours of *Dora the Explorer* or had a frustrating afternoon trying to grocery shop with a toddler. She may not have heard a sentence with more than two words in it for an entire day. When you're home, she'd like to hear words arranged in sentences and paragraphs with questions and answers. Or she may simply need you to listen. Our quiet, attentive presence is often the best support we can provide.

Our wives do not necessarily need us to play Mr. Fix-It when they share their problems. If a wife exclaims with a sigh, "I got stuck in line for forty minutes at Wal-Mart!" she may be looking for something like, "How frustrating for you," from her man, not "Next time shop at Albertson's, then." She may need to feel heard, to be held, to know she's loved in the midst of her frustrations. More than advice, a wife may merely need her husband's "ministry of presence" in times of grief, in times of joy, and through the sheer monotony of daily living.

What do we mean by emotional, relational needs? We all need to know we are significant, that we are important, that others value us as individuals. Do you help meet those needs for your wife? Sometimes "being strong for her" is not the solution. We may have to demonstrate our emotional sensitivity and vulnerability so our wives can see how much they mean to us.

Then there are physical, sexual needs. The Scriptures speak boldly and clearly about these. To pretend they don't exist is foolish. The marriage relationship can meet physical needs in a wonderful, glorious way. The world may do all it can to distort, pervert, and twist our views about sexuality, but God designed sex as a beautiful expression of joy between a husband and wife and of His love and feelings of intimacy toward us.

To summarize the Ephesians passage, a husband must love in a way that's sacrificial, sanctifying, and satisfying. As a result, his wife will have an ideal environment for growing in godliness. There's no contingency or escape clause. Love honors God.

Notice that the text doesn't say, "Love her sacrificially if she submits to you." A husband cannot demand or even expect submission.

In obedience to God, he loves his wife and entrusts her to the Lord. I think of a friend who faithfully visits his wife, an Alzheimer's patient. He loves her; he feeds her; he walks with her. Yet she does not know him. Sometimes she yells statements that humiliate him. He expects nothing of her, and daily he fully gives of his love without any hint of hope that she will respond. That's the kind of love to which God calls us, and it is possible by His supernatural grace.

Another husband, Bobby, is married to a woman who battles mental illness. She frequently spends all day in bed and feels threatened and angry if he tries to do housework; she struggles against bouts of depression that keep her inside the bedroom for days at a time. It's been years since they had any sort of physical relationship. "I'd gladly trade places with someone whose wife is physically limited," he shares. But Bobby chooses daily to show sacrificial love to his wife while his needs remain unmet.

God calls men to love sacrificially, even if they find themselves in a less than ideal situation. Are you willing to display this kind of love even if you go years without having any of your needs met, perhaps waiting on the Lord to soften her heart? Many marriages fail because we are unwilling to pay the price of self-sacrifice or we've never considered the biblical guidelines for marriage. We let our own desires take precedence over our created purpose, which is to worship and obey God.

When two sinners marry each other, you can bet they'll have moments of unhappiness ahead. At some point, your spouse will treat you badly. All marriages face stress and trials. Our bodies fail us. Our job security falls through. Life happens. Yet it's the total, unswerving, God-centered commitment to one another and to the marriage that provides the glue that holds a couple together.

Husband, study your wife. When couples come to me for counseling, I ask a seemingly simple question: Name three things that your spouse likes. The women can usually rattle them off. In fact, most could rattle off ten. But the men may ask, "Me? Are you talking to *me*? Three things she *likes*? Okay, me, myself, and I." If I ask the men to list their wives' favorite hobbies, their favorite places to go, what snack foods they really like, and so on, some of them who've been married for decades sit there dumbfounded and without a clue. Men, we must communicate better, more frequently, and more deeply to understand the precious gift God has given us in our wives.

We might sometimes do this by simply paying attention. When I went on vacation with my wife one year, I learned that she collected thimbles. So now whenever I travel, I try to find thimbles. To my surprise, I later learned that she also likes collecting onyx turtles. I search for those now, too.

I read one study that said husbands and wives communicate an average of thirty-seven minutes a week. That's five and a half minutes a day. Communication doesn't mean reading the paper while you pretend to listen with, "Uh-huh. Yeah. Yeah. Uh-huh." It doesn't include flipping the channels and saying, "Honey, can I have a Coke?" "Honey, what's for dinner?" "Honey, the kids are making noise." We score no communication points at all for these utterances. To get points we have to set down the paper, physically turn to face her, and communicate with body language, "I'm listening and interested." Good communication doesn't require agreement, but you must hear and understand what is said.

The inspired apostle Paul shared some great wisdom about marriage. So did the apostle Peter. He provides some brief but powerful instructions: "Live with your wives in an understanding way, as with a weaker vessel" (1 Peter 3:7). We may read "live with" or "tabernacle with" or "share the tent with" and assume that as long as we provide the place to live, we're fulfilling this Scripture. Wrong! As alluded to in Ephesians, the Bible directs us to share our time and lives and hearts. To live with a wife in an understanding way, or according to knowledge, means you actually have to know something about this woman with whom you live. Ignorance is dangerous! The phrase "live with" has sexual connotations, too. In addition, understanding our wives requires conversation, communication, the ability to sense and recognize needs, share joys, and bear sorrows.

Peter tells husbands to live with their wives "as with a weaker vessel." This does not mean weaker intellectually; it doesn't mean weaker spiritually; and it doesn't mean weaker emotionally. It is a comparative term that suggests weaker in a physical sense. Think of the difference between a husband and wife like the difference between a shatter-resistant car windshield and stained glass, or between a stainless-steel pot and bone-china vase. Peter says the wife is precious, a jewel: "Handle with care!"

A wife is a treasure in God's sight, female by divine design. She is a woman, crafted by God in His image. God says to grant her honor as a fellow heir of the grace of life. She's a coheir and coequal in essence and value. Both husbands and wives submit to the Lord. A wife does so by respecting her husband; the husband does so by treating his wife as a precious treasure, to be continually enjoyed.

How do you talk to her? Do you speak of her as a wonderful companion, a helper for whom you are grateful to God? Are you willing to give up your life for her? Or do you speak of her with sarcasm and disrespect in front of others? Do you whine at her requests with, "Yes, dear!" or worse yet, treat her as if she weren't there? Do you act as though she were your personal slave and attempt to justify your actions by saying that's her biblical role?

While sex is the number one expressed need for most men, the corresponding need for most women is relational interaction that includes talking, affirmation, and affection from their husbands. If you feel frustrated that your wife is not "giving" you sex often enough, ask yourself, "Am I giving her my focused, undivided attention as often as she desires it?"

To live in an understanding way means you have to listen well, to talk and ask questions. One member of my church said, "Our marriage works great; I find out what she wants me to do and I do it." While he said this tongue in cheek, I suspect many marriages operate under the "Don't rock the boat" philosophy: pretend all is well—don't ask, don't tell—and keep peace at any cost. That's not what Scripture says men should do. Husbands need to strive for unity with their wives, but they should also retain their individuality and initiative, seeking ultimately to do what God wants them to do.

Peter pictures husbands consistently granting their wives honor, respecting them, treating them as precious treasures. Thus, Scripture is clear on this—there is *never* an excuse for physical, verbal, or emotional abuse. If unresolved anger remains between you and your wife—if you have not settled your differences to the fullest extent that you're able—you're out of fellowship with God and, Peter writes, your prayers will be "hindered."

Scripture says, then, that my relationship with my wife impacts my relationship with God. Our marriages affect our prayer lives. Are your prayers being heard or hindered? If you have a problem with anger, bitterness, or slander, you're not allowing the Spirit to control your life. Praying, except to seek forgiveness and reconciliation, is wasted breath.

So in Peter's passage, as well as in Paul's, we see a call for husbands to love selflessly. That could mean laying down your life, but it could also mean something that may be, for you, even more difficult: it could mean laying down the remote. It might mean giving up the bigger bowl of ice cream . . . or the Rose Bowl game on New Year's Day!

I grew up dreaming what it would be like to have a family. Back then I imagined that when I married, I'd be a great husband who would treat my wife like a queen. But royal families historically have little to commend them. I came to realize I'd better find some better models. A healthy dose of a book penned by a different king—Solomon's Song of Solomon—shows us that believers have the potential to have the best romances in the universe. Husbands, do others who observe you comment about how much you love your wife? In Song of Solomon 2:4, the bride says this:

> He has brought me to his banquet hall,
> And his banner over me is love.

In Solomon's time, when the troops needed to regroup, their leaders raised a wide banner so that all could see where to go. It was like a gigantic traveling billboard for the company whose insignia it bore. Solomon's love for his bride was like this banner. It was public and easily seen by anyone observing. Rather than being ashamed of her, he openly delighted in her.

Think of times when you've seen a man treating his wife tenderly in a public place. Maybe he opened her car door, took her hand, and said kind words to her. Maybe he leaned forward over dinner to whisper something sweet. You probably said to yourself, "That guy really loves his wife."

Much of the lasting joy in a marriage comes from little things—the small courtesies, the day-to-day doing of the stuff that you might consider insignificant. We may think that if we pull it together for Christmas and anniversaries and maybe even Valentine's Day, we are "Husband of the Year" material. Yet we cannot erect a magnificent monument on a poor foundation. Those one-time "big deals" do not compensate for a lack of daily kindnesses.

When I practiced obstetrics/gynecology, I frequently asked women about their homes and their husbands. I learned that wives generally are unimpressed with the many hours their husbands put in at work. They actually prefer more time with their men at home. When we get to the end of our lives and stand before the Father, I doubt He will assign "mansion space" according to the number of hours worked. God will, however, hold us accountable for whether or not each of us loved his wife sacrificially.

The flip side, which is equally destructive, is the husband who refuses to work or insists on keeping a failing business afloat. He declines to provide adequately for his family's material well-being. This does not honor the Lord.

Work-related distractions are not the only environmental hazards that can erode relationships. Factor in hobbies and sports. I know guys who play softball five nights a week, bowl four nights a week, and have nights out with the guys two nights a week. That's more nights than there are in a week! So I'm guessing they're not home a lot. None of these activities, of course, is inherently bad, but we've got to keep them in balance. How do you know if you're overdoing it? Ask your wife. If you come in and say, "Hi, honey!" and she asks you to show some photo identification or state your full name, you've probably been out too much.

Just ask, "Do you feel like I spend enough time with you?" If the answer is no, do something about it without delay.

You can improve your marriage. No matter how good it is, it can always be better. So start where you are and make a commitment now to cultivate the relationship, to think creatively of ways to bring more joy to your wife. Be forewarned: if you've been a lazy slob for a long time and start to love your wife sacrificially, she may faint from shock. But go for it anyway—at least she'll be a happy woman as you rush her to the hospital. Communicate love that is tender, compassionate, and sacrificial.

Marriage is full of adventure, and change is a significant part of that journey. We grow; we learn more; actions that were great yesterday may not be so great today. You may do something caring and compassionate one day, and she appreciates it; yet you try it again and it falls flat. That keeps life interesting.

One evening my friend Danny picked up a damp bath towel and, oblivious to the implications, exclaimed, "Ummmmm! Charlotte, this smells like you!" His wife of many years replied, "Ooooooooooh, Danny, that's the most romantic thing you've ever said!" Although not fully grasping how his recognizing the scent of her body lotion on the towel constituted a romantic remark, Danny seized the moment. A wonderful, romantic evening followed.

Almost gleeful about his incredible discovery—the key to his beloved wife's inner fire—Danny could hardly wait until the following night. Once again, armed with passion unquenchable, he declared, "Charlotte, this towel smells like you!" His remark was met with silence. He repeated in the most seductive voice he could generate, "Charlotte, this smells like you." Her response dashed his hope: "Yes, I just used that to dry off." No romance, no passionate embrace. Just a matter-of-fact reply. An educated man with a doctoral degree, Danny concluded, "Women: a mystery." Few would argue with his astute assessment or with the ageless truth that the key to unlocking the heart's passion remains elusive.

Each marriage is unique, but all marriages experience growth and change. And people resist nothing more than they resist change. Sometimes change may mean, as in Ron and Cindy's case, adapting to the shocking revelation that your marriage is going to require a lot more work than you anticipated. Circumstances sometimes develop that stretch us to the limit of our ability to give, requiring us to rely more on God's all-sufficient grace. But we honor God as we rely on His strength to live our lives as godly husbands, and in the process we create a beautiful living, breathing portrait of the love of Christ for His church.

12

A Word to Wives

I am the rose of Sharon,
The lily of the valleys.
—SONG OF SOLOMON 2:1

Just for fun one night, my (Sandi's) married sister, Mary, and her single friend, Angie, spent an evening doing an Internet search of Christian dating services. They both groaned when they saw one advertisement that read, "Christian male looking for buxom woman with biblical view of submission."

In the same way that a "Christian beefcake with a biblical view of self-sacrificing love" would be less than the whole picture of God's ideal man, a Barbie look-alike with a servant heart is less than the sum total of God's ideal woman.

What does the Bible say about what a good woman looks like? God has a lot to say. It all starts in the garden of Eden. God created Adam's wife as a helper. To understand what that means, we consider the type of help we see in these non-marriage examples:

- A daughter asks her mom for some *help* with math. The mother understands algebra and can explain and guide her daughter through working the formulas.

- One friend *helps* another by showing her how to use the computer so that she has the necessary skills to change jobs.
- An obstetrician involved with a complicated delivery calls out for his partner to *help*. He wants someone who knows what needs to be done without being told.

In each of these cases, the helpers have strengths they use to aid the ones needing help. Unlike an apprentice who helps from an untrained or unskilled position, these "helpers" give assistance from a position of ability. Now consider Genesis 2:18:

> The LORD God said, "It is not good for the man to be alone;
> I will make him a helper suitable for him."

In the past, many have suggested this word "help" involves subordination, indicating that woman is lesser than man. At first glance this word is, frankly, a little less than exciting if we link it with common uses of the term—such as Hamburger Helper or "plumber's helper." Yet when we consider how biblical writers used this word, we see that it carries a strongly positive meaning linked to words like "aid" and "support." It's frequently used in reference to God helping His people in the face of enemies. For example in Psalm 54 the psalmist writes, "Strangers are attacking me. . . . Surely God is my *help*; the Lord is the one who sustains me" (vv. 3–4 NIV, emphasis added). In the Bible we read no fewer than fourteen times where God is said to help humans.

To demean the woman's God-intended task of helping her husband by insinuating (or outright declaring) that hers is a somehow less important rank or "role" ignores the biblical use of the word elsewhere. As helper to the man, the woman meets his insufficiencies with her own sufficiencies. Perhaps this is why opposites tend to attract. Together you reflect the image of God as your strengths and weaknesses complement each other. Think of the money-whiz wife helping her impulsive husband; or the spontaneous wife helping her highly regimented man; or the reserved husband married to a woman who loves adventure.

In addition to being a helper, the woman is described in Genesis as "suitable" or "according to what corresponds to him—equal and adequate to himself." Thus, the woman is an aid equal to and corresponding to the man, a helper who will enable him to achieve the blessings of God that he cannot fully achieve on his own. Her presence in creation was the only addition needed before God could pronounce his creation "very good."

You might ask, "How can I help my husband?" Begin by figuring out his strengths and weaknesses and then weighing them against your own. During a marriage conference someone asked, "Who should balance the checkbook?" The answer: whoever the two of you decide can best handle it.

Contrary to what's been taught in many churches and seminars, the husband does not have to "buffer his wife from the stress of finances" by handling all of the money matters. Consider Paula, a CPA, who is married to a man who asked, "So I actually have to have income before I can deduct expenses?" If this man handled their money, he would not buffer her from stress; they would be *in* the buff, because they'd have no money.

Another asked, "Who washes the dishes?" Again, that depends. Are you both employed all day? Do you need to divide the domestic tasks so you'll have time together? Or is one of you a homemaker? Or unemployed, and thus available to do a greater percentage of the domestic tasks? Nowhere in the Bible does it say, "The man earns the money, takes out the trash, and handles the lawn and cars; the woman changes all the diapers, provides all the parental instruction, does all the shopping, washes the dishes, and keeps the laundry done." Some believe this is the biblical division of labor. Does your husband love to cook? We see biblical examples where Jacob made stew, Stephen and a small group of men served food to widows, and Jesus prepared fish for His disciples.

Paul does say he wants wives to be "homeworkers" (see Titus 2:5), but bear in mind that he's speaking to women in a culture in which most of the commerce happened in the home.[1] So both husband and wife contributed to the economics of the household, as is still necessary for most families in the world today.

Questions about how to fairly distribute the weight of household tasks are some of the greatest struggles couples encounter in their first years together. The Bible does not list tasks separated by gender. But it does say that two become one. Together husband and wife work it out so all necessary tasks get done, both deal justly with one another, and both are affirmed.

And as we mentioned earlier, in the first years of marriage one major cause of marital discord is sex. Men generally rank sex as their number-one need; women generally rate sex below their top five. How can you be a helper to your husband in the satisfying of his sexual desires?

As the years pass, discord may arise from other sources. Some men wish their wives would keep pace with them intellectually. Others are concerned that they won't be able to keep pace with their wives' professional competence. Or a husband may struggle with his wife's cavalier attitude about her appearance: "What does an extra fifty pounds hurt?" she may think.

For couples who have children, it can become even more difficult to maintain the daily communication that is so important for deepening intimacy. With kids going to soccer and drama class and band, the love life becomes a low priority.

Statistics show, however, that the average couple who has children will spend more than half their lives without kids. Why are divorce rates so high between ages forty-five and fifty-five? Because people "run out" of children. They've hung together because at least they could argue about the kids: "You're not doing that right!" or "You should be teaching that kid some manners." It ties them together. But that's not what makes a marriage.

What, then, does he consider his greatest perceived needs? How can your priorities reflect your acknowledgment of what's important to him? How can you use your strengths to bless and complement your husband, to be the kind of "help" to him God intended?

In Genesis and the garden of Eden, God gave us *helper* as one model for wives. Proverbs give us another glance at God's ideal for wives:

> A wife of noble character who can find?
>   She is worth far more than rubies.
> Her husband has full confidence in her
>   and lacks nothing of value.
> She brings him good, not harm,
>   all the days of her life.
> She selects wool and flax
>   and works with eager hands.
> She is like the merchant ships,
>   bringing her food from afar.
> She gets up while it is still dark;
>   she provides food for her family
>   and portions for her servant girls.
> She considers a field and buys it;
>   out of her earnings she plants a vineyard.
> She sets about her work vigorously;
>   her arms are strong for her tasks.
> She sees that her trading is profitable,
>   and her lamp does not go out at night.
> In her hand she holds the distaff
>   and grasps the spindle with her fingers.
> She opens her arms to the poor
>   and extends her hands to the needy.
> When it snows, she has no fear for her household;
>   for all of them are clothed in scarlet.
> She makes coverings for her bed;
>   she is clothed in fine linen and purple.
> Her husband is respected at the city gate,
>   where he takes his seat among the elders of the land.

She makes linen garments and sells them,
   and supplies the merchants with sashes.
She is clothed with strength and dignity;
   she can laugh at the days to come.
She speaks with wisdom,
   and faithful instruction is on her tongue.
She watches over the affairs of her household
   and does not eat the bread of idleness.
Her children arise and call her blessed;
   her husband also, and he praises her:
"Many women do noble things,
   but you surpass them all."
Charm is deceptive, and beauty is fleeting;
   but a woman who fears the LORD is to be praised.
Give her the reward she has earned,
   and let her works bring her praise at the city gate.

31:10–31 NIV

One woman insisted, "I can't stand that Proverbs 31 lady. I feel tired just thinking about her." This woman is so competent, so intelligent, so industrious and strong that she certainly challenges any suggestion that the "little wife" has no independent thoughts, that she's less intelligent than any man, or that godly women must be passive, timid, dainty, or fearful.

Perhaps it would help you to know that a king named Lemuel wrote this passage of Scripture in Hebrew. It forms an acrostic poem, with a line for each letter of the Hebrew alphabet. The contemporary English equivalent might be something like, "An Excellent Wife—from A to Z." It has also been suggested that this passage is not a snapshot of one day in this woman's life. Only Superwoman could in one twenty-four-hour period find and purchase exotic foods, make a real estate purchase, plant a vineyard, operate the spinning wheel, make and sell clothing, and help the poor. The mere reading of it is enough to cause heatstroke.

Rather than a snapshot, this is more like a movie depicting the phases of this woman's life. And at the end of her days her children rise up and call her blessed. After her youth is gone and wrinkles line her face, she still is a woman to be praised because she has the qualities that outlast physical beauty.

The word translated "noble character" could also be rendered "excellence" or "strength." It's used in other places to describe both physical strength and strength of character—so this woman is virtuous, noble, or possessing valor. This is no helpless waif who depends on her husband to make every decision. Within a context of mutual trust characterizing this woman's relationship with her husband, she possesses so much competence that she can go buy a field on her own. She completes him, taking all her abilities and developing them to the fullest.

She is also a woman of relationships. Her servants, the needy, her children, and her husband all depend on her strength and character. Yet her key relationship is her vertical one—with the Lord.

So a godly wife is a helper and a woman of strength. But there's another word that keeps showing up in the Bible when wives are described: *submission*.

Submission? Whoa! The "s" word! Mention it and people think of slave girls who nod "Yes, Master." They're pictured as the kind of women whose meekness enables domestic violence and makes them "doormats"—and who are sought on "Christian" Internet ads.

Yet *submit* is a biblical word. Husbands usually are instructed to love their wives and wives usually are instructed to submit. There are places where wives are told to love their husbands (Titus 2:4) and husbands are directed to honor/respect their wives (1 Peter 3:7), but the emphasis usually is the other way around. Four times God instructs wives to submit:

> Submit to one another out of reverence for Christ. Wives, submit to your own husbands, as to the Lord. For the husband is the head of the wife as Christ is the head of

the church, his body, of which he is the Savior. Now as the church submits to Christ, so also wives should submit to their husbands in everything. (Eph. 5:21–24 NIV)

Wives, submit to your husbands. (Col. 3:18 NIV)

Likewise, teach the older women to be reverent in the way they live, not to be slanderers or addicted to much wine, but to teach what is good. Then they can train the younger women to love their husbands and children, to be self-controlled and pure, to be busy at home [lit. "homeworkers"], to be kind, and to be subject to their husbands, so that no one will malign the word of God. (Titus 2:3–5 NIV)

The fourth "submission" passage is 1 Peter 3, and we'll look at that one a little later.

First, though, I've heard it said that the wife's "role" is to submit. Yet submission is not a role. Being a wife is a role. Submission is an expression of Spirit-filled maturity. When God gives His development plan for intimacy, He tells wives to submit, but He usually does so within the larger context of sharing lives together in fellowship with the Spirit of God.

Because the word *submit* carries so much baggage, perhaps it would help to begin by clarifying what submission does not mean.

Submission Is Not . . .

- giving up all efforts to influence your husband, giving in to his every demand.
- letting him think he's better at something than you are when he isn't.
- waiting on your husband. (The woman in Proverbs 31 has servants; she is not herself a slave.)
- obeying. Submit differs from obey, which is given as instruction to children and slaves—and is certainly our duty to God.
- letting the husband make the final decision.

- tolerating abuse. (Submission never means tolerating abuse. The best way to be a "helper" to an abuser is to expose him.)
- going along with your husband even if he wants you to sin (as Sapphira did in Acts 5), or if he endangers your life (as in the case of Abigail, described in 1 Samuel 25).

Finally, submission is not the sum total of what a wife is to be. It was one aspect of first-century biblical instruction for her. She is a helper, an able woman full of character, and she needs to respect her man (Eph. 5:33). The New Testament writers talking about marriage most often tell husbands to love sacrificially and wives to submit. These are two sides of the same coin.

Jesus Christ demonstrated submission perfectly. As a result, Paul exhorts us in Philippians 2:5–8,

> Your attitude should be the same as that of Christ Jesus: Who, being in very nature God, did not consider equality with God something to be grasped, but made himself nothing, taking the very nature of a servant, being made in human likeness. And being found in appearance as a man, he humbled himself and became obedient to death—even death on a cross! (NIV)

The Son is equal with the Father, yet He chose to place Himself in a position to serve the Father. Wives are equal with their husbands, yet they choose to serve their husbands. All Christians are to submit themselves to God.

Jesus demonstrated that submission is not to be feared or avoided but embraced. Submission involves "emptying ourselves." Imagine the Philippians 2 passage restated from the wife's perspective: "Even though you are equal with your husband, do not consider equality with him something to be held on to, but empty yourself." It involves having the same kind of attitude Jesus demonstrated toward the Father in the garden of Gethsemane: "Not my will, but yours be done" (Luke 22:42 NIV).

So What Is Submission? Submission Is . . .

- being willing and ready to renounce our own wills and ways for that of another.
- the opposite of striving, rebellion, self-assertion; and of loud, pushy, obnoxious, or boisterous opposition toward another. It involves deference and surrender, inner stillness, and peace.
- *willingly* yielding our rights.
- a *voluntary* attitude of respect and cooperation.
- restricted to a woman's actions toward her own husband (as opposed to the belief of some that all women should submit to all men).
- an act of God-worship. Submission demonstrates our love for the Lord.
- entered into with a gentle, quiet spirit. This does not necessarily mean silence, although sometimes silence may be necessary to demonstrate a kind and gracious attitude that radiates peace.

As the Bible teaches over and over, "the way up is down." The way to be great is to serve. The submission wives are to demonstrate is a voluntary attitude of cooperation, of assuming responsibilities. If you look at this list, it's not much different from sacrificial love, is it?

And what happens if your husband doesn't show you that kind of love?

Although evidence may seem to prove your husband is less than ideal, your responsibility as a godly woman in obedience to God requires submission. You may say, "Submit to him? He's a jerk; you don't know him." That may be true. Perhaps submission becomes more necessary, in fact, if your husband is the kind of man who spends the vacation money on a satellite dish and then sits belching as he channel surfs, yelling, "Hey, woman! Bring me a beer!" If he's thoughtful, she can focus more of her energy on helping and supporting him with her strengths; if he's difficult, she must expend more energy working at demonstrating respect when she wants to lash out with, "Would you like that beer with strychnine in it?"

Peter included wives married to difficult men when he gave these instructions:

> Likewise you wives, be submissive to your own husbands, that even if some do not obey the word, they, without a word, may be won by the conduct of their wives, when they observe your chaste conduct accompanied by fear. Do not let your beauty be that outward adorning of arranging the hair, of wearing gold, or of putting on fine apparel; but let it be the hidden person of the heart, with the incorruptible ornament of a gentle and quiet spirit, which is very precious in the sight of God. For in this manner, in former times, the holy women who trusted in God also adorned themselves, being submissive to their own husbands, as Sarah obeyed Abraham, calling him lord, whose daughters you are if you do good and are not afraid with any terror. (1 Peter 3:1–6 NKJV)

We have to understand the culture of the day. When Peter wrote this, he was writing to Christians living in a pagan culture. Members of false religions went to a temple where they expressed worship by engaging in sex with temple prostitutes. In those times the wife assumed her husband's religion; to do otherwise was considered unfaithfulness. So Peter wrote to Christian women, wives who had come to know the Lord yet remained married to spiritually lost men. Can you imagine what that would be like?

It came as a real shock for these men when their wives became Christians. They would arrive home from worship at the temple of Aphrodite (or that city's equivalent) only to find that their wives had become believers in Jesus Christ and were trying to live godly, pure, reverent lives. These wives might then take exception to their husbands' excursions of "worship," creating major conflict. When these wives came to know the Lord, the first thing they wanted to do, of course, was tell everyone else about salvation in Christ.

Missy, a new believer in our own time, shared that she wants to exclaim to her husband, "I can live again; my life is complete because the Spirit of God now lives in me!" Yet because she's married to a man who doesn't know the Lord, she knows this sort of enthusiastic talk would alienate him from the gospel. Scripture says the way to win a "lost" husband is to demonstrate chaste, pure, reverent behavior—and to do so without uttering a word of correction. What you do is more important than what you say. In ongoing intimate relationships, quiet actions communicate truth best.

Peter goes on to write about external appearance: "Do not let your beauty be [merely] outward adorning." Avoid making yourself attractive only on the outside—by braiding your hair, wearing gold jewelry, and wearing pretty dresses. (Neither should your adornment always amount to baggy gray sweats and pink curlers.) Concentrate on the inner person, the hidden person of the heart, working to develop the imperishable quality of a gentle and quiet spirit, which is precious in the sight of God. This does not mean a wife can't have an extroverted personality; it means she has a quiet *spirit*.

You as a wife are your husband's peer, his equal in value to God. You glorify God by complementing your husband. You can create, imagine, emote, reason, and process information. You can buy, sell, diagnose, build, design, philosophize, and write epics. Together you share life as equals, as joint heirs of the grace of life.

This is God's ideal. Yet we do not live in an ideal world. So we ask, "How can I submit, especially if he's not loving me?" The only way we can do *any* of this is by God's grace. Lemuel gives us a hint of this at the end of Proverbs 31, where we read, "A woman who fears the LORD, she shall be praised." Jesus said, "Apart from Me you can do nothing" (John 15:5). Living in a quiet spirit requires supernatural enabling. It means having a moment-by-moment walk with the Lord in which you draw on His power to be all He intends you to be. The greatest thing you can do for your partner is to be controlled by the Spirit, participating in a worshipping community to support you.

The apostle Paul summarizes (Eph. 5:33), reminding the Spirit-filled husband to love and the wife to respect. Neither is conditional. He is to love her sacrificially, even if she is unloving. She is called, as an act of Christ-worship, to respect her husband, even if that means respecting the "role" of husband that he might mature into it. Recall how the wife in 1 Peter lives in a way that draws her unbelieving husband to Christ. The husband is to honor his wife as a joint-heir, so his prayers won't be hindered. Such loving and respecting make for perfect symmetry, possible only with the enabling of the Holy Spirit.

A woman who reflects godly qualities—a helper, a woman of strength, a wife who willingly "empties herself" and demonstrates respect for her husband, and above all else fears the Lord—has "worth that is far above rubies." She will influence more than her husband and family. In the larger community, people will often sit up and notice. A fourth-century, non-Christian Roman who opposed the gospel still exclaimed enviously, "What women these Christians have!"[2]

13
A Call to Purity

I adjure you, O daughters of Jerusalem,
By the gazelles or by the hinds of the field,
That you will not arouse or awaken my love,
Until she pleases.
—SONG OF SOLOMON 2:7

An unmarried couple goes "too far" and she winds up pregnant. She has the baby, but conceals the father's identity to protect his reputation. A scenario from *Desperate Housewives*? An old episode of *Grey's Anatomy*? Actually, it was the plot of Nathaniel Hawthorne's book *The Scarlet Letter*, published more than 150 years ago. Some things never change.

I (Dr. Bill) spoke at a pastor's conference overseas, and the spiritual leaders of the nation I was visiting expressed amazement over the sexual problems facing their Christian singles—a trend toward immorality running about twenty years behind a similar trend in America. Sexual immorality is public and prominent today, but sexual issues have probably plagued every culture, just as they did in Corinth two thousand years ago. (To refresh your memory, you may want to read 1 Corinthians, particularly chapters 5–7.)

God's Word is as relevant today as it was to the Corinthians then. We have sexual desires that God created, and the Scriptures charge us, if we are married, to meet each other's needs. If unmarried, we are to remain sexually pure. That means more than abstaining from vaginal intercourse. It involves abstaining from fondling genitals, oral sex, and physical pleasuring that leads to orgasm. The biblical word is *porneia*, which is often translated "fornication," but involves a wide range of sexual practices.[1] It bears repeating that the question to ask is not "How far can I go?" but "What standard of purity honors God?" Such a standard is not what we will view on TV or at the movies or read in magazines or on blogs. Yet it is clearly what God desires and has determined as best for our well-being.

God speaks boldly about sexuality. He created us male and female, so our sexuality is no surprise to Him. And He made us with sexual desires.

It all starts at conception, when God determines whether we will be male or female. Biology demonstrates that maleness or femaleness begins in the chromosomes at the very moment our DNA lines up. The Bible reveals this in Psalm 139: "For you created my inmost being; you knit me together in my mother's womb. . . . All the days ordained for me were written in your book before one of them came to be" (vv. 13, 16 NIV). God knows us as individuals while in the physical realm we're little more than composite masses of molecules.

Soon, a young child grows and reaches that dreaded time called puberty, when a hormonal storm hits; hormones can overwhelm young people. At puberty the body starts to change, and the child's maleness or femaleness becomes more pronounced. Puberty is a difficult, confusing time, a period of great transition. During puberty a person has a full range of feelings, including sexual drives and impulses. This is not wrong. Our sensuality, our feelings based in our sexuality, is from God. The fact that humans begin to feel physically attracted to each other does not shock or surprise Him. But the time of raging hormones can bring confusion about exactly what or whom a young person is attracted to. It's a delicate time. That's why mature, Spirit-filled adults must point our kids toward what's right while communicating to them that it's okay to have strong desires and feelings. Otherwise, they're going to get plenty of distorted instruction from the world.

Once we survive puberty and make it to adulthood, we find that we still have feelings—strong feelings. We tend to underestimate the power of hormones, the pull of visual stimulation, and the shrewdness of the media. Advertisers use sexual imagery to sell everything from cars to cosmetics because it works. As a society, we fall for the idea that if a pretty girl or a studly guy drinks a certain brand of soft drink or drives a particular type of car, we need one, too. Madison Avenue knows our susceptibility, and they sell us their products by taking advantage of it.

When it comes to sex, we may notice two extremes—anywhere, any time, with anyone, or to be avoided at all costs in any situation. Those who don't lean toward promiscuity may view sex as Count Leo Tolstoy did. A married man and professing Christian, he wrote the classic *War and Peace*. He advocated abstinence within marriage, advising husbands and wives to sleep in separate rooms. The Shakers, an early American sect, preached the abolition of sexual relations. After reading some of their literature, Tolstoy wrote to a friend, "I shall not overcome this problem in a hurry, because I am a dirty, libidinous old man!" What a tragedy that he considered his God-created desires for his wife to be dirty. Tolstoy considered marriage nothing more than legalized prostitution. His biographer wrote,

> For him the enemy was woman; and the reason was that he was too strongly sensual not to be continually led into temptation. In physical pleasure he abandoned some part of himself; when the act was over he hated the woman who had gained that moment of power over him and he scurried back into his shell, determined not to come out of it again.[2]

Either extreme about sex—the view that the marriage bed constitutes legalized prostitution or the belief that "anything goes at any time"—is wrong.

In the seventh chapter of his first letter to the church at Corinth, the apostle Paul answered specific questions the church had sent to him about sexuality and celibacy. He was not writing an unabridged manual on the subject; he wrote specifically to one set of issues. For this reason it is important that we not limit our understanding of God's teaching on marriage and singleness to this one portion of Scripture. Still, it's important to consider what and to whom Paul wrote.

Corinth stood at the center of a religious system that fostered sexual immorality. People went regularly to pagan temples and had sex with temple priests and priestesses as a part of worship. Because immorality ran rampant in their city, the Corinthian Christians asked Paul, "Isn't it better just to totally forget about sex? Wouldn't it be smarter, even as married Christians, to abstain from that stuff?" These early Christians were willing to embrace such an extreme position because they'd been strongly influenced by the Greek thinkers of their day, who commonly believed there was something inherently sinful in the flesh. The Corinthian Christians adopted the Greek idea that the flesh was lower and dangerous, and must be avoided completely.

In response, Paul wrote this: "Now concerning the things about which you wrote, it is good for a man not to touch a woman" (1 Cor. 7:1). "Touch" in this context is a euphemism for sexual intercourse; it's used here in the same way we use "sleep with" to refer to sex. It's like saying you want a "bite to eat" when you really mean you want a whole sandwich. Paul goes on to say, "But because of immoralities, let each man have his own wife, and let each woman have her own husband" (7:2). Paul was advocating gender equality, a ground-breaking concept in his culture—a culture that imposed on women the status of property with no rights.

"Let the husband fulfill his duty to his wife," he said, "and likewise also the wife to her husband. The wife does not have authority over her own body, but the husband does; and likewise also the husband does not have authority over his own body, but the wife does. Stop depriving one another" (7:3–5). Paul uses the word "duty" here, which includes the obligation to meet the physical needs of the spouse. But, as mentioned, his words are not the entire biblical treatment of sex. Remember when God told Abraham that Sarah would conceive Isaac? She asked, "Shall I have *pleasure*, my lord being old also?" (Gen. 18:12, emphasis added).

Paul's next statement, the idea that each marriage partner has authority over the other's body, represents for some one of the least popular sections of Scripture. These people want to believe, "I have my rights. I can do what I want with my own body." But if you have chosen to marry, you've yielded that right.

When I practiced medicine, I used to teach a "soon-to-be-married" class at church several times a year. I taught about sex. Many churches and most Sunday school teachers don't want to talk about sex. This uneasiness and insecurity resulted in many invitations for the "doctor" to address this issue. Each time I did so, I handed out cards so attendees could write questions, because nobody would actually raise their hands and ask, "Do you have to have sex when you're upset or 'not in the mood'?" or "Do I have to give it to him every time he asks?" Yet at least one person has asked these questions at every conference. (The questions submitted form the basis for the Q & A sections of this book.)

Apparently we've ignored a key distinctive of marriage. The Scriptures say the marital union is a relationship in which we no longer have final say about our own bodies. When we marry, we voluntarily relinquish those rights, giving that authority to our wife or husband. We take what God has entrusted to us—the temple of His Spirit—and in turn entrust it to our husband or wife. One counselor we know recommended that a client deprive her husband of the sexual relationship for months, until she decided she "wanted it." This counselor reasoned that it would be damaging to have sex just to meet her husband's needs.

Paul suggests otherwise. He tells us not to deprive each other. The word "deprive," like the word "defraud," was commonly used in relation to debt. His idea is that when you marry, you owe a debt to your partner. You obligate yourself to meet his or her sexual needs. To deprive that person, to defraud him or her, fails to keep that promise; it amounts to defaulting on a debt.

As we study Scripture, we see that Paul gave only one reason for allowing physical needs within marriage to go unmet. That one exception was when a couple agreed together that, for a short time, they would abstain to devote themselves to prayer. But it is only "for a time" and "by agreement," according to Scripture. This clearly counters the erroneous view that God created sexual expression solely for the purpose of procreation.

The Corinthians wondered if real, spiritual Christians truly need physical sexual interaction. They thought that perhaps celibacy, even within marriage, was a much higher moral good. But Paul argued, in essence, "No, that's dangerous thinking. You start depriving one another and Satan will get a foothold." That's what he is saying when he writes, ". . . lest Satan tempt you because of your lack of self-control" (7:5). We live in a day when this may be the most popular of Satan's footholds. Of all the areas in which he can attack us, our morality seems most vulnerable. *Before* marriage the great temptation is to engage in immorality, and *after* marriage Satan tempts us to deny each other sexual relations.

God designed sex for oneness in marriage; He didn't intend it to be a weapon of interpersonal warfare. Nor did He intend its use as leverage for bargaining. He designed it as a means of intimate communication between a man and a woman who have committed themselves to each other for life. In any other context, the purpose of sex gets twisted.

God says marriage is a good thing; but marriage isn't the only thing. In the larger context of life, our obedient service to God is more important, and we can offer that service as single people. Paul goes on to address singles: "Yet I wish that all men were even as I myself am. However, each man has his own gift from God, one in this manner, and another in that. But I say to the unmarried and to widows that it is good for them if they remain even as I" (7:7–8). He brings up at this point the topic of celibacy, and he uses the word "gift," which in Greek is *charisma*. It's the same word he uses in later chapters to describe the spiritual gifts with which we serve the church. Some believe the "gift" of which Paul speaks is a special enabling from God that allows the unmarried person to be content as a single. Others believe the "gift" is whatever one's marital status is. In this vein, David Hoffeditz, author of *They Were Single Too,* writes, "The true issue is not to determine one's gift, but rather to faithfully serve God in whatever position He grants. While neither the gift of marriage nor singleness is permanent, we accept our personal marital status as a gift given by God."[3]

That being the case, "without a partner" does not necessarily mean "without a ministry." Clearly God uses single people. Jesus never married. John the Baptist never married. Add to that Mary and Martha, Jeremiah, and Nehemiah, not to mention the widowed Anna and Ruth.[4] Paul was probably married at one time but was single at the time he wrote this epistle. (Paul was a rabbi and perhaps a member of the Sanhedrin, which required its members to be married. The leaders may have made an exception for Paul, but it's more likely either that his wife died or she left Paul when he became a Christian.) Referring to his single status, he wrote, "I wish [you] were even as I." He goes on to explain why singleness is of great value, using the word *charisma,* or "grace gift." Celibacy is a gift from God. The single can go about doing God's business unhindered by family responsibilities.

Paul had more to say on the subject: "I want you to be free from concern. One who is unmarried is concerned about the things of the Lord, how he may please the Lord; but one who is married is concerned about the things of the world, how he may please his wife" (vv. 32–33). This advice is practical in its meaning. Paul was saying that, in the day and time in which his original readers lived—in a distorted and confused culture—it was easier to devote oneself to ministry as a single, focusing on God's will without worrying about events at home. Why? Because, as he told them, marriage is precious, and married people have pressing responsibilities to their families. It's as though Paul was giving orders to the troops before they went out to combat, and he said, "You can fight the fight better if you don't have your mind and heart at home." To be unmarried is no tragedy; in fact, it can often be quite useful for the Lord's work.

An unmarried person must consider how God wants to use him

or her. In Matthew 19, Jesus teaches that some are born eunuchs, some are made eunuchs by man, and some are eunuchs by choice. Jesus was saying that some people by birth are unable to marry and bear children. Some become that way through surgical procedures, or as a consequence of weapons or warfare. But some, for the sake of God's kingdom, embrace celibacy so they can more fully devote their lives to God by giving up what is good.

While that's true, single people still have sexual desires. And we should encourage deeply affectionate but nongenital relationships among singles. They can express their sexuality through warm, satisfying friendships, and the church can help by providing a context for these friendships to develop. Even though singles should abstain from sex, they need touch. In fact, they probably need it more than many married people do. And it's important to emphasize that singles aren't waiting because sex is *bad*. They're waiting because it is *good* in its God-given context. In his award-winning *Dallas Morning News* article, "Movie Aside, Virginity at 40 is Worthwhile," Paul Buckley wisely writes, "Waiting is hard. But we see it as the fast before the feast."[5]

The number of singles is continually on the rise. As of 2000, the most common household type in the U.S. was people living alone. Twenty-seven million American households consist of a person living alone, compared to 25 million households with a husband, wife, and child.[6] But what if you find yourself single and you don't have the "gift" of celibacy? You feel consumed with the idea of finding a partner—your heart longs for that soul mate. Pray for God to provide that special one. Pour out your heart to Him. But "seek first His kingdom and His righteousness," and value the gifts that come with the single life.

Perhaps you are at an "in between" stage. You're single, but you're involved in a romantic relationship that may result in marriage. How can you reflect both your purity and your sexuality within that relationship?

First, recognize that God has designed us with sensual appetites but He has also given us the commands and the ability to control them. He says to walk in the Spirit and you won't commit the deeds of the flesh (see Gal. 5). Jesus as Savior has delivered us from the penalty of sin by His death, and from power of sin by the Spirit, although He has not yet delivered us from sin's presence. He has sent the Holy Spirit to indwell us, counsel us, comfort us, and convict us of wrongdoing. The Spirit also enables us to live a holy life that's pleasing to God.

If you don't know Christ, if you haven't yet trusted Him as your Savior, then you don't have the power to live a holy life. We live in a fallen world that has surrounded us with sensuality and temptation. But God offers a way to access His power. He also offers us forgiveness and cleansing when we fail Him. Receiving Him as Lord involves praying, acknowledging our inability to save ourselves, accepting our need for cleansing from sin, and placing our faith in Christ's work on the cross as being sufficient to save us. Only after placing our faith in Him in this way will we have the supernatural power to overcome evil.

According to the Bible, sexual relations are to be engaged in regularly, but only by those with lifelong marriage commitments to each other. Yet today, premarital and extramarital sex are common, even between couples who have no intention of committing their lives to each other. Sex is enthralling—make no mistake about it. Yet it also distorts these relationships outside of one's own marriage, detracting from what God would have them to be. It stunts spiritual growth, alienates the sexual partners from God, and erects a barrier to true intimacy in the future.

"It's possible to love deeply and not fall into bed—and I know it from experience," writes Leigh McLeroy in *Moments for Singles*:

> First, . . . Sexuality is a God-given and beautifully wrapped "present" that can be opened for the first time only once. I prefer to savor this gift at the right time, under the right circumstances, because I believe what its Giver has said about its worth. Second, I'm absolutely certain I am loved. If there were a serious love deficit in my life, the temptation

to fill it with sex would almost certainly feel overwhelming. But the relationship that I have with Christ can fill my deepest longings for love and intimacy if I will allow it to and as much as I will allow it to. My choice to reserve sex for its intended home of marriage has much more to do with love and desire than it does with obedience and dread.[7]

If you've failed here, remember that God provides a way of spiritual reconciliation. Confess your sin to Him and receive the forgiveness He promises. Change your thinking by filling your mind with Scripture. Make a new start. In *Real Sex: The Naked Truth about Chastity*, Lauren Winner writes, "One who, like me, had sex before marriage can rightfully mourn and grieve the loss of virginity." But, she says, "The critical question for Christians is *what are you doing now?* Not *have you sinned in the past*, but *if you sinned in the past, how are you dealing with it? How has Christ's blood redeemed you, and how are you obeying now?*"[8]

The dating believer who wants to remain pure must go out only with other believers who are committed to maintaining the biblical standards that limit physical expressions of intimacy. Although lust expressed may be pleasurable, it is momentary and it falls well short of the full experience of marital sex because it also denies committed relationship. Jesus condemned lust because it cheapened sex, making it less than God created it to be. One non-Christian man who actively engages in multiple sexual encounters wrote, "I am wondering—will sex be better when I am actually in love?"[9]

Next, find someone or a group outside of the relationship to whom you can be accountable. One of my (Sandi's) single friends wrote this to me:

> We broke our rule about doing nothing intense while lying down. Except for the fact that we broke our own rule, we didn't do anything morally wrong, so don't worry. We are very aware that it will be easier next time to want to bend the rules again. That was Saturday night, on our date—which

was a picnic in the woods, with a fire and everything. So you could probably call that a compromising situation as well. Boy, I'm not doing too well here, am I?

Just knowing she would have to later give account for her actions helped to keep this young woman from "going further."

"Long distance relationships help," Tara, a single woman, said laughing. She went on to add more seriously, "I think integrity and respect for the other person as a creation of God are strong incentives against violating him or her. You have to learn to focus on the other person's good, and not personal selfishness, or what feels good for *you*. Also, you have to keep the long-term goal in view. Women need to realize that they do things that cause guys to want more, and that guys do things to cause women to want more. *Both* have to take responsibility in restraining the physical relationship."

John, who is currently engaged, said, "We set some rules: Nothing below the neck, under a blanket, or lying down. It's just too hard otherwise." Another single suggested, "We never get into the car together unless we've decided ahead of time where we're going. That helps us avoid the temptation to cruise around and end up at the lake in the back seat. We know that if we demonstrate selfless love in our physical relationship before marriage, we're more likely to demonstrate that same kind of love to each other after we are married."

We know of Christian parents who believe their sons will have sex before marriage but not their daughters, because "guys do." This is wrong! Both men and women are fully responsible for their own actions; *both* must take full responsibility for "slowing down."

One single woman shared, "It's sometimes beneficial to know and communicate when the other person is hitting hot buttons and to stop at that point, instead of going to the 'point of no return.'" She laughed and went on, "I like the 'beep, beep, beep' warning approach myself. It lets the other person know that he is going in the wrong direction, yet does it in an amusing way." She continued, "It's easy for us women to think we owe men for the dates and food and the stuff they buy us. A lot of women don't think enough of themselves to say, 'I should be pursued for *me* alone and not what I can give with my body. I'm worth getting to know, *period*.' I've had trouble with this."

Another suggestion is to keep the engagement period short. By the time a couple reaches engagement, they are entering levels of intimacy that should not be sustained for long without expression in sexual intercourse. As Paul advised, "It is better to marry than to burn" (1 Cor. 7:9).

Today, wise people follow God's directives to abstain from sexual relations outside of marriage and relinquish bodily rights within marriage. While it's true that if couples do engage in sexual immorality, no one has to wear an external scarlet *A*, yet what we do with God's gift of sex leaves its mark internally. Nevertheless, even scars from sexual sin can point to the goodness of God. As Philip Yancey observes in a chapter titled "Designer Sex,"

> Jesus set the example for the rest of us by responding with great tenderness to those who had failed sexually. Recognizing the depth of their pain, he offered forgiveness and not judgment. The pain that lingers after sexual failure is, oddly, an indirect proof of sexuality's original design. Those who test that design, and fail, in the process gain some haunting sense of what we are missing. We want desperately to connect, to grow in personal intimacy even as we progress in sexual intimacy. We want to be fully known, and fully loved. When that does not happen, or when the fragile link snaps, it simply proves that in sex, as in every area of life, fallen humanity gets in the way and keeps us from realizing the ideal.[10]

14
Protect Your Sexuality

If she is a wall, we will build towers of silver on her.
If she is a door, we will enclose her with panels of cedar.
—SONG OF SOLOMON 8:9 NIV

Imagine waking up every morning, looking out over the pyramids, and eating leeks and onions. Your brothers have thrown you in a pit and sold you into slavery, so you've gone from having servants to being one. You're lonely and alone with no future. Your boss, Potifer, is in charge of Pharaoh's bodyguards. The brightest, most educated, most powerful, most articulate, most attractive people surround you, yet you have nothing. Then your boss's wife, a beautiful woman, makes it her life goal to seduce you. In fact, she tries daily. Finally one day, she throws herself at you, and you have to literally run out of the room.

This is Joseph's story, right out of Genesis 39. Talk about temptation!

A group of four Christian wives who were employed in various businesses met with me (Sandi) for a weekly Bible study. And as we worked our way through the Word, we focused on its great and not-so-great women. During the session in which we considered the story of Joseph and Potifer's wife, each one of those women confessed that she had struggled with the temptation to cheat on her husband. Each at some time in her marriage had met "someone else" to whom she felt strongly attracted. For these women, the struggle had not begun with lust but with emotional attachment. In every case, those wives said that they were happily married, so the pull was not because their husbands had failed to meet their needs.

In his book *Torn Asunder: Recovering from Extramarital Affairs*, Dave Carder identifies three kinds of adulterous relationships. He labels them as follows: (1) The one-night stand. An otherwise faithful husband or wife meets someone at a movie matinee and they end up sleeping together. The liaison has never happened before and it never happens again; (2) The entangled affair. A woman and man who work together for a long time grow into a deeply intimate relationship that leads to regular sex; (3) The sexual addict. A man or woman has a pattern of engaging in sexual acts outside of the context of any relationship.

Carder labels the second as the most problematic and one of the most difficult to rehabilitate due to the extensive emotional involvement: "In the entangled affair, the man and woman have a relationship—often akin to the marriage relationship."[1] In addition, the "innocent spouse" has a harder time dealing with this type of sin on many levels. "A prostitute shows a woman there's something wrong with her husband; an affair suggests that maybe something's wrong with [the wife] herself," explained the now-divorced wife of a Clinton administration official, whose adultery was exposed by a tabloid.[2]

Many of the books and magazine articles we found in our research tended to blame adultery on bad marriages that failed to meet needs. Yet while a difficult marriage can certainly make temptation more enticing, such thinking ignores the fact that marriage, by its very nature—with its cornerstone covenant of committed love and security—will not offer the mystery, the conquest, the rush of "live for the moment" that some seek in illicit relationships. Couples have seen in movies—or have experienced but can't match within the confines of marriage—the thrill of the chase and the added excitement that comes from fear of exposure. Unfaithfulness has strong elements of selfishness and ego satisfaction. And the third party can offer a thoughtful listening ear along with sexual variety. Or as a *Newsweek* writer described it, a new partner can provide "the kind of respect and admiration that wives find it hard to give their husbands after watching them fall asleep in front of reruns . . . for the last twenty years."[3]

Every married partner—whether happily married or not—must take steps to protect his or her fidelity. It's difficult to find credible statistics on how widespread adultery is, but the General Social Survey (funded by the National Science Foundation) has asked about adulterous behavior repeatedly in surveys since 1991. In 2004, it found that 15 percent of those who had ever married said they'd had sexual relations outside of their marriage, and that more (currently or formerly married) men (20 percent) than women (12 percent) reported this behavior.[4] An earlier survey found that 21.2 percent of men and 11.3 percent of women admitted to being unfaithful to their spouses at least once in their lives.[5] (The key word here is "admitted.") Another report found that, within the twelve-month period preceding the survey, 3.6 percent of men and 1.3 percent of women reported infidelity. Those who attended church were roughly half as likely to cheat.[6] We should probably note that those who attend church are also less likely to *admit* they have committed adultery, but adultery is also truly less likely to happen if someone is a committed Christ-follower.

These statistics represent physical adultery. But what about emotional affairs? And lust? All things considered, all married people will find themselves tempted in some way at some time in their lives.[7] In premarital counseling, some couples are incensed that I (Dr. Bill) would caution them in this area. Yet making the assumption that we're going to be tempted at some point keeps us from thinking, "I am immune" or "I am never going to fall." Countless people have confessed to me their moral failures, explaining, "I never thought it would happen."

The Bible has plenty to say on the subject. We have Joseph's example of literally running away. We read Paul's exhortation to

Timothy to "flee youthful lusts." We know Jesus Christ's teaching on the subject: "You have heard that it was said, 'You shall not commit adultery'; but I say to you, that everyone who looks on a woman to lust for her has committed adultery with her already in his heart" (Matt. 5:27–28). We also find a father's warning to his sons in Proverbs 5:3–5:

> For the lips of an adulteress drip honey,
> And smoother than oil is her speech;
> But in the end she is bitter as wormwood,
> Sharp as a two-edged sword.
> Her feet go down to death,
> Her steps lay hold of Sheol.

If adultery is such a common problem, what can we do about it? First, let's look at how we think about extramarital relations.

Myth #1: A little fantasy never hurt anybody.

Consider how it hurt Jeanette. She writes:

As a believing wife and mother who had an affair several years ago, I want to warn others that if they first yield to mental adultery, it could easily take them the whole way down the wrong road. If there's time to be alone with the other man, the two of you will most likely confess your struggles to each other. After allowing wrong thoughts, this is the most dangerous step to take. If he is a fellow believer, you will say you must conquer this thing together in prayer. You'll feel such a tenderness toward each other that you'll need to express your affection with warm embraces and "holy kisses." It is a short road from there to the point where you allow yourself the pleasure of more and more sensual temptations. Finally, you quit trying to resist.

If you're truly a believer who is used to enjoying fellowship with God, you are in for a lot of misery. You'll long to go back to the time when you could sing, "I Love You, Lord" and mean it. You will cry over songs like "He Is Lord," knowing that now He is not Lord of your life. You will become unable to give testimonies or share with other believers on anything but a surface level. You will be unable to concentrate on anything else. Then, to cover your sin, you'll lie.

At the same time, you'll be involved in a passionate, romantic relationship. You'll feel beautiful and part of life will seem wonderful. While you know it's sinful, you'll find yourself helplessly in love and enjoying part of it.

Eventually the two of you will talk of ways to end the relationship. You may even take some very painful steps. You'll feel like you're going through a divorce without being able to tell anyone. The pain is so strong, and the pull is so strong, that these steps will not last long. The longer it all goes on, the more a part of each other's lives you become, and the more you'll have stored in your memory. You'll realize how much easier it would have been to stop it all at the "thoughts" stage. You would give anything to go back and do it all over differently.

You will have lost your relationship with the Lord. And you'll realize you've also lost your relationship with your husband. Either you'll go through the rest of your life keeping something from him or you'll eventually confess it to him and destroy him in the process.

Your memories will be your worst enemies. You will both cherish them and hate them. You will long for the days when your husband's lovemaking was the only way you knew, when certain scents, songs, clothes, places, and words did not stab you with reminders. In the strongest way I can say it, *you'll be sorry, sorry, sorry.* Yielding to the excitement will never be worth what you have to reap.

I'm not suggesting that a person who has had an affair must live in bondage and condemnation forever. Yes, God can bring spiritual and marital healing, even of the painful memories. But it will be very hard.

If you've already yielded and know it must stop, take the risk of praying, "Lord, do whatever you have to do to make me willing to stop." Then be prepared for what He brings. In my case, it was an unplanned pregnancy. I had to confess to my husband. Years later, we're still working through it.

All of this did not start or end overnight. It was gradual. It starts with thoughts. And those wrong thoughts should be avoided at all cost.

Another woman, Kathy, shared how she had to change jobs and move to another city to get away from an extramarital relationship. "It all started with what I thought were some harmless thoughts. It ended with me praying and praying that God would take away my feelings for this man. I became angry with Him that He didn't. It took me a long time to realize that you can't always expect God to bail you out of a situation you lived yourself into."

More people are staying together after unfaithfulness these days. At one time people generally considered the offended spouse "weak" if he or she reconciled; but it's becoming more socially acceptable to "work it out." Some do it for the kids; others do it for the sake of *access* to the kids. They also don't want to be single again, to be, as one person put it, "out there with germs and creeps." Sexual betrayal is painful, but so is divorce.

Myth #2: I can have a little liaison without consequences.

For the past fifty years we've lived in a society of "free love" in which indiscriminate sex has become the premarital norm. People consider monogamy mundane, and biblical standards have been discarded. Yet divorce rates are sky-high. Premarital sexual involvement places couples at higher risk in the future; if you can't hold to God's code of conduct before marriage, it gets harder to draw the line later.

Both premarital and extramarital sexual involvement is wrong, although acceptable in our society. Just because you may not contract AIDS, become infected with other sexually transmitted diseases, get pregnant, or suffer the humiliation of embarrassing discoveries, doesn't mean you endure no consequences.

Before King David sinned with Bathsheba, he experienced nothing but blessing from God; after his sin, he suffered consequences for the rest of his life. In the short term, he lost an infant. Long term, his sin had far-reaching effects, including tension in his family relation-ships—his children followed his example and engaged in immorality. Apparently what is true today was also true several millennia ago: if parents are unfaithful, they place their children at a higher risk for infidelity.[8] Later, David lost respect in the eyes of the nation, and he had nothing but political trouble from that time forward. Even though David experienced forgiveness, he never again returned to his previous levels of relative tranquility.

Many adulterers who have been scorched would attest to this.

Myth #3: Marriage will cure lust.

During my senior year at a Christian college, one of my (Sandi's) professors told our class that he battled lust more since his marriage. "Now that I have a more 'informed' view of what goes on behind closed doors, I lust more specifically," he said. So clearly marriage does not cure lust.

Lust can be a problem, too, if a spouse's needs are ignored. In 1 Corinthians, Paul seems to indicate that a failure to mutually meet sexual needs within marriage can lead to temptation. So marriage is not a cure-all—even a good marriage. It doesn't cure lust any more than regularly eating healthy meals cures cravings for choco-late cheesecake, particularly if such a "sweet tooth" was cultivated before marriage. If you crave pepperoni pizza, no amount of quiche will do.

In another book, *The Jesus I Never Knew,* Philip Yancey writes, "During a period of my life when I was battling sexual temptation, I came across an article that referred me to a thin book, *What I Believe,* by the French Catholic writer François Mauriac. Mauriac dismissed most of the arguments in favor of sexual purity that he had been taught in his Catholic upbringing. . . . 'With self-discipline you can master lust': Mauriac found that sexual desire is like a tidal wave powerful enough to bear away all the best intentions. 'True fulfillment can only be found in monogamy': this may be true, but it certainly does not *seem* true to someone who finds no slackening of sexual urges even in monogamy. . . .

"Mauriac concluded that self-discipline, repression, and rational argument are inadequate weapons to use in fighting the impulse toward impurity. In the end, he could find only one reason to be pure, and that is what Jesus presented in the Beatitudes: 'Blessed are the pure in heart, for they will see God.' In Mauriac's words, 'Impurity separates us from God. . . . Purity is the condition for a higher love—for a possession superior to all possessions: that of God. . . .' That is the motive to stay pure. By harboring lust, I limit my own intimacy with God. The pure in heart are truly blessed, for they will see God. It is as simple, and as difficult, as that."[9]

We never permanently "quench" our sinful selves by substituting holy activities. By God's grace we conquer lust on a moment-by-moment basis as we love Him, walk with Him, and desire to see His face above all others.

Myth #4: If I fall into sin, it's because my spouse has somehow failed to meet my needs.

This is the lamest of all cop-outs. Don't believe it.

After twelve years of a strong marriage, Sue and Dick wondered what had happened to them. Dick had begun taking medication for a medical condition, and they didn't realize one of its side effects was depression. It was nearly a year before they determined the cause. In the meantime, they struggled with how to deal with Dick's altered personality. They still had a loving, supportive relationship with an active love life, and they experienced no additional conflicts, but they both felt sad a lot, and they found it difficult to cope with Dick's negative outlook. Although their marriage was "happy," it was at risk.

During that time, Sue began to feel attracted to a man in her office. Finally she sat down with Dick and told him, "I don't want to add to your depression, but I think we need some counseling. I don't know how to deal with your pain. And I'm finding other men—one in particular—a lot more attractive than before."

Confiding her secret feelings relieved some of the pressure for Sue. And Dick immediately found a counselor for them to begin seeing. Even though the depression had a physical cause, they both needed help in dealing with the emotional fallout.

Gordon MacDonald, a widely respected Christian pastor, speaker, and author of *Ordering Your Private World,* wrote, "I am a broken-world person because a few years ago I betrayed the covenants of my marriage. For the rest of my life I will have to live with the knowledge that I brought deep sorrow to my wife, to my children, and to friends and others who have trusted me for many years."[10] MacDonald relates a conversation that happened several years earlier:

> I gave a speech at a college commencement. Before the festivities began, a member of that school's board sat with me in the president's office. We'd never met before, and we were asking questions of each other that might help us get better acquainted. Suddenly my new friend asked a strange question. I've thought about it many times since then. "If Satan were to blow you out of the water," he asked, "how do you think he would do it?"
>
> "I'm not sure I know," I answered. "All sorts of ways, I suppose; but I know there's one way he wouldn't get me."
>
> "What's that?"
>
> "He'd never get me in the area of my personal relationships. That's one place where I have no doubt that I'm as strong as you can get."[11]

MacDonald now warns, "An unguarded strength and an unprepared heart are double weakness."[12]

"The heart is more deceitful than all else and is desperately sick;

who can understand it?" we read in Jeremiah 17:9. The Bible tells us that even the best of humans are masters at deceiving themselves and others. No one is immune, and if we think we are, we are that much more vulnerable. Put another way, "Let him who thinks he stands take heed lest he fall" (1 Cor. 10:12). If David, a man after God's own heart, can fall, we can, too.

If even happily married people are at risk, there's no way to absolutely "affair proof" a marriage for a lifetime. Rather, a day-to-day, minute-by-minute decision to remain faithful to God and one's spouse is required. Nor is there a way to so totally satisfy your mate that he or she will never stray, because even the best feeling of satisfaction is short-lived. Yet neither is remaining faithful a hopeless struggle. In the next chapter we'll talk about some safeguards and ways to minimize risk.

Myth #5: If I spend time with God every day, I will not be "at risk."

It's true that your relationship with God is the strongest factor in maintaining moral purity. But it has to be a moment-by-moment relationship. If we purify our hearts daily through a quiet time of confession, repentance, and redirection, we've taken a big step. Do spend time with Him daily. But don't assume that because you spend time with God each day, you can relax. Consider a Bible college professor who had an adulterous affair and left his wife and ministry, but once reported, "I ride my bike ten miles daily, attend church, and have a scheduled Bible study time." One man involved in an adulterous relationship resolved never to "cheat" on Sunday—and he kept his promise!

On the other hand, if you're neglecting daily time with God, you are at *far* greater risk of falling into sexual sin. That regular time of reflection and self-examination is essential to maintaining God's standard of purity.

Angela felt a strong attraction to a man with whom she was working on a multimillion-dollar business project. So as part of her prayer time, she would think through the specifics of how she expected to be tempted that day. She'd commit to avoiding "extra" trips to the man's desk and determine not to make unnecessary phone calls to him. She would think through and choose ahead of time to do the right thing that day in every specific way she could anticipate. "You have to make many decisions throughout the day," she confided. "It's not something you just decide once and for all and never have to face again. Fortunately, after two years the project ended, and though I felt really sad, I knew that God knew what He was doing to take me out of that situation."

Joseph knew as well as anyone that remaining morally pure and faithful to God sometimes takes every ounce of moral fiber we have. The women with whom I (Sandi) met for Bible study all remained true to their spouses. So by God's grace and enabling, a high standard of moral purity within marriage is certainly possible—yet not without prayer and determination. As those who have extensively researched monogamy can attest, "We must devote more conscious effort to ensuring that we stick to what we have promised. Monogamy isn't like breathing, and the realization that we need to work at it may help keep us focused."[13]

15

Developing a Loyal Heart

Put me like a seal over your heart . . .
For love is as strong as death.
—SONG OF SOLOMON 8:6

I (Sandi) was sitting in on a Bible class one afternoon as we were discussing David and Bathsheba. A student raised his hand and asked the teacher, "I read that thirty percent of evangelical pastors have moral failures. I don't want to be in that statistic. But I think I'd be naive to think it couldn't happen. You've been married for four decades. How have you managed to remain faithful to your wife?"

Perhaps for the sake of simplicity, the instructor answered, "You do three things. You tell your wife every day that you love her; you never touch your secretary; and you never go to lunch with another woman."

In one way he was right, but on another level he wasn't. Secretaries are not the only danger; neither are male/female lunches unpardonable sins. Yet he was right in encouraging us to invest our affections and energies in the right relationship, as Proverbs 5:15–19 encourages:

> Drink water from your own cistern,
> And fresh water from your own well.

Should your springs be dispersed abroad,
Streams of water in the streets?
Let them be yours alone,
And not for strangers with you.
Let your fountain be blessed,
And rejoice in the wife of your youth.
As a loving hind and a graceful doe,
Let her breasts satisfy you at all times;
Be exhilarated always with her love.

God gave us biological desires, and in the book of Proverbs we get a glimpse of how He views the beauties of sexual love within marriage. God's Spirit enables us to channel our drives responsibly. Proverbs 5:20–23 continues,

For why should you, my son, be exhilarated with an adulteress,
And embrace the bosom of a foreigner?
For the ways of a man are before the eyes of the LORD,
And he watches all his paths.
His own iniquities will capture the wicked,
And he will be held with the cords of his sin.
He will die for lack of instruction,
And in the greatness of his folly he will go astray.

This is important advice.

Our instructor left out an essential encouragement: *We must win the battle where it starts: in our thoughts.* What begins as legitimate appreciation of physical beauty or character can turn into selfish desire. James wrote, "Let no one say when he is tempted, 'I am being tempted by God'; for God cannot be tempted by evil, and He Himself does not tempt anyone. But each one is tempted when he is carried away and enticed by his own lust. Then when lust has conceived, it gives birth to sin; and when sin is accomplished, it brings forth death" (James 1:13–15).

In her book *Quest for Love*, Elisabeth Elliot wrote, "The battleground is the mind. To pray, 'Deliver us from evil,' lays on us the responsibility to struggle against the evil in our minds, for that is where trouble begins and where it must be conquered."[1]

When Janice, a single woman, worked in the media department at a Fortune 500 company, she often helped with video editing. This involved sitting with the door shut in a darkened room with the video editor, who in this case happened to be a married man. Janice and Ed spent hours looking at the screen, throwing around creative ideas, and developing projects together. Sometimes they'd walk down to the corporate cafeteria and continue talking about the project over food. Having lunch together, which some might label as "dangerous," was actually the safest time of day for them because of its public setting. When the mind is right, location is not a great worry. When Ed's parents died, Janice hugged him. "To do otherwise would have seemed inhuman," she explained.

There were moments in their relationship when they'd be working together and Janice would realize, "Whoa. This is a member of the opposite sex. This is not a girlfriend I'm hanging out with." She explained her thinking: "He had many wonderful qualities. And the fact is, just about every Christian (and most non-Christians) of the opposite sex have qualities that, if you got to know them well enough, you'd find attractive and unique." She added, "But by God's grace I made a choice to think and feel as I was supposed to. I handled it at the level of my thoughts, continually checking my context, my motivation, and my attitude. We worked together for more than a decade before moving on to other careers. Today we remain good friends."

Liz, a university student, was asked to intern for a male professor. She spent the year sitting across from him in his private office, joining him at his appointments, going to meetings with him, attending his off-campus lectures, and sometimes even heading down to the campus food service building with him to grab a bite to eat.

"He's a wonderful man, and I love him as a dear friend," Liz shared. "He has many appealing qualities, including the fact that he's unashamed to be my friend. Yet I don't remember ever having

one wrong thought about him that entire year. It's not that I couldn't
have been tempted. But I made daily decisions to think of him as a
brother, and by God's grace I stuck to it—I wasn't going to let my
mind *go there*."

In the past twenty years, an increasing number of women have
entered the work force, so we need guidelines that encompass the
changing situations in which we find ourselves. Shanelle, for example,
had always said, "I will never get into a car alone with a man who is not
my husband." But one night her husband needed to stay at church to
counsel someone, and she needed to get home to do some work. One
of the guys in their college department—someone with whom she felt
no particular "chemistry"—offered to drive her home. At that point,
she realized that declining his offer would be ridiculous. So she had an
uneventful ride home with him. She later shared, "I had made rules
to safeguard myself in situations that were not dangerous. I needed
to make them closer to the heart: I would never ride in the car alone
with a man I was *dying* to be alone with, and I would never have lunch
with somebody who made me feel like I was as sexy as J-Lo."

External rules alone can prevent a few problems, but many people
have "fallen" without ever compromising their external rules. It's
possible to love your spouse, never go to lunch with a member of
the opposite sex, and never touch your coworkers, yet still become
embroiled in an adulterous relationship. Besides, some guidelines
can make us rigid where we need to show flexibility, as was the case
with Shanelle. Externals are easy to skirt, but if we set righteous
internal guidelines, if we continually reject all wrong thoughts and
feelings, we cannot "get around the rules."

Dr. Frank Pittman, the author of a book on infidelity, says unfaithfulness, while it is a sin of the body, is even more a sin of the heart.
Most affairs are conducted primarily on the telephone: "The essence
of an affair is in establishing a secret intimacy with someone"—a
secret that necessarily must be defended with dishonesty. Infidelity,
he says, is not *just* about "whom you lie with. It's whom you lie to."[2]
The availability of the Internet, e-mail, and text messaging have made
it increasingly easy for such secret intimacies to develop.

Frances was working with the associate pastor of her church on a project for the church youth. It didn't take long for them to realize they worked well as a team. They enjoyed working together, and the time flew by when they met to brainstorm concepts and make decisions. Before long this pastor, Ronnie, was calling her at work for her help with incidental decisions. She began faxing him Garfield cartoons that she knew he would enjoy. Then he began confiding that he was unhappy in his marriage. Frances, being a compassionate person by nature, felt deep sympathy for Ronnie and wanted to help. Before long, she realized she was involved in a mental affair. She begged God to take the feelings away, but He didn't. She found herself leaving out parts of conversations when recounting them to her husband, knowing he would be upset if she told him the whole truth.

Finally, recognizing that in her own strength she stood powerless against her feelings, Frances met with a friend and confessed that she needed some accountability. Her confession helped to break the obsession. Together Frances and her husband worked out the steps needed for her to unravel the web of relationship she had woven in her mind. Eventually she decided that, because she was "in so deep," she had only one option: to remove herself from all situations where she had contact with the man to whom she was attracted.

Cindy and Patrick had been married for ten years when they began partnering with Bob and Glenda at a drug rehabilitation center for juveniles. They were all best friends, working together and supporting each other in a difficult ministry. After several years, Cindy felt drawn to Bob, and she was fairly sure he felt the same way. Soon they were exchanging notes, running errands together, and looking for each other in crowds.

When the relationship intensified, Cindy took a bold step in the right direction. She confided in her husband that she needed his help in keeping Bob at a safe distance. Patrick, though, ignored the warning, even sending his wife on more errands with Bob. This made Cindy feel that her husband did not cherish her enough to help her stay faithful, so she rationalized that her temptation was his fault.

It wasn't long before she and Bob became physically involved. The affair went on for months before someone caught them.

Patrick was bewildered. "I thought it was wrong to be jealous!" he insisted. Both couples resigned from their jobs and tried to rebuild their marriages. Several months later, Cindy called Bob, seeking to build a secret liaison. But he told her that he wanted to rebuild his relationship with his wife and that he didn't want to hear from her again.

Elements of these scenarios are all too common. In his book *His Needs, Her Needs,* Willard Harley describes a typical affair as consisting of two people combining sexual lovemaking with feelings of deep love.

> The relationship that combines sex (usually very passionate sex) and very real love threatens the marriage to its core, because the lovers experience real intimacy, and it meets at least one need of the spouse outside the exclusive marital relationship. . . . An affair usually begins as a friendship. Frequently your spouse knows your lover; not uncommonly the third party is the husband or wife in a couple you both know and consider "best friends." In another common pattern the outside lover comes from your spouse's family—a sister or brother. Or you may have met your lover at work.
>
> [Often] the attraction is not necessarily physical, but emotional. What really turns you on is not your new partner, but the fantasy. . . . The longer it goes on, the more difficult you will find breaking it off. In some cases the above process may take only a few months; in other cases it will take many years.[3]

Many warn that because of the danger of cross-gender friendships, men and women should never be friends. Some suggest that male-female friendships will always develop into something more. Comedians joke that men have no female friends—they just have women they haven't slept with yet. And they say women have no male friends—they merely have men they keep around "just in case."

While inappropriate affection should be handled with extreme measures, the solution is not to avoid relationships with members of the opposite sex. Often there is little we can do to keep friendships from happening anyway. Meetings, projects, and ministries throw us together. Besides, God made men and women in His image, so both genders working together, using their unique gifts, bring a balance to any project.

Consider some examples of male-female relationships in Scripture. Paul called two women in Philippi his "co-laborers"; he also sent greetings to women named Lydia and Priscilla. In Romans 16 he warmly greets a long list of coworkers, many of whom are women. Jesus entered a house occupied by two unmarried women and talked with them on a below-the-surface level about spiritual things, showing utter disregard for custom in doing so. He praised Mary over Martha for sitting at His feet and engaging in deep communication. He touched women, and He received touch from them—such as the time He received Mary's worship when she anointed Him with costly perfume.

"We must be human; we need intimacy, touch, meaningful conversation, and much more outside the marriage bonds," writes Richard Foster in *The Challenge of the Disciplined Life.* "Otherwise we will be asking the marriage to carry more than is reasonable for even the healthiest relationship."[4]

During an interview with Eugene Peterson, translator of *The Message,* I (Sandi) asked Peterson, who had been a successful pastor for thirty years, "How do you handle friendships with women?"

"Is sex a contagious disease?" he asked. "Sex is a danger, but money is a danger, too. Do you refuse to take a salary because money is a danger? I've not lived cautiously. I have friendships with women. They are my friends. Touch is a human thing, not just a sexual thing. It is dehumanizing to deny touch. I'm convinced that the so-called failures in ministry are not motivated sexually. For both men and women, they're motivated by arrogance, pride, power, and a hunger for intimacy. It doesn't happen overnight. They have long histories before them. The failures don't happen because you touch somebody; they have to do with character development—part of learning to be a man and learning to be a woman. It's part of spiritual maturity and spiritual formation. If you pour all your energies into trying to avoid sexual sin, you will fail in another area. There are other failures that are terrible, too. Life is messy."[5]

So how do you tell the difference between friendship and romance? Your thoughts and motives give you away. We read in Proverbs, "Watch over your heart with all diligence, for from it flow the springs of life" (Prov. 4:23). Here are some questions to help us identify misguided affections:

- Do you make special trips past her desk or his house?
- Do you manipulate situations so you can be alone in secluded, private settings?
- Have you started taking special care of your dress, your physique, and overall appearance? Are you wearing an alluring scent?
- When you are around him or her, do you feel like you're sixteen again?
- Do you find yourself thinking of this person frequently outside of the usual context of your contact?
- Do you purposely withhold some conversations, letters, or events from your spouse?
- Do you dread accountability times? Do you not even *have* a person to whom you are accountable for your thoughts and actions?
- Do you find yourself thinking of this person instead of your spouse when you watch romantic movies?
- Do you think of this person during romantic activities with your spouse?
- Do you talk about him or her more than about your spouse?
- Is the love you feel for this person infatuation that wants to

possess or is it true love? Real love wants the other to be all he or she can be in Christ—a love that would never lead the loved one down a treacherous path away from God. Are you acting with his or her best interest at heart?

Let an application of the Golden Rule help determine the state of your relationship. Ask yourself: *Would I want someone else to treat me as I'm treating this person's spouse, even if only in my heart?*

Here's another factor to consider. Foster, who earlier suggested that we should not expect all our needs for intimacy to be met in marriage (we're talking here about our need for acceptance, respect, value, and appreciation at a personal level, *not* physical, romantic, erotic intimacy), qualifies his statement with the reminder, "We really must be sensitive to how our actions and even our thoughts affect our marriage."[6]

It may be easier for husbands to appreciate their wives' cross-gender friendships than it is for wives to accept their husbands' friendships with other women. In one piece of research on cross-gender relationships, when men imagined their wives committing sexual infidelity, their heart rates took leaps of a magnitude typically induced by three successive cups of coffee. They sweated and their brows wrinkled. Yet when they imagined a nonphysical, emotion-oriented friendship, they calmed down, although not to their normal level. For women, things were reversed—redirected love, not supplementary sex, brought the deeper physiological distress.[7]

In Song of Solomon 8:6 we read the bride's words to her groom:

> Put me like a seal over your heart,
> Like a seal on your arm.
> For love is as strong as death,
> Jealousy is as severe as Sheol;
> Its flashes are flashes of fire,
> The very flame of the LORD.

A king's seal was commonly used as a sign of ownership, similar to the way cattle ranchers brand their livestock or our mothers wrote our names in our clothing before sending us off to camp. Solomon used his seal to mark something priceless, and therefore something from which he would never part. Solomon's bride desires to be set as a seal on her husband's heart in the place of his affection. In other words, she is asking, "Let me own your heart."

In that context, we read, "Jealousy is as severe as Sheol." Sheol was the place of the dead. How strong is death? In the same way that death is permanent, the lover would not give up her beloved. This jealousy is a godly kind, the kind that would never allow the loved one to continue down the wrong path without issuing a warning. It is the opposite of indifference.

So are we saying a mate should be jealous? Yes and no. Jealousy that desires to control one's spouse stunts the relationship's ability to grow and mature. We're not talking about a jealousy that stifles. Nor are we encouraging the competitive jealousy we might feel when another receives a promotion or is honored in some way. We're talking about the side of love that guards that which God intended to be exclusive. It protects the relationship's security. Sometimes an "outsider" can see the warning signs more clearly than the person in the midst of a situation. Consider that one of God's names is "Jealous God." Even Erica Jong, the siren of sexual liberation in the 1970s, has conceded, "The great experiment of my generation was that people tried to abolish jealousy. It never worked."[8]

Yet aren't we supposed to trust each other? In 1 Corinthians 13, we read that love "is not jealous" and that it "believes all things." Here, though, Paul is speaking against having a controlling jealousy, not a protective one. Nor is he talking about the blind sort of belief that ignores the evidence. One pastor explained it like this:

> "Love believes all things": Then what if I'm disappointed?
> "Love bears all things": Then what if there's no change?
> "Love hopes all things": What if there's still no change?
> "Love endures all things. Love never fails."

The positive side of jealousy desires to protect something that is irreplaceable. What is love worth? Again, Solomon writes in Song of Solomon 8:7,

> Many waters cannot quench love,
> Nor will rivers overflow it;
> If a man were to give all the riches of his house for love,
> It would be utterly despised.

Back in the 1990s, Robert Redford starred in *Indecent Proposal*. The character Redford plays offers a million dollars to a husband and wife, who agree to let the wife commit adultery with him. The movie's message: to show that in the end it's not worth a million dollars to risk losing the exclusive husband-wife bond.

How do we stay faithful to our promise? It starts in our *thinking*: "Whatever is true," writes Paul in Philippians 4:8 (NIV), "whatever is noble, whatever is right, whatever is pure, whatever is lovely, whatever is admirable—if anything is excellent or praiseworthy—think about such things." The battle to keep your marriage exclusive is won or lost in the brain long before it has any chance of proceeding to a bedroom.

16

When Delight Becomes Obsession: Sexual Addiction

There are sixty queens and eighty concubines,
And maidens without number;
But my dove, my perfect one, is unique.
—SONG OF SOLOMON 6:8–9

Many in the counseling field recognize a condition labeled as sex addiction, obsession, or compulsion. It involves a cycle of preoccupation and fantasy moving to the "hunt" for satisfaction. This is followed by the act, whether viewing porn and masturbating or seeking out a prostitute or other sexual expression. Guilt and shame for the sinful behavior follow. Most then vow never to fall again. Yet without accountability and encouragement following repentance, the cycle will begin again with the fantasy trigger. In my (Dr. Bill's) practice, I'm seeing more and more men *and* women getting caught in this desperate cycle of sin. Research suggests that many who lock into this process have deep feelings of isolation, abandonment, and loneliness. While such feelings certainly don't excuse the sin, the church must act compassionately with the resources of the gospel and godly fellowship to help those with sexual compulsions to establish life trajectories of holiness and accountability.

Consider this true story about a man we'll call Tom. Eventually he was bound to be caught. For years Tom committed adultery with co-workers. Then he started using the Internet to feed his appetite. Before long he was meeting strangers for sexual encounters. Like one of the nearly 7 percent of married clergy who use pornography, this man fell further and further into sin. When by accident he corresponded in a porn chat room with a woman who knew him from church, he confessed his behavior to the senior pastor. He was shocked to find himself out of a job. His argument: "But I *confessed!*"

Tom's wife, whose suspicions others had discounted for years, joined a spouse's support group. There she found great encouragement through the process of rebuilding their marriage and establishing personal accountability.

We often hear it said that "every sin is the same in God's eyes—they're all bad." And while it's true that the blood of Christ covers all, 1 Corinthians 6:18–20 suggests that sexual immorality is uniquely damaging for two reasons: first, it's a sin against the body; second, we take the Holy Spirit with us when we commit sexual sin.

> Flee from sexual immorality. All other sins a man commits are outside his body, but he who sins sexually sins against his own body. Do you not know that your body is a temple of the Holy Spirit, who is in you, whom you have received from God? You are not your own; you were bought at a price. Therefore honor God with your body. (NIV)

The gravity of sexual sin is pointed out not only in God's special revelation of His Word, but is also noted in the world around us. A writer for *Elle* magazine made this observation:

> Of all our appetites, it seems to me, sex is the most anarchic. It's where we feel our keenest sense of sin. The sexual impulse rides roughshod over our ethics and our desire to be just to other people. All over the world, people build these fragile structures called relationships and the single biggest fault

line that can destroy nearly all that hard-won trust is the issue of sexual wantonness, or infidelity—the idea that one of the partners will look outside the relationship to satiate a sexual appetite he or she cannot control.[1]

With every other kind of sin we receive instruction about putting on spiritual armor so we can stand and fight (Eph. 6). Yet when it comes to sexual immorality, the scriptural advice is much different: Flee!

When describing the intimate relationship between Christ and the church, Paul uses the bride and groom relationship as the most fitting earthly analogy. God has chosen the most loving, intimate metaphor in the world to picture His relationship with us. He has apparently designed sexual intimacy as much for pleasure as for procreation (see Song of Solomon). So we can learn much about our Creator and His desire for us to experience delight from how He made us. Human sexuality represents a powerful aspect of our being that can bring some of life's greatest joys, but it can also generate enormous pain. And for people like Tom it brings an ongoing struggle with what many label as sexual addiction.

Some question whether such a "condition" even exists, or if it's really simply a series of bad choices. Medically speaking, the word *addiction* has a specific meaning—that substances taken into the body act on the brain in such a manner that their removal brings withdrawal symptoms. In that sense excessive sexual activity is not addictive. Yet we'll use the term "addiction," as is done at the popular level, to describe sexual obsessions, compulsions, dependency, or increasingly unhealthy involvement.

Using this broader definition, experts in the field of Christian counseling, some speaking from personal experience, suggest that the impact of such a condition is considerable. Russell Willingham in *Breaking Free* defines sexual addiction as "an obsessive-compulsive relationship with a person, object, or experience for the purpose of sexual gratification."[2] His broad definition could include many behaviors, both pre- and extramarital.

Self-described recovering sex addict Dr. Mark Laaser identifies loneliness as the driving emotion behind such behavior. He prescribes Christian fellowship as the "antidote." His research as a counselor suggests that traumatic episodes in early life play a significant role in the development of sexual addiction. According to his work, *Faithful and True: Sexual Integrity in a Fallen World*, 81 percent of sex addicts were sexually abused as children, 74 percent were physically abused, and 97 percent emotionally abused. He says most addicts have as a commonality the abandonment of "touch, love, nurture, and affirmation." Abandonment, or even the *sense* of abandonment through divorce or death of a parent, can represent significant risk factors for sexual addiction.[3]

The progression of symptoms suggests that such addiction comes close to meeting the criteria for a true addiction, not only in the frequency of acting out, but also in the escalation of activities to find sexual gratification. Like most addictions, "tolerance" develops as the conscience is seared, necessitating more powerful experiences to reach the same effect. Like a drug addict needing increasing amounts of drug, the sex addict falls into increasingly sinful sexual behaviors to achieve the same thrill. Sex becomes a means of escape from reality as it provides a temporary sense of feeling "normal." For the afflicted person, the result is a double life that includes denial and often despair.

Exposure or public discovery, causing pressure from family or legal issues, may provide the needed motivation for the sex addict to seek help. And as with any addiction, the consequences of exposure may include financial problems, relational upheaval, job loss, and community shame.

The book of Proverbs provides graphic imagery about the consequences of sexually immoral behavior:

> Can a man scoop fire into his lap
>   without his clothes being burned?
> Can a man walk on hot coals
>   without his feet being scorched?

> So is he who sleeps with another man's wife;
> no one who touches her will go unpunished.
> —Prov. 6:27–29 NIV

The sobering recognition of consequences can lead to a period in which the addiction seems under control, but a relapse will occur unless ongoing help is sought.

Most sex addicts are male, but a rising percentage of women are similarly afflicted. They often relate stories of abandonment or abuse and lack of affirmation by the males in their family of upbringing, followed by acting out. Their resulting response may include seductive behavior, adulterous acts, and serial sex partners. Some sex addicts move in the direction of homosexual behavior or fetishes to get the craved endorphin fix that comes with orgasm.

Certain core feelings surface in recovering sex addicts, according to Patrick Carnes in his book, *Out of the Shadows*. Such feelings include these thoughts: "I am basically a bad, unworthy person"; "If you really knew me, you wouldn't love me"; "I can't depend on others to meet my needs, so I must meet them myself"; and "Sex is my greatest need." The resulting depression can put the addict at risk for a relapse in sexual "acting out" and even thoughts of suicide.[4]

As with any of God's good gifts, sexuality—created as a wonderful expression of covenant love and intimate bonding—can become a painful trap and a seemingly irresistible force. Its immense power finds its full expression within marriage—a committed, covenant relationship. When people seek sexual pleasure devoid of commitment, accountability, and responsibility for personal actions, they often find themselves in a downward spiral of self-destruction.

Some activities as part of this spiral are socially acceptable in many contexts. And the spiral may begin with frequent use of sexual humor and innuendo. Turning every conversation in a sexual direction may be the first discernible clue of an underlying problem.

Consider the male choir member who made crude jokes about his wife's anatomy. A fellow believer asked him, "Jay, are you into pornography?"

Stunned, he said, "What makes you ask that?"

"Because you seem desensitized to what is appropriate."

His wife later confided, "He keeps a stash of magazines in a drawer beside the bed."

Easily accessible sexually explicit material draws an ever increasing number of willing participants by way of catalogs, magazines, TV with cable and satellite feeds, and now—one of the greatest dangers—the Internet. One couple who had enjoyed a relatively good marriage for more than two decades split up after their grown son used his father's computer. There, the son found a long list of pornographic favorites on the record of his dad's recently visited Web sites.

Access to the World Wide Web has the advantage of providing speedy access to all sorts of information, but it has proven dangerous to those prone to sexual addiction. Whereas one might hesitate to go to an X-rated movie or buy inappropriate literature, the easy, in-home availability of online pornography is as tempting as setting an open bottle of whiskey in front of an alcoholic. According to the *New York Times*, the sale of sexually degrading images has become a $10 billion-a-year industry, compared with the $10 million-a-year industry it was thirty years ago. The paper goes on to report that it's now easier to order porn into the home than to have a pizza delivered.[5] Hollywood throws fuel on the fire by releasing 11,000 adult movies per year—more than twenty times the mainstream movie production.[6] But movies wouldn't get produced if there weren't a market. And a market there is. Americans spend as much on porn as they spend attending professional sporting events, buying music, or going out to the movies.[7]

The addict can at first rationalize about the progression of symptoms because the viewing of pornography and masturbation "doesn't hurt anybody." Many people fantasize about sexual activities. Yet according to Scripture, to engage in sexual fantasies about someone other than one's spouse constitutes adultery—clearly a sin to avoid if one is to "walk worthy" of Christ and His payment for our sins. Victory requires drawing on the divine power to demolish strongholds, "tak[ing] captive every thought to make it obedient to Christ" (2 Cor. 10:5 NIV), which becomes quite a discipline for the one immersed in sexual thoughts.

This involvement in sexual activity escalates over time, and individuals with sexual compulsions become "hooked on a feeling" that can only be chased, never permanently obtained. We read in Ephesians 4:27 (NIV) the exhortation to keep from giving the devil a "foothold" through our anger. The same could certainly be said for denying that foothold through sexual immorality.

Many progress to voyeurism (gaining sexual pleasure from watching others engage in sexual behavior), exhibitionism (gratification from self-exposure), and fetishes. Those with fetishes derive sexual pleasure from a wide variety of objects, including women's clothing or shoes.

Most sex addicts follow a fairly predictable cycle of behavior, outlined by Stephen Arterburn and Fred Stoeker in *Every Man's Battle*. The cycle begins with a visual/emotional trigger usually followed by a struggle between the longings for sexual release and the desire to "do good." The fantasy may serve temporarily as an escape from emotional pain, but eventually a "plan" begins to develop to turn fantasy into reality.[8] We find in the book of James an explanation of how such a progression happens:

> Each one is tempted when, by his own evil desire, he is dragged away and enticed. Then, after desire has conceived, it gives birth to sin; and sin, when it is full-grown, gives birth to death. (James 1:14–15 NIV)

Planning may involve complex rituals, whether driving to get pornography, casing a store to verify that no familiar people are around, or driving great distances to avoid being recognized. The ritual provides a heightened sense of satisfaction while waiting for the opportune moment. The addict stalking his prey acts as a predator and, in some instances, he or she is precisely that.

Then the addict reaches the "goal"—the pornographic material, the affair, or the appointment with the prostitute—and sexual release takes place. Yet suddenly, deep shame and remorse replace the sheer thrill of the act itself as the bleak reality of the post-orgasmic state sets in and with it a sense of acute loneliness. Life has remained unchanged with only a brief escape, and now thoughts center on the risk of exposure—the legal, moral, familial, and health consequences. Additionally, for the Christian, the spiritual reality of moral failure can feel overwhelming. Consider David's description in Psalm 32 of how his bones wasted away and how guilt sapped his energy.

The addict then believes his or her own promises: "Never again. If I don't get caught or contract some venereal disease, I will never fail again." Such promises, even couched in Christian jargon about forgiveness and restoration, are almost certainly doomed to failure without consistent Christian fellowship, personal accountability, and often, professional support. In the absence of these, the fragile addict awaits the next visual stimulus, and the awful cycle begins again.

The Bible speaks clearly about some issues, declaring certain behaviors sinful. These include premarital and extramarital sex, incest, bestiality (sex with animals), and necrophilia (sex with the dead; see Lev. 20:15ff.). One must assume Scripture includes these prohibitions because there was a need to prohibit them. Romans 1 tells us that God's judgment sometimes involves His giving sinful people over to their sin. That is, sometimes His discipline allows people to continue in the downward spiral of sexual degradation. History confirms this. In the great cultures of Egypt, Greece, and Rome, sexual immorality became a large part of the social fabric and contributed to the dissolution of their prominence.

Today, the intense sexual emphasis in American culture (music videos, movies, and TV sitcoms) and even the example set by some political and church leaders help encourage a skewed perception of sex. Some unmarried Christian couples can get caught up in chasing the endorphin rush with an attitude of "take it to the limit." They erroneously believe that they can keep the "letter of the Law" by drawing the line at intercourse. They feel that as long as they abstain from vaginal penetration, even if they engage in something as intimate as oral sex, they have obeyed God's prohibitions against "sex" outside of marriage. While these couples don't necessarily fit the profile of sex addicts, their times together can easily begin to revolve solely around sexual stimulation. As mentioned, couples who are truly following Christ from the heart, however, will not ask, "How far can I go?" but, "What is God's standard for sexuality and how can we most glorify God in this relationship?"

The problem, then, originates in wrong thinking. For the Christian, the solution begins with right thinking. Those who counsel sex addicts recommend that they start by being honest with themselves that they have a problem. Then they must tell someone they trust about their addiction (Eph. 5:21; James 5:16). Next, the addict is encouraged to destroy all pornographic material, including sales catalogs if those pose a problem. One young man even held a magazine-burning event with his accountability partner. If videos bring temptation, video stores of any kind must be avoided.

In my counseling sessions with those struggling in this area, I've found that some of the most pertinent truths for this type of bondage are found in Romans 6. Consider, along with Paul, the questions "Are we to continue in sin that grace might increase?" and "Shall we sin because we are not under law but under grace?" (vv. 1, 15). Paul's powerful answer? "May it never be!" Paul argues that all who are in Christ have been baptized into His death (v. 4). That means none of us has to live the way we used to, because we aren't who we used to be. When Christ died to sin, we in Christ died to sin as well. So we are no longer slaves to sin (vv. 6–7). We must *know* that we have new life in Christ, consider it to be true, and live consistent with this reality (vv. 3, 11, 13). The Scriptures say, "Do not go on presenting the members of your body to sin as instruments of unrighteousness; but present . . . your members as instruments of righteousness to God" (v. 13).

Paul explains in the last half of the chapter that we are either slaves of sin or slaves of righteousness (vv. 16–20). God has made it possible in Christ to live holy, godly lives. We must choose, and present ourselves, even as a soldier salutes and presents him- or herself to

God for service. According to Paul, we are dead to sin, but alive to God in Christ Jesus—a remarkable, lavish outpouring of grace on the basis of His forgiveness.

A husband who had struggled with pornography for years—one of the nearly twenty percent of married men who do—shared his recent experience of sitting outside a convenience store listening to the end of a favorite song on the radio after filling his car with gas. Suddenly he realized that he'd not even felt tempted to go in and buy a pornographic magazine. On his long journey toward godliness, he knew he had not yet "arrived," but he breathed a prayer of thanks for the small victory.

17

Sexuality and Aging

I am my beloved's and my beloved is mine.
—SONG OF SOLOMON 6:3

She was sixty-seven years old when she gave birth to twin girls, thanks to in vitro fertilization with donor eggs. That made Adriana Iliescu of Romania the oldest woman to give birth in the world[1]—the modern world, that is. Luke 1:7 tells us that Elizabeth and Zechariah were both "well advanced in years" (NKJV) when their son John the Baptizer was conceived. Sarah was ninety when she birthed Isaac (Gen. 17:17). And these folks had nothing on Methuselah, who fathered is first child at age 187 and had other children before he died 782 years later (Gen. 5:26).

Regardless of how many decades we medically extend the "child-bearing years," the aging process—for all the money spent fighting it with facelifts, tummy tucks, and liposuction—is still occurring. Unless someone discovers the "Ponce de Leon" gene or another "fountain of youth" in the various wrinkle creams and herbal remedies, we'll show signs of advancing age as the body's mechanisms for repairing itself fail.

Yet much of the news about *sex* and aging is good. Studies have shown that "physical capacity for male erection and male and female orgasm continue almost indefinitely, . . . and, for many, sexual satisfaction increases rather than decreases as individuals enter into their senior years."[2] And here's another piece of good news: if one's sexuality is constant throughout life, "the biological changes associated with aging are less pronounced and sexuality is usually less affected."[3]

While we Westerners tend to view aging as an enemy to be fought, the book of Proverbs lends a different perspective, describing gray hair as "a crown of splendor" (Prov. 16:31 NIV). Aging, in fact, provides the opportunity to grow in many areas. In 2 Peter, we find exhortations to grow in knowledge, self-control, perseverance, godliness, brotherly kindness, and love. The Scriptures teach us that as long as these are increasing, life has purpose and meaning. While some medical problems may arise, a life with purpose through deepening love for God can be joyful and satisfying.

As we age, then, we can grow in wisdom and kindness. Certainly we need these traits to face the accumulated years' changes, particularly the ones that affect sexual functioning. Recognizing that satisfaction and performance have enormous mental components, it's easy to see that, for both men and women, the changes that aging brings can generate some new challenges or bring old ones to the surface. Yet these challenges can provide wonderful opportunities to deepen intimacy and discover ways for a man and woman to delight each other in an atmosphere of ever-deepening unity.

Many women feel unattractive and fear loss of sexual *desirability* as they age. In contrast, men, though some do obsess over their looks, usually are most fearful of the loss of sexual *ability*. Performance anxiety issues, even impotence, develop for men who in the past have rarely struggled to "rise to the occasion."

Yet midlife, as the research has revealed, can also be an exhilarating time for marriage partners. What couple in love doesn't talk of growing old together? And many husbands and wives draw closer, as the shared years and life experiences have "smoothed out the rough edges." As character, charm, and understanding flourish, couples find that physical appearance alone doesn't define attractiveness. Lois and Oscar, for example, both in their nineties, have spent many years together as husband and wife. They demonstrate a deep commitment and affection, developed through the complex pressures they have faced together.

An interesting difference between aging men and women was reported in *Psychology Today*.[4] There seems to be a tendency for men, as they grow older, to retain a mental preference for the image of the "woman I married"—the young, attractive, blushing bride. With the passage of time, that girl of their dreams has morphed into a middle-aged woman, and men can experience difficulties in arousal and performance as a reaction. The same study suggests, however, that the average woman, as she matures, finds in her mate attributes that *become* "the ideal." That is, if her man puts on a little weight and thins out on top, she modifies her ideal to include a "plump, balding guy"—a nice adaptation.

This difference in ideals can have significant impact in the bedroom. The man in a "midlife crisis" might leave his wife for a younger woman or have extramarital affairs to meet his perceived need to feel young and virile again. At the same time, although the wife feels content with her partner, she senses his distance and becomes hypercritical of her own appearance.

It doesn't have to be this way. Many couples find middle life quite satisfying. With the fear of pregnancy gone, years of history built together, and deep communication developed through years of observing each other, many couples report this as their best time. Feeling unencumbered with all the cares of youth, they enjoy lovemaking. It may take them longer, but no stopwatch ticks off the minutes. They have time to enjoy, to explore, and to learn more about each other. One woman in her seventies, after nearly fifty years of marriage, read a book on marital intimacy and told us, "I learned something new—but I'll be danged if I'm going to tell you what it was!"

"Midlife crisis" is not, then, a mandatory stage. Men don't have to fit the stereotypical picture of the guy with the red sports car, shirt unbuttoned to the navel, leaving his marriage for a twentysomething blonde. Women aren't destined to be depressed, miserable, and hypercritical about their own appearance. Aging poses certain complex challenges, but with the support of spouse, family, church, and good medical care, midlife and beyond can be wonderful.

Perimenopause

Midlife alters the woman's hormonal cycle. The prepared woman knows changes are coming and that they're part of the divine design. The complex synchrony of estrogen and progesterone wavers. Perimenopause, which typically lasts several years preceding menopause, includes unpredictable estrogen production. Other hormones change too, so women in their late thirties and forties may experience symptoms that have an impact on their sexual responses. These include hot flashes, those bursts of "core meltdown." Add in the possibility of sleep disturbances, night sweats, generalized moodiness, and at times profound depression, and you have a fragile condition.

With fluctuating estrogen production, the vagina loses elasticity, lubrication fails (necessitating the use of artificial lubricant), and sex can become painful. Bladder function becomes less predictable, and ultimately, some sexual sensations change. The size of clitoral, vulvar, and labial tissue decreases, along with the size of the cervix, uterus, and ovaries. However, the sensitivity of the clitoris remains the same as when a woman is younger.[5]

Libido is a complex combination of many factors, and many of them can be changing in perimenopausal women. A thorough medical exam and proper treatment can resolve most of these issues, and women will find hormonal stability again. Various therapies, some available over the counter and some by prescription, can significantly alleviate these problems.

A health care provider can help suitable candidates by prescribing estrogen replacement therapy (ERT) or other treatments. While some women can begin estrogen replacement therapy, others cannot or may choose other treatment strategies. Despite occasional complications, normal sexual function is not only possible in the forties and beyond for most women, but it is a vital part of life in good, healthy marital relationships. In fact, women often report increasing sexual pleasure as they mature.

Menopause

Menopause brings with it some predictable obstacles. As we said, without estrogen, decreased elasticity and lubrication may cause painful intercourse, bleeding, and tearing of the vaginal tissues. Painful sex is not limited, however, to estrogen deficiency in a woman, but can be related to a number of vaginal conditions. Thus, a thorough gynecological exam yielding an accurate diagnosis must precede therapy. Pain should never be considered normal, and a well-informed physician can present a variety of options.

Surgery and Medications

In addition to difficulties that accompany chronic medical illnesses, surgical procedures can affect sexual expression in midlife. Male sexual dysfunction can happen as a direct result of radical prostate procedures and some abdomino-pelvic vascular procedures. In other cases problems may be less direct, such as those that may arise following abdominal surgery. For men whose impotence is purely anatomical, prosthetic devices, pumps, vacuums, and an assortment of appliances may restore sexual function. For those with secondary issues (such as fear following a heart attack), the medical team can assess the true risks and make suggestions of ways the individuals should best approach sexual expression.

In women, a number of specific gynecological procedures may affect sexual comfort and responsiveness. Removal of the ovaries, for example, has an impact on female sexuality. And discomfort from pelvic inflammatory disease can also inhibit function and cause discomfort. With orgasm, many experience the gentle contractions of the uterus; for patients with fibroids or endometriosis, such contractions may actually cause pain. But after a hysterectomy the sensations change. Most post-hysterectomy women are fully responsive and adapt quickly without problems.

Medications may require some adaptation as well. One husband, when his wife was on tamoxifen following breast cancer surgery, noticed during a romantic interlude that his wife was becoming physically hot. He could feel the heat within his arms and noticed the sweat on her lips. Thinking he was perhaps the world's greatest lover, he was thoroughly disappointed to find that these responses were the result of a hot flash, not hot love. Couples—especially those armed with a sense of humor—can certainly learn to express their love after the myriad procedures people face over the decades in countries where good medical care is available.

Men and Midlife

From an actuarial standpoint, the segment of the population age forty-five and over is the healthiest age group in the United States. If the AARP, a nonprofit organization for people over fifty, were to become a nation, it would be the thirtieth most populous in the world, slightly under the population of Argentina. More than half of the people in history who have reached age sixty-five are alive today.[6]

Due to today's improved health care and living conditions, normal sexual function for men is possible not only in their forties but well beyond, continuing as a vital part of life. While men in midlife have no dramatic hormonal flux equivalent with "the change" in women, they often undergo some psychological changes that affect marital intimacy. Some suggest that, in the forties or fifties, men come to recognize they will never win an Olympic medal or even advance in their own vocation much beyond their current status. While this is certainly a broad generalization, those who focus on such a realization may feel depressed and disappointed, which may affect their sexual functioning.

Yet with such a sense of limitation can also come freedom. The couple who has worked hard to raise their family well begins to enjoy the long-term effects of wisdom, experience, and truly "knowing" each other. Men who work to keep the romance alive, to woo their wives with tenderness, can find midlife a terrific time to be in love. Most husbands find lasting contentment in their faith and commitment to their family. Those who go looking outside the marriage bond usually find themselves feeling more empty than they did when they started looking. God alone can truly fulfill the deepest needs and bring peace and joy to the soul.

Occasional impotence—the inability to achieve or sustain an erection sufficient to permit satisfactory intercourse—becomes increasingly common as the years pass. But greater sexual control and better understanding of his wife's needs and preferences often makes the older lover more satisfying to his spouse. Assuming good health and a strong relationship, many men can achieve erection and reach orgasm into their eighties and beyond. Although sexual arousal and climax may require more time, pleasurable sensations can be heightened for both partners. Satisfaction and gratification do not always have to be defined as "climax." Couples can find joy in the journey of relational intimacy and spiritual oneness.

Medical factors, though, can have an impact on sexual performance and pleasure in midlife and beyond. Erection and ejaculatory problems may have a neurological cause, so a thorough examination might clarify any problem and generate practical suggestions for keeping romance alive. Medications interfere with normal functioning, particularly some targeted at hypertension and psychiatric difficulties. Alternative drug therapies may make an impact, so consult your physician if you develop sexual problems.

At a recent conference, several wives shared with us that sex for them had been "short, sweet, and fall asleep"—for *him*. Yet as their husbands aged, the women reported new pleasures. Their men seemed less in a rush to get to the ultimate experience, having learned how to bring pleasure to their wives. These women were genuinely happy over the new heights that they had achieved. Some even found that they were more responsive sexually than they had ever imagined they could be.

Men and Low Desire

Many books and marriage conferences emphasize the common problem of the disparity between the husband's and wife's interest in sex. While they usually focus on men with high levels and women with low libidos, some couples have the opposite problem—he is much less, if ever, interested. Continually hearing that they are "different" in this way only adds to the frustration these couples feel.

"I'll never forget the first time my husband rejected my sexual advances," writes one woman who now volunteers helping other women whose partners have low-desire issues. "He hadn't been in the mood lately, so I slid my naked body into bed next to him and began to make my move. He began laughing, pushed me away, and asked me what the heck I was doing! I was devastated and humiliated. I had always been under the impression that the man was supposed to be the sexual powerhouse, the one in the relationship who was insatiable. The woman was supposed to be the one turning down sex—that's the way it had always been portrayed in books and on television! I was confused, sad, and angry. My husband and I began fighting about sex every weekend, and I would find myself retreating to the sofa and resorting to self-pleasure."[7]

Another woman, Lanette, is one of the most attractive women I (Sandi) have ever known, but it didn't take long to find out why she paid so much attention to her beautiful hair, flawless makeup, and stylish clothes. Her husband ignored her. She changed her hairstyle—sometimes the color, sometimes the cut—about six times a year, hoping that somehow she would find the right combination to catch his interest.

Laura sat across from me in her company's cafeteria. She picked at her food and periodically wiped tears. "I caught him masturbating," she told me. "I've gone six months without having my needs met. I've begged him to pay attention to me. And now this!" Laura's husband had a long history of alcohol abuse, causing periodic impotency. His insecurity about it made him avoid intimacy altogether, so she lived as a married celibate. While other women complained that their husbands were always after them for sex, Laura listened longingly.

Candy called me on the recommendation of a friend. "We've been married for six months," she told me, "and the only time we did anything was on the first night of our honeymoon. The rest of the trip, he said he was too worn out from all the festivities. That was just the beginning of the excuses. Most recently I bought a new sexy nightgown for Valentine's Day. We had a special dinner together, but when it came time to 'be together,' he fell asleep on me. It must be so wonderful to be married to someone who expresses physical love. I can't imagine how special that would be."

A little more than a third of married women complain that "he's rarely interested."[8] Men can experience lack of interest in sex for a variety of reasons. Usually the greatest fear that enters a wife's mind is that her mate is having an affair with another woman, or worse—as it turned out for Candy—that he's a practicing homosexual.

Communication Is the Key

If decreased desire in a husband or wife becomes a problem, couples need to begin the solution by having a heart-to-heart talk outside of the marriage bed. Some feel they are wrong to expect their marriage partners to have sex with them. Yet 1 Corinthians 7:3 makes it clear that the husband and wife have a responsibility to meet each other's sexual needs. If your partner lacks interest, begin by praying for help in having a difficult but necessary conversation. Then together explore the possible cause or causes.

Ask your spouse, "Is there anything I can do to help you be in the mood more often?" Perhaps he's bored with the routine. Perhaps she needs help with the kids. Consider together whether lack of interest in sex is a new problem, or if it's been this way since day one. Is he getting his needs met elsewhere? Does she seem to have no desire at any time? Is work particularly stressful lately? A man will often avoid sex because he's having potency problems and is afraid of risking failure. This is why it's so important to discuss his lack of interest in a supportive and loving way.[9]

Seek medical help if the lack of desire is not a temporary difficulty. Physical reasons for low sexual interest in men include conditions such as diabetes, cardiovascular disease, extreme stress, and, as with both Lanette's and Laura's husbands, a history of alcohol abuse. Often the medication history can give clues, as a variety of drugs can impact libido and function. Antihypertensive medicines, medications used for migraines, and most of the SSRIs (Prozac, Paxil, Zoloft), so useful for certain anxiety and depressive disorders, can dramatically lower libido. If brain serotonin levels are relatively high—as is true for many patients on antidepressants—sexual dysfunction may occur.[10]

People with high-stress jobs or very physical jobs can, indeed, be physically tired. A phenomenon that appears unique to men, though, and that seems similar to a general depression, involves an unsatisfying work experience, or a sense of "failure to accomplish" something significant in a lifespan. For many men, job performance and sexual prowess are tightly linked. In addition, failure to perform up to his own "standards" can begin a downward spiral of ongoing failure. If a man tries to have sex when tired or distracted by job or other concerns and can't maintain a satisfactory erection or reach ejaculation, it can plant deadly seeds of doubt in his mind. These can be powerful enough to cause him to prefer not trying rather than trying and failing. Encouragement, support, and "another time, another place, another try" without pressure may resolve the issue.

A husband who experiences these episodes is hardly alone. The e-waves and airwaves are inundated with advertisements for erectile dysfunction aids—both prescription and nonprescription approaches. This change in publicity is striking. Erectile dysfunction has, in fact, surfaced as a major male issue and is frequently followed by seeming lack of interest in sexual expression. Erectile dysfunction along with premature ejaculation cause considerable male sexual difficulties. However, there are many successful therapies ranging from biblical counseling to specific medications for particular patients.

Hormonal issues can play a role for both men and women. As a man ages, the testosterone slowly decreases which may cause a noticeable change in libido, size and firmness of the erection, as well as force of ejaculation. For the man who has been able to perform "on demand," these changes can be anxiety-producing, even frightening aspects of the normal aging process.

For aging women (see sections on perimenopause/menopause,

pp. 229–30), besides the hormonal effects, body image seems to play an enormous role. As a woman feels less attractive and less secure, she may resist advances and be more reluctant to initiate sexual expression. So we find husbands with failing confidence in their ability and wives that are insecure in their appearance—a recipe for decrease in the number of intimate encounters.

For men, obesity may also be a factor. In a study of nearly 2,000 men at the Harvard School of Public Health, "those with 42-inch waists or larger were twice as likely to have problems getting an erection as those with 32-inch waists. Researchers suspect that's because they had risk factors for heart disease—high blood pressure, high cholesterol, and inactivity—which compromise not only blood flow to the heart, but also to the genitals. The solution? Frequent workouts and a low-fat diet."[11]

Seek competent counseling

One woman wrote, "When my husband takes his arousal pills—about four times a month—we have great sex. But I'm angry at his need to take 'something' to have sex with me." Her words demonstrate how easy it is to take his low desire personally, but if he needs medication to achieve an erection, his lack of drive is probably out of his control. The available medications increase blood flow to the pelvis, and perhaps boost his confidence. Her anger would seem to be misplaced in this situation. This couple could probably benefit from a third party to help them have some difficult conversations in a supportive atmosphere. It's not easy to talk with someone else about your love life, but sometimes a neutral party can help a lot.

Many counselors and most pastoral counselors, however, have no experience in sex therapy or dealing with these intimate issues. So try to find someone with training and expertise in treating sexual problems. Checking with your physician might be a good first place to start.

When the wife has a lower sex drive than her husband, she can still usually help him experience sexual release in a relatively brief time. Providing sexual release is more complex, however, when the one with the lower libido is the husband. Because sexual satisfaction for her generally takes longer, requires more concentration and ambiance, and is a reflection of the intensity of her feelings toward her man, the uninterested husband must involve himself for much longer to satisfy his wife. And her partner's enthusiasm is more closely linked to her ability even to experience orgasm than it would be for many men with less interested wives. Nevertheless, it's still worthwhile to have intimate contact, if only to assure her of his love, affection, and concern for her welfare.

Bear in mind that there are alternate ways to achieve orgasm (see chapter 8) even when the husband suffers from erectile dysfunction. Couples should feel free to explore and experiment in these areas. Perhaps once the husband is successful in these ways, his lagging libido will be less of an issue.

Some husbands *are* trying to be sensitive, but they often find themselves having painful conversations that go something like this:

HIM: "Do you need me to meet your needs tonight, sweetheart?"

HER: "It would be nice if you actually wanted me."

HIM: "Hey, I'm doing the best I can."

HER: "I don't want some sort of sympathy session—doing it because you have to. You'd just be pretending."

HIM: "Then what do you expect me to do? Lie and tell you I can't wait? I'm willing to meet your needs. That's the best I can do right now."

The neglected wife will probably feel insecurities such as, "If only I were more beautiful" or "If only I were more sexy." Even if doctors can identify a medical cause for the husband's seeming indifference, these feelings are difficult for her to overcome. Yet it's important for her to remind herself that God created her in His very image, so she is a beautiful creature, fully desirable, despite her husband's medical or emotional issues.

Because a spouse's lack of interest usually brings feelings of rejection and even insecurity for the more interested partner, he or she may be especially vulnerable. First Corinthians 7:5 gives the clear command not to deprive each other for this very reason—because it leaves one's spouse more vulnerable to sexual temptation. If your spouse refuses to or can't help you achieve sexual release, you as the deprived spouse must recognize the additional moral vigilance that must accompany such difficulties in your life.

The way your spouse decides to respond to your need, though, is largely out of your control. If he or she ignores your pleas despite attempts at communication and intervention, seek the help of a third party. If your spouse remains unresponsive, you must live with the devastating reality of life as a celibate married person. The ongoing support of a trusted friend will be essential to helping you deal with such a loss.

In this case our Savior's submission to the Father serves as a source of enablement and encouragement: "When they hurled their insults at him, he did not retaliate; when he suffered, he made no threats. Instead, he entrusted himself to him who judges justly" (1 Peter 2:23 NIV). That is not to say you silently bear it, opting never to bring it up. Periodically express your ongoing desire for marital oneness. Yet recognize that if your spouse fails to respond, it's out of your control.

For many women, their husbands' lack of interest is a source of ongoing grief, as sexual oneness was created as an essential piece in the marriage equation. If this is true for you, express your emotion to God, knowing He will honor you for exhibiting a quality that reflects the heart of God Himself—loyal, faithful love that cares for those who cannot reciprocate.

This can go both ways. Many wives are no longer available to their husbands after the kids are grown and gone. A man in such a situation must learn to live godly in the midst of her selfish approach, as well.

Jesus Christ understands the difficulties of the celibate life. In Ronald Rolheiser's book *The Holy Longing*, he notes, "When Christ went to bed alone at night, he was in real solidarity with the many persons who, not by choice but by circumstance, sleep alone. And there is a real poverty, a painful searing one, in this kind of aloneness. The poor are not just those who are more manifestly victimized by poverty, violence, war, and unjust economic systems. There are other less obvious manifestations of poverty, violence, and injustice. Celibacy by conscription is one of them."[12]

As we've said before, the number-one sexual difficulty couples experience is the inability to talk about it. This appears to be a pattern that continues through the years unless couples make a specific effort to communicate about their intimate lives. Physicians estimate that nearly half of their menopausal patients suffer from a loss of sexual desire or satisfaction. And while approximately two-thirds of the men have noticed a decrease in sexual activity since their partners entered menopause, only half of the couples have discussed these changes together.

So the first line of defense is communication. The second is knowing what to expect. The third is knowing to seek help any time you experience discomfort or ongoing anxiety. Finally, focus on the benefits of loving well at each age. In their time of youth, couples experience new, exciting sensations, and awaken to worlds of self-discovery. With maturity comes skill, confidence, and deepening intimacy. In old age, couples bring to each other the wisdom and joy of love learned over a lifetime. As the authors of *Love and Sex After Forty* remind us, "Love and sex are twin arts, requiring effort and knowledge. Only in fairy tales do people live happily ever after without working at it . . . but sex does not merely exist after the middle and later years; it holds the possibility of becoming greater than it ever was."[13]

Like the bride in Song of Solomon who felt free to say, "Dark am I, yet lovely" (1:5 NIV), we face growing old together by working to create a secure atmosphere for each other. In that place, loving eyes look beyond physical imperfections and exclaim, "This is my lover, this my friend" (Song 5:16 NIV).

18
Questions from Our Readers

May he kiss me with the kisses of his mouth!
For your love is better than wine.
—SONG OF SOLOMON 1:2

Questions About Desire

What natural herbs or foods can I take to increase my desire?

Many companies market herbs as aphrodisiacs or sexual-response enhancers despite legal restrictions. Although some long-touted aphrodisiacs are being tested—including a derivative of chili peppers now in legitimate trials[1]—to date there is no such thing as a science-verified aphrodisiac. In 1989, the Food and Drug Administration officially banned the sale of "any product that bears labeling claims that it will arouse or increase sexual desire or that it will improve sexual performance."

If you believe that eating oysters or exotic herbs will put you in the mood, they probably will, considering the fact that the brain is the most powerful sex organ we have. The same is true of vitamin E and other highly touted supplements. While drinking alcohol—for those who imbibe—may make you feel sexual, it actually impairs performance. A better way to stay sexually healthy begins with relational intimacy built on a strong foundation of spiritual unity.

Perhaps the best way to stay sexually healthy is simply to have sex.

Will an oral contraceptive take away my sexual desire?

One patient wrote, "I'm pretty sure that the oral contraceptive I'm taking has decreased my desire. I'm a lot less frisky than I was two months before the wedding, and I noticed it before the wedding. I think my husband is afraid I'll go off the pill and get pregnant. So he's convincing himself that I'm just nervous from the stress of not getting the sex thing perfect. Basically, he thinks I need to relax—not just my muscles, but my mind."

The pill combines two powerful hormones, but at low levels. Ideally, these artificially produced hormones shut down the woman's own ovarian production of estrogen—a major contributor to her level of interest. There is no real surge in progesterone, and the small amount of testosterone made in the woman's ovary can be diminished. A fair number of women have noted a decreased sex drive while taking oral contraceptives. For these women, physicians can switch prescriptions to a combination that includes a slightly more "androgenic" (male hormone) type of progesterone. Using this pill may cause acne, oily skin, and weight gain, so it may take a few months to find the "happy median."

More Questions About "The Pill"

When I'm on an oral contraceptive, should I take a periodic break?

Many pill takers believe they need to take a periodic break from oral contraceptives. This is unnecessary. Medical evidence suggests that if women take their pills correctly, taking time off from them does not lower the risk of complications or disease, and it may result in a surprise pregnancy.

Do oral contraceptives cause weight gain?

Some but not all oral contraceptive pills cause weight gain. As many women gain weight as lose it while taking "the pill." How one woman might interact with a specific oral contraceptive is anyone's guess, but diet and nutrition always play a role. The pill can't be responsible for a fifty-pound weight gain!

Do oral contraceptives cause abortion?

Oral contraceptive pills are designed primarily to prevent ovulation or egg release. Most pills are a combination of an estrogen and a progesterone derivative that cycle a woman artificially without allowing ovulation. In addition to preventing egg release, the pill thickens cervical mucus, making sperm penetration more difficult. It also changes the motion of the cilia (tiny hairlike structures) within the fallopian tubes, altering egg transport. Finally, it thins the uterine lining (endometrium). And many believed that a thinned uterine lining was less favorable to implantation should fertilization occur. The most recent research suggests otherwise. While each one of these effects actually increases the effectiveness of the pill in preventing pregnancy, the latter, in theory, could possibly have an abortive effect if breakthrough ovulation were actually to occur.

Nevertheless, we must avoid oversimplifying this complicated scenario. Those who argue that the uterine environment is hostile to implantation while the woman is taking the pill are correct. Yet if breakthrough ovulation does take place, this would mean that hormone levels have been sufficient to allow ovulation. In that case, the pill has *failed* to do its job, because the estrogen level *has* to be higher in the first place to permit an egg to reach maturity. And, remember, the same hormone—estrogen—that allows ovulation also grows and thickens the uterine lining.

To continue the above scenario, once breakthrough ovulation has taken place, progesterone would be secreted in normal, high amounts, even if the woman continues to take the pill. Thus, in the roughly seven days it would take for the fertilized embryo to reach the uterus and implant, the hormones would also prepare the uterine environment to be more "friendly" to implantation. So in this scenario, it's extremely doubtful that the uterine lining would be too hostile to allow implantation should breakthrough ovulation occur. Current medical data do not support the theory that birth control pills cause abortion, but each woman should be informed as new research adds to our understanding of this complex process.

In addition, reliable studies have used vaginal ultrasound to monitor ovarian egg maturation, as well as monitor blood hormone levels in women on the pill. These studies have not supported the claim that significant rates of breakthrough ovulation occur. The data would suggest that people regularly taking the pill rarely, in fact, ovulate at all. Thus, the potential risk of the pill's causing abortion seems very low, although the possibility does exist. It is significant that the majority of Focus on the Family's Physician's Resource Council concluded in 1997 that there is no direct evidence that the pill causes abortions.[2] The official position of the Christian Medical Association as of 2006 states that there is no direct evidence currently that the pill causes abortion.

In a personal conversation I (Dr. Bill) had with one of our nation's leading experts in the field of hormonal contraception, he astutely observed that in the decades the pill has been around, if the "hostile, thin endometrium theory" were actually true, we would have seen an increase in the number of cases of "placenta accreta," a condition of the placenta burrowing too deeply into the wall of the uterus. We sometimes see this complication in women who at one time had a C-section, and the scarred area of the uterus has a thinner endometrium. There has been no increase, though, in this complication of pregnancy, despite the thousands upon thousands of women/years of pill use. I find this a compelling argument and believe that, for appropriate patients, the combination birth control pill remains an ethical option.

What should we do? Know the medical risks as they are currently understood. Be willing to be teachable if new data reveals different risks. Then prayerfully decide if you can use pills until the question is more fully resolved. If you take oral contraceptive pills, do so carefully as we *know* consistent use will diminish the risk. And be gentle with others who make choices that differ from yours.

Questions About Intercourse

What can we do about the fact that I ejaculate before she is ready for me to?

In the workbook, we include the "squeeze technique," although we don't necessarily recommend it. Another suggestion was to have sex twice in one night. Here's another.

Know this first: once a woman has had one orgasm, should she wish to pursue a second one, the time between the first and the next is relatively short compared to how long it takes from excitation to orgasm with the first. So seek to bring your wife to climax apart from intercourse, whether through touching with your palm or fingertips, oral stimulation, external contact with the penis, or a combination of these. Take your time and enjoy the trip. As was said so succinctly in a *Newsweek* article, "Nature did not design most women to climax reliably through intercourse, especially in the missionary position."[3] Many couples prefer to save intercourse for after her orgasm—or after her first orgasm—so she is more lubricated and engorged.

Once she has reached orgasm and expressed that she is ready again, move to penetration and thrusting, with additional manual stimulation for her if she requests it. The length of time required for the male to exercise self-control should be much shorter. In addition, if you ejaculate apart from satisfying her, she has already had one orgasm. Inquire about whether she would like you to proceed with manual stimulation or just enjoy the afterglow with cuddling and caressing.

Enjoy each other. If it works out that she has an orgasm via penetration, wonderful. But if not, enjoy the fullness of your own experience and realize you can both be satisfied.

What are some of the special challenges unique to virgins?

One reader wrote, "After going to the doctor two months before the wedding, I came away thinking I was good to go. All the running, tampons, and the fact that I'm over thirty made me think my hymen was very flexible, if not gone. So I didn't do any stretching exercises. I could always feel my body responding when we kissed, so I imagined we'd have no trouble at all on the wedding night. I was shocked when it was so painful.

"I know everybody has baggage, but I think I pride myself on being a 'free from bondage woman' who understands God's perfect plan for beautiful sex within marriage. But it still really hurt at the initial entry.

"Even now, if he thrusts too deeply, it's painful. I know I'm headed for trouble if I can't get into this 'penetration thing.' I'm already getting an aversion to sex. I want to be close to him and sexual with him, but not intercourse."

Another wrote, "I used to cry and cry out of frustration for my loss of interest in sexual intercourse because it's so painful. But now I think it's hopeless to cry. We both are desperate. It may be something mental or physical with me. Now I become angry with myself for desiring something that may never come back (orgasm). Should I just forget about it? Should I just endure painful intercourse? Am I going to be part of the statistics of women who don't respond?"

Yet another said this: "We ended up having a sexless honeymoon because the pain was so great for me. We called the doctor and he prescribed a numbing cream, but that didn't help when it numbed my husband on contact! When we got home, the doctor gave us dilators and that helped a lot. I would insert them for about thirty minutes to stretch me before intercourse. I felt a lot of fear and guilt. I had always dreamed I would be this satisfying lover for my husband and I feel as though I've been one big disappointment. We had a great relationship before, but after all this we started arguing a lot. I never realized how sexual intimacy would be such a core part of our relationship. Our love life is much better now, but it has taken time to make the adjustment."

The first patient in these three scenarios probably has a tight hymeneal ring, even if she can insert two fingers. Or perhaps she has a slight skin flap inside the vagina, possibly caused by a congenital problem. It's important to know that pain is abnormal except at the beginning when couples are adapting to one another, and for some a deeper pain occurs at the time of ovulation when the ovary is swollen and a bit tender. Discomfort associated with intercourse is medically treatable. Find a physician who will listen, and then with exercises, dilators, lubricants, and even surgery, the pain can be resolved. Don't just endure pain! The medical term for painful sex is dyspareunia, and anything that has its own name has to be serious! Figure out whether it's physical/anatomical, or muscular spasm because of either fear or past experience. Sometimes pain is related to a lack of lubrication or elasticity because of hormones such as the pill. Figure this out. It will be totally worth it for your entire married life.

Our runner friend said, "Now when I talk to other women who are entering marriage as virgins, I tell them that having low expectations is key—don't set yourself up for failure by thinking you have an exceptionally loose vagina. Also, hands and mouth are great alternate ways of stimulation. I encourage couples not to get caught up with 'I must get intercourse good before moving on to the rest.' Lubricant on top of the condom has helped—no dry condoms! In addition, it's been great to talk with women who are willing to talk. I've found that especially helpful."

Another shared something else that came as a surprise for her. "I always imagined 'entry,' but I never thought beyond that to think that 'what goes in must come out.' This is messy, smelly business. In our first experiences, the bodily fluids from our lovemaking spilled all over the bed, and we'd end up trying to edge each other out for the dry spots when it was time to go to sleep.

"No matter how often a person might shower . . . well, tell the type-A virgin that this is messy business, but 'the boy' doesn't seem to care.

Who do you think thought up gelatin and mud wrestling? I'm sure it was guys! Now we keep a hand towel in the nightstand by the bed for spontaneous encounters. When we plan ahead, we bring a warm, moist, scented washcloth and make cleanup part of the interaction. A few scented candles can mask the faint seminal smell, too."

Apparently, these ladies are not alone. In a survey of two thousand Christian women, the results of which are published in Archibald Hart's book *The Secrets of Eve*, he reported what women do not like about sex. Thirty percent complained about the mess, 6 percent listed "partner's smell" as a turn off, 16 percent didn't like the inconvenience. For 8 percent, it hurts.[4]

To minimize the adjustment to sexual intimacy, isn't it better to live with someone first to make sure you're compatible?

According to the U. S. Census Bureau, between 1960 and 2000, the number of unmarried couples in the United States increased tenfold—that's close to one thousand percent! Here are some additional figures for Americans from the 2000 census:

- About 11 million people live with a person to whom they are not married. This includes both same-sex and different-sex couples.
- 9.7 million Americans live with an unmarried different-sex partner and 1.2 million Americans live with a same-sex partner.
- 41% of American women ages fifteen to forty-four have cohabited (lived with an unmarried different-sex partner) at some point. This includes 9% of women ages fifteen to nineteen; 38% of women ages twenty to twenty-four; 49% of women ages twenty-five to twenty-nine; 51% of women ages thirty to thirty-four; 50% of women ages thirty-five to thirty-nine; and 43% of women ages forty to forty-four.[5]
- The number of unmarried couples living together increased 72% between 1990 and 2000.

The Houston Chronicle reported that couples who live together before marriage have an 80 percent greater chance of divorce after they are married than those who don't cohabit first. A Washington State researcher discovered that women who cohabit with a man are twice as likely to experience domestic violence as are married women. The National Center for Mental Health revealed that the incidence of depression among cohabiting women is four times greater than that among married women, and two times greater than depression among unmarried women. In a survey of more than 100 couples who lived together, 71 percent of the women said they would not live-in again.[6] In practice, cohabiting couples who marry—many of whom already have children—are about 33 percent more likely to divorce than are couples who don't live together before their nuptials.[7] Virgin brides, on the other hand, are less likely to divorce than are sexually experienced women who entered marriage. Evidence strongly suggests that, while test driving a car might be a good idea, "trying out" one's future partner is not.

Since God prohibits intercourse before marriage, what's wrong with sexual release that doesn't involve intercourse?

An increasing number of couples—including many Christians—are engaging in mutual orgasm, sometimes including oral sex apart from intercourse, so as to technically keep God's law against fornication. Consider one woman's statement: "My high school boyfriend and I wanted to save intercourse for marriage, but that didn't stop us from having ecstatic sex. We explored ourselves and each other and learned how to fantasize and kiss and touch in very imaginative ways. Those intense sessions left us feeling like we'd been transported to hyperspace."[8]

It's important for these couples to know that the prohibition against "immorality" that occurs numerous times in the New Testament comes from the Greek word *porneia*. This broad term encompasses premarital and extramarital intercourse and also any intimate sexual activity outside of marriage. (We discussed these in greater detail in chapter 13, "A Call to Purity.")

In addition to the sin issues involved, couples engaging in such sexual behavior are at risk for contracting sexually transmitted diseases (STDs). Together, more than twenty-five of these diseases are infecting at least 12 million Americans annually. One in four sexually experienced adolescents acquire a sexually transmitted disease each year.[9]

19

Relational Intimacy in Marriage

How beautiful and how delightful you are,
My love, with all your charms!
—SONG OF SOLOMON 7:6

When we marry, we each bring our own temperaments, character strengths and weaknesses, abilities and disabilities, cultural backgrounds, family backgrounds, and sexual histories. Perhaps you are an extrovert married to an introvert, or vice versa. Maybe you're a "messy" married to a "neatnik." Some of the very differences that once attracted couples to each other can wear on them in the day-in and day-out of marriage. The good news is that it's not the differences that cause the most marital stress—it's how we handle them, how we *communicate*.

Communication involves transferring thoughts, ideas, emotions, and passions from the mind of the communicator to the mind and heart of the listener. Most communication is nonverbal, but how we talk is also essential. And so is how we listen. Think of it this way: although high-definition color television images are broadcast through the airwaves, if your only receiver is a tiny black and white TV set, you'll never catch the beauty of the programming. In marriage, your ears and eyes are your primary receivers of communication messages. By improving your capacity to take in the full picture, you

250

can enjoy a full-color relationship. Such a relationship requires the total engagement of both husband and wife. And full engagement takes time and energy—precious commodities.

Deeply satisfying sexual intimacy occurs in an environment of deep relational intimacy, which includes safe and secure conversation. You'll be talking about what arouses you, why you can't seem to get aroused, or how you feel when you're more interested in lovemaking than your partner is. You'll talk about how many children you want and what sort of contraception—if any—you should use. These and the many other conversations you must have are all deeply intimate topics that bring great potential for growth but also for deep hurt. The exercises below are designed to help you practice the fundamentals of positive communication to minimize injury and maximize joy in your oneness.

In the preceding pages, we described in detail both physical and spiritual intimacy. But we touched only briefly on relational intimacy. The middle of the pyramid (see illustration) will now be our focus.

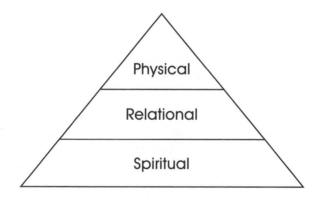

Relational intimacy is comprised of all the days, hours, and minutes during which you as a couple connect through messages—whether in person, by phone, e-mail, text messaging, body language, or attitudes. Clearly, relational intimacy constitutes a major portion of marital life.

Extensive listening skills will not necessarily be required to decide whether you want tacos or burgers for dinner, but issues such as the ones mentioned above will require full engagement from both of you. Whatever the decision or resolution for each issue, one of the goals is for your consensus to match God's best for you in the situation. It doesn't matter who comes up with the idea that prevails; what matters is finding God's will as a couple and honoring your spouse.

True intimacy is the state of being fully known, fully and truly loved, without fear of rejection or abuse. Kind and considerate communication can and should build intimacy. Ordinarily, one of the two of you tends toward the relational sphere as your primary path of intimacy. It's often the wife, but not always. Many highly verbal men enjoy long, relaxed conversations. For the other spouse, communication may feel more like work than pleasure. But such work has enormous benefits as you become a lifelong student of your husband or wife and appreciate his or her unique qualities. The result will be deep intimacy.

We start with listening. As a general rule, seek to understand before seeking to be understood.

How to Listen

Effective listening is *active*. It requires energy and work. Most people do not listen skillfully or intentionally. Consider that doctors interrupt patients on average within seven seconds of asking a question!

Refrain from interrupting or jumping in, even when you're sure you know what your spouse is going to say. Interrupting fails to honor your partner and cuts short the process of developing intimacy. So, while you may have a good sense of where the conversation is going, be patient. You may be surprised as the discussion changes, or that in speaking of the problem, new ideas or angles come to mind. The "perfect answer" you were itching to offer may address the wrong question!

To listen well you must be fully present to your spouse, connected by your love, your commitment, and your desire to hear and understand. Demonstrate attentiveness with body posture, facial expressions, and/or affirming remarks. The point is that you're focused, not daydreaming or mentally arguing but fixed on every word, every gesture, seeking the most minute clue to fully understanding your spouse. As you would study a fine work of art, or engage in a beautiful piece of music, be alert to the thoughts and feelings articulated by the mate God gave to you.

Listen graciously; that is, assume the best motivation by your spouse. When your beloved is talking to you, believe that he or she has something important to say.

Ask questions

Asking questions means drawing out details with appropriate inquiries, nods, smiles, and words of appreciation. Use pertinent questions to draw out the deepest truth. Do you really want to know what he's thinking? How she feels? What makes him tick?

Once you think you know, summarize what has been said, and see if you really did get it right. Can you put it all together? If so, speak it back to your beloved as a question: "So you're saying you don't want to do natural family planning because it would require abstaining during the only time of your cycle when you're ever aroused?" or "You're asking me to have the lingerie catalog sent to my office instead of here at home because the images are too tempting when you're home alone?" This allows for clarification, because you probably won't get it all on the first run through. Don't be discouraged. Listening *is* hard work.

Acknowledge and affirm

Acknowledging your spouse—whether verbally or just with eye contact, a nod, and a smile—demonstrates love. It does not imply agreement. You are modeling godly character when you engage with your whole self as your spouse shares deeply. Listening requires focusing on the speaker, not interrupting, not wandering, and not preparing to mount a counterattack.

For example, even if you envision a mess created by having the lingerie catalog sent to your office, acknowledge that your spouse is trying to think of ways to remain pure in heart and mind. By nodding, you are not necessarily agreeing to the proposed plan of action.

Affirming as you listen can be as simple as adding a soft, "Yes, I see" or "I understand" and perhaps, "Tell me more about that." The speaker should sense by your body language and words that you are committed to the conversation and to resolving the issue at hand. Other ways of affirming may include touch, a pat of the hand, a caress of the shoulder, or just a body posture leaning toward your spouse comfortably, demonstrating you desire to know more and are in no hurry to leave. Affirming makes acknowledgement positive and active. Not only do you recognize your spouse as he or she shares, but your encouraging words and gestures make the discussion safe and unifying.

In some marriages, conversation has no balance. One unloads a firestorm of data—what I think, what I want to do—and the other gives up, gives out, and gives in. A familiar joke is that the key to a successful marriage is two words: "Yes, dear." In reality, that may represent withdrawal or disengagement from the conversation and ultimately from the marriage. Such a sad imbalance prevents the couple from ever discussing the perspective of the silent partner. All the gifts and abilities that God has given to that one will remain untapped and unused. That's like rowing a boat with one oar, or flying a plane with one wing.

How do you know if you are communicating well? If the listener hears and understands (remember this does *not* require agreement), you have communicated. If you can do that without making your spouse feel threatened or devalued, you have communicated well.

The Process of Communication

With such strategies for effective listening in mind, consider how to process together some of the sensitive issues mentioned throughout this book. Doing so requires six E's—Elicit data, Explore your spouse's heart, Entrust your heart, Express desires, Examine options, and Embrace your solution. When you communicate deeply, when you engage in deep soul conversation, you enter into a place where trust is vital. In an atmosphere of deep trust, you will find safety, security, and the freedom to speak with genuine candor—all indicative of true relational intimacy.

Elicit data

In pursuing intimate dialogue, gather the data pertinent to the discussion. What are the facts surrounding your issue? What do you know? What does your spouse know? What remains to be known before the two of you can determine an appropriate solution? If you suffer from arousal difficulties, what medications are you taking? What are their potential side effects? Are you under stress at work? Get all the facts on the table.

Explore your spouse's heart

Gently probe, reflect, and question to discover what your partner thinks and feels about the issue at hand. What does she know about oral sex? What does she feel about engaging in it? What has he heard about vasectomy? What are his feelings about having one? Before arriving at any conclusions, draw out your spouse's intellectual and emotional perspectives on the matter.

Entrust your heart

Once you've sought to understand your spouse, share what is deeply true about you. "When you want to use the vibrator, I feel like I must not be exciting enough." "When you laughed at me for buying a leopardess nightgown, I felt stupid." Revealing such intimate feelings requires trust. You offer a bit of your heart, a little piece of your deepest self, and entrust it to your beloved. As you share your heart, recognize that you tread on sacred ground.

Express desires

Each of you has desires. What are they? Clarify how you would like to resolve the issue at hand. Explore what each of you is willing to do within a reasonable timetable or to be responsible for on a list of possibilities. For example, "We don't have to use the vibrator, but so often I feel rushed—like I need to hurry, and it speeds the process for me. I'm not suggesting you're doing anything wrong, but maybe if you could help me to know through your words and your hands that you're in no hurry, it would help."

Examine options

Often during the exploration of the heart and articulation of the desires, various options come to the table. ("We don't have to receive that catalog at either location.") This frees you as a couple to discount "who" originated the solution you may pursue and focus on the unity that brings together your diverse gifts and abilities. As the information comes to light, you can view new solutions or consider and weigh hybrid ideas.

Embrace the solution

Ultimately, resolution must come to each issue. Choose a course of action based on the data, thoughts, feelings, and desires of each. Your goal is to prayerfully arrive at what you sense, together, represents God's best for you as a couple, His Spirit's leading for you in the matter. Together you decide; you embrace your decision figuratively even as you embrace one another literally.

Foundations for Conversation

Prayer

Surround your significant marital conversations with prayer. You'll be amazed how this one step alone will enormously impact the success of any deep discussion. Commit yourself, your spouse, your marriage, and your words to the Lord, asking Him to direct your conversation. Pray silently if you're not yet comfortable praying aloud.

Prayer and a unified goal can set the right mood and keep you on track. Communication should draw you together, not push you apart. It isn't about winning or losing, it's about oneness in Christ.

Whether you make a good decision together or not, you're in it together. When the argument is over, you are still married, so going for the "win" at all cost will, indeed, cost more than what the short-sighted victory is worth.

And as you talk about any significant issue, the Holy Spirit may bring to your mind a related Scripture or a principle that will help you. You will likely face some tough decisions. Sometimes none of the options look too promising and you have to decide between unpleasant alternatives.

Many Christians were taught the memory device "ACTS" as they learned to pray: Adoration, Confession, Thanksgiving, and Supplication. Perhaps your marital communication would benefit from the same acrostic.

- *Adoration*. Do you first communicate your love and adoration?
- *Confession*. Is there anything between you and your beloved that needs to be confessed and forgiven? Perhaps the topic at hand has been discussed time and again and one of you still bears the scars of past hurtful words. Confession and forgiveness may be appropriate steps to open the channels of heart-to-heart connection.
- *Thanksgiving*. Are you thankful to God for your spouse? Does your spouse *know* this? Do you regularly affirm him or her and verbally rehearse the things for which you are most thankful?
- *Supplication*. Supplication involves asking for specifics.

Scripture

Many issues are settled by Scripture. When it comes to being honest or lying, a Christian always speaks the truth in love. Even if it's costly financially, academically, or otherwise, honesty and integrity are foundational to intimacy. Should you lie and say you had an orgasm when you didn't? Should you pressure your wife to engage in a sexual practice that violates her conscience? Should you rent an X-rated movie in an effort to jump-start your sweetie's low desire? Some answers are clear.

Yet many issues you will discuss are less so. Is natural family planning for us? How far apart should we space our children? With these you must bring a biblical perspective. Do you honor one another? Your love and conduct toward one another as man and wife will be a testimony to those around you, so learn to do things well.

Counsel and reflection

Perhaps you would benefit from godly counsel, medical counsel, or a certified sex therapist. And keep in mind the marvelous resource of the church, the Body of Christ. Often you can locate godly mentoring couples or individuals who have experience in your particular area of need. Why not seek out somebody who knows those areas where you are struggling and can give you some guidance?

Maybe you both need some time for reflection, which may be overnight, several days, or even weeks, depending on the type of decision. Decisions such as how many children to have, and when, merit the kind of deep discussion we're talking about. With mutual respect, considerate listening, and thoughtful speaking, solutions can surface in a way that draws you together, with the commitment and energy to do what you've decided to do.

Don't allow an impasse to dissolve marital intimacy. There will be some areas where you don't see eye to eye, or the decision doesn't come right away. Don't give up! Cling to one another and pray for unity and insight into the dilemma.

Physiology

Fatigue and emotions can negatively affect your ability to communicate. If you're really tense about some issue, if something is really under your skin, you're unlikely to communicate well or constructively. One significant finding of John Gottman's research involves the physiological response to disagreement. Dr. Gottman and his team noted that when a participant had a rise in pulse to more than 100 beats per minute, regrettable words were spoken.[1] An individual's ability to think well and articulate clearly and calmly disintegrates with major emotional response. So if you're nervous or angry and your pulse and breathing rate are climbing, you may very well blurt out something you'll regret—or that you *should* regret. Why would you want to do that to your spouse? How many of your conversations over key and important issues have been lost in a maze of emotional verbiage? Not only is such communication unhealthy; it also fails to get you to the point of good decision-making.

Surely there's a better way! Chill out, wind down, relax, take a time out, and plan for a resumption of the discussion when you're both ready, willing, and able. It's legitimate to say, "I'm just a little bit on edge. Let me go for a walk." Or "Let me sit down," or "Let's go for a walk together." Whatever it takes for you to get your pulse and respiratory rate back under control should precede the resumption of the discussion. Sometimes, sleep is essential to intelligent conversation and listening with a "Spirit-filled" ear.

Relaxation breathing can be helpful in normalizing the pulse rate. (Inhale slowly, silently counting to six, then exhale slowly also to a six count.) Such breathing will generally restore a greater sense of calm and ability to think and speak kindly.

So what's the ultimate goal? God's glory; two becoming one. It's been said that opposites attract. It's also been said that opposites attack. Which of these is true in your marriage is up to the two of you. God has given you a relationship full of mixed strengths, weaknesses, temperaments, backgrounds, disabilities, and abilities. And apart from Him you can do nothing (John 15:5). A marriage without God can be a prescription for disaster. Yet with Him at the center of your priorities and interactions, the opposite is true. With Jesus Christ as Lord of your marriage, you will find yourselves embarking on a lifetime journey of ever-deepening spiritual, relational, and sexual intimacy. "Imbibe deeply, O lovers."

20
Some Final Thoughts

Beneath the apple tree I awakened you.
—SONG OF SOLOMON 8:5

Ginger had had no sexual experience before she was married. Several months before her wedding she began taking birth control pills; they decreased her desire for sex. In addition, for the first ten years of her marriage, Ginger endured painful sex due to a physical problem that would later require surgery to correct. Both husband and wife wondered about her lack of interest in sex, thinking there must be some deeply rooted psychological causes they didn't understand. The situation was further complicated when they read several popular Christian books about sex that wrongly stressed simultaneous orgasm should be a couple's goal, and also insisted, again incorrectly, that vaginal orgasms are "the only way to go." Because vaginal penetration caused Ginger pain, all these factors collectively led to a painful experience overall.

Eventually, further education about sex helped reshape this couple's thinking about "how it must be done," and surgery corrected Ginger's medical condition, which proved to be the final solution. After ten years together, Ginger and her husband began to have a dynamic, active love life. This is one of many examples in which physical intimacy develops after years of difficulty.

Sexual intimacy is one of God's most beautiful gifts to us, but learning to enjoy this gift fully is a process that requires time and experience. Together the two of you can reach heights in your relationship that most cannot even imagine. If you're married or considering marriage, we hope this book has supplied the encouragement and biblical instruction you need to find great fulfillment in your relationship. If you're a physician evaluating and working with couples, we have tried to make this book a useful tool. And we've endeavored to create a frank and, at times, even entertaining resource for pastors and counselors, with an underlying theme of hope.

No matter where couples find themselves on a scale measuring relational health, there is every reason to believe life together can improve. Couples can develop intimacy by gaining knowledge, and knowledge in turn can improve our thinking and living. My (Sandi's) younger sister jokingly volunteered to write an introduction for this book stating as much. She wanted to say, "My sister has come a long way since her prepuberty days when she told me it was illegal to have sex any way other than in the missionary position. She also told me a special brand of MP (missionary police) made it their job to check." Yes, I told her these and more myths. While we blame television for a lot, we certainly should never count out "The Sibling Factor" as a contributor to our ignorance. I'm not sure my sister's husband has ever forgiven me. (Fortunately, a little education has corrected the damage her "sexpert" sister had inflicted.)

A couple's depth of physical pleasure and lasting heart intimacy is founded on spiritual growth and maturity. God created us to know Him and worship Him, and our earthly relationships stand or fall on the security and intimacy we find in our relationship with our heavenly Father. A couple in our church who had a basically decent marriage believed all-out commitment to the Lord would mean a less exciting sex life for them. As they both began to grow spiritually and increase in sensitivity, kindness, and compassion, they entered into a whole new dimension in their lovemaking. To their surprise, they discovered that the opposite of what they'd expected had happened: their spiritual growth led to a more fulfilling, more thrilling sex life. As couples grow spiritually, they grow in their ability to give themselves more completely to and for one another. This selfless giving, as opposed to less intimate sex that amounts to little more than a sharing of body parts, is a key to developing sexual intimacy.

We included a lot of Scripture in this book, believing God is the ultimate expert. And we incorporated a lighthearted tone at times, convinced that a sense of humor is essential in unraveling popular notions about romance. Some of those notions were reflected in comments at a recent conference. A woman observed, "Thank God for 'quickies.' But you sure never see them in the movies. The only on-screen couples who have quickies are under the age of fifteen and worrying about getting caught. And honesty? Do you ever see a woman who's left unsatisfied?"

We encourage a healthy sense of curiosity and mystery about male and female sexual preferences and the more important individual husband/wife differences. So if you're experiencing sexual difficulty now, know that there's hope. You can adjust. Sexual drives change over time, and disparity between your desire and your spouse's may equalize. You adapt. You grow. The important thing is to keep seeking and exploring options, keep loving your spouse, and as one Texas-born friend insisted was the key to sexual happiness, "Y'all be *nice* to each other!"

Workbook
Exercises for
Developing Intimacy

A major sex survey commissioned by _Redbook_ magazine included responses from approximately 100,000 women. The findings? Among the most important: strictly monogamous women experienced orgasm during sexual interludes more than twice as often as promiscuous women. And it found that highly religious women were more likely than moderately religious or nonreligious women to describe their sex lives as "good" or "very good." Later, in what is probably the most scientific, comprehensive study yet, researchers found the same results: The women most likely to achieve orgasm each and every time (32 percent) are conservative Protestants.[1]

A healthy marital relationship and a high level of commitment to one's marriage partner seem to play a major role in the extent to which a person is satisfied sexually. This is why the best foundation for a satisfying sexual relationship is a loving, Christ-centered marriage.

In addition to that, we can learn things about each other that can help to enrich sexual intimacy within marriage. But first, it's helpful to understand why a husband and wife don't always "connect" when it comes to sex. For starters, each person is sexually unique. Your partner's likes and dislikes aren't available on a computer printout that can be obtained on the Internet. (If they were, it could be a sign of some really serious problems!) So we take our individual preferences and combine that information with the fact that God made men and women with differing sexual-response timing. It soon becomes clear that it's impossible to "intuit" what will satisfy your partner; you must communicate with your mate. Developing sexual intimacy requires transparency—being honest about the person you really are.

Have you ever seen the book *How to Satisfy a Woman Every Time and Have Her Beg for More*? If all men were marrying that author, I (Dr. Bill) would tell them to buy her book. Since they're not, I don't necessarily recommend it. Why? Its author operates on the assumption that all women want the same thing, the same way. God has made all women and men unique, with varying needs, interests, and "erogenous zones." What works for one person may be a disaster for another. In the movies, when a man kisses a woman on the ear, she swoons; your partner may giggle. We're all unique in our responses to stimulation.

To help your spouse understand what you do and don't like sexually, you have to communicate. If something pleases you, learn to say so; if you find something unpleasant, let your partner know. Recognize, too, that your desires may vary from year to year, or even from day to day (or night to night). So leave room for "updates." A key element in learning to be sexually intimate is learning to be verbally intimate.[2]

Some people find it easier, initially at least, to write their thoughts than to verbalize them. You may be trying to figure out how to say tactfully, "Honey, this is really dull; there *must* be more to it than this." Your wife may tend to be critical when you try to be honest. Or your husband may think he knows it all and could satisfy anyone with an array of sexual techniques derived from junior high locker rooms, *Playboy* magazine, or by watching lots of movies. Writing out your preferences, and having your mate write his or hers may help.

The workbook that follows is to help you identify important matters such as what you like and what satisfies your spouse. When you have completed this workbook, you'll have your own personalized version of *How to Satisfy Me*. Talk about it. And recognize that through your years together much will change, so leave plenty of room for growth.

We'd like to offer some suggestions about how to use the workbook. First, *do not try to do all these exercises in one sitting*. Give yourselves time to process what you've learned. You may want to try doing one exercise per week. Also, you don't need to do them in the order given. And finally, while engaged couples can complete *some* of these exercises, we have designed this section primarily for married couples.

Physical Intimacy Exercises

Knowing My Own Body (for Women)

Explore your body

To help your husband give you pleasure, you need to be acquainted enough with your own body so you can guide him. What you discover when you are alone can relieve some of the uneasiness that may be present when you are together. Get to know yourself and what you enjoy so you can communicate it. Incidentally, men generally have more knowledge of their genitals than women have of theirs because men are so "handy."

We recognize that you may not consider it "okay" to touch yourself and explore your own body for the purpose of improving your intimate times together. It appears, however, that medically, theologically, and socially this is helpful rather than harmful.

1. Hold the hand mirror and spread the outer lips (labia majora) so you can examine the rest of your external genitals.
2. Find the labia minora, or inner lips.
3. Next, look for the clitoris. If you are unsure of its location, touch where you think it might be. It is very sensitive to touch. (During lovemaking, some women prefer that their husbands touch around or near it, avoiding direct stimulation.) The

VULVA

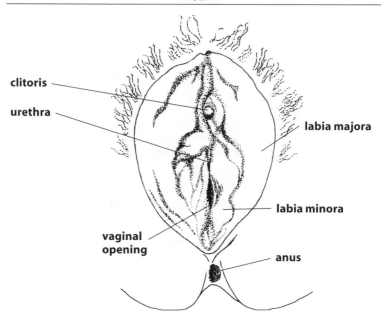

clitoris

urethra

labia majora

labia minora

vaginal
opening

anus

purpose of this is to learn where the most pleasurable feelings occur for you. If you are more comfortable, find your clitoris while you're standing in the shower. When you're standing, it is at the "front most" point of your genitals. Remind yourself that God designed it only for receiving pleasure. Gently caress it and notice what sensations it brings. Remember that many men learn "this is what rings the bell," so your husband may rub or press too hard or too vigorously or too directly. What feels good to you?

4. Find your vagina. This is where you insert tampons, if you use them. Using the moistened tip of your finger, try to find the opening. It may not be possible, as we shared in the story about the woman who had no vaginal opening. If not, make an appointment with your physician. If so, insert your finger into your vagina. Gently press on the vaginal wall. If you think of the opening of the vagina as a clock, start at the twelve o'clock position (nearest the front of the body) and slowly move around

the wall of the vagina, pressing and stroking at every point of the clock. Try varying degrees of pressure and types of touch. Be especially aware of any points of pain or pleasure.

5. Now explore for sensation in the so-called G-spot area. With your finger in your vagina, tighten the muscle you use to stop urinary flow. Keeping that muscle tight, move your finger in a little farther, just beyond the inner ridge of that muscle. Press, stroke, and tap toward the front of your body as though you are pressing the inside of your vagina toward your pubic bone, or "upward." This is the "G-spot." Continue to massage using varying degrees of pressure. Note any sensations you might experience. Many women do not notice any different sensation here from that which is experienced in any other part of the vagina, and some feel pleasure here only when they are already aroused. What you feel or don't feel is neither right nor wrong. Your goal is to become aware of these sensations to help both you and your spouse to understand and discover.

6. Thank God for making you a sexual creature.

Now that you have a better idea of what does and does not feel pleasurable, set aside a time for doing this again with your husband present, guiding his hand to what does and does not feel good.

Do a stretching exercise

In the gynecologist's office the general standard is that a vagina should comfortably accommodate two fingers up to the second knuckle for comfortable intercourse. If this can't be done, we suggest gentle stretching while sitting in a tub of warm water. A warm massage with oil can also be used. Using your thumb or two fingers, you should apply gentle pressure in the posterior direction—that is, toward the tailbone—and maintain it for fifteen to thirty seconds; then relax and repeat.

You should repeat this exercise each day for about ten minutes, until you can do it comfortably using two fingers. Six to eight weeks of daily diligence will usually allow for comfortable intercourse and mastery at contracting and relaxing these muscles. If you still have difficulty after marriage, your husband can help by incorporating this exercise into your time of foreplay.

If you feel uncomfortable touching yourself, you can use a plastic tampon applicator. Commercially available lubricants such as K-Y Jelly, Maxilube, Sensilube, and Replens are also useful.

Exploring Pleasure for Men

After a bath or shower, focus together on his pleasure. Guide your wife's hand and communicate what you like best—how hard, how soft, best locations for her touch, and types of motion preferred. Try to leave preconceived notions behind. Take, for example, a woman who read that the most sensitive part of a man's body is the head of the penis. As a result, she focused all of her attention there. Her husband had already told her this form of stimulation was too intense and that he didn't care for it. But she ignored him because a book had told her otherwise. Later, this man gently repeated his instructions, and he finally convinced his wife that even though it's the most sensitive place, the head of the penis has such sensitive nerve endings that for him, stimulation there brings a sensation not unlike pain. Most men prefer less-direct contact at least sometimes.

One of the women mentioned earlier told of her husband saying to her, "You're doing it wrong" when she tried to give him pleasure through oral sex. Many men have this complaint. If oral sex is a practice in which you both want to participate, gently share with her how you want her to go about giving you this kind of pleasure.

Controlling Pleasure for Men

For men who tend to ejaculate before either the husband or wife is ready, many recommend "the squeeze technique." Before sharing the "how to" on this, I want to say that I (Dr. Bill) do not consider this the ideal solution for premature ejaculation.

One study suggests that men have difficulty "holding back" for

MALE REPRODUCTIVE SYSTEM

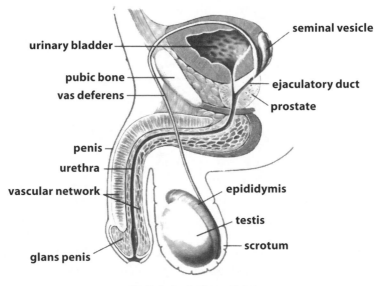

urinary bladder

pubic bone

vas deferens

penis

urethra

vascular network

glans penis

seminal vesicle

ejaculatory duct

prostate

epididymis

testis

scrotum

© by Grolier, Inc. Used by permission.

more than three minutes once they have penetrated the vagina. Age certainly plays a role here, as does experience. Yet it's possible for a man to learn control that will enable him to hold back for as long as necessary to regularly satisfy his partner. Still, for a young man having first sexual encounters with his gorgeous bride, I consider it more helpful for him to tell her, "You are so overwhelmingly exciting to me that I can't hold back, so let's make love twice. The first time, feel free to overwhelm me. The second time around I'll be there to satisfy you." Not only is this true and flattering to her, it allows him to mentally "stay with her," as opposed to distracting himself by rehearsing baseball scores to keep from getting too excited. (I especially want to avoid the type of "aversion therapy" one wife described: "When my husband gets 'too close,' I say, 'Green Berets.' This suggestion makes him imagine horrifying scenes of Vietnam so he can 'cool down.'") Having sex a second time also allows her to be more expressive in her arousal without concerning herself that she will "make it too hard for him to control himself."

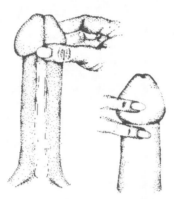

Now let's look at now the squeeze technique works. The woman sits, straddling her aroused husband's legs as he lies on his back. She places her thumb on the frenulum of the penis (see diagram) and her index and middle fingers just above and below the coronal ridge on the opposite side of the penis. She exerts a firm grasping pressure for four seconds, then abruptly releases her hold. She should always apply pressure front-to-back and not side-to-side. (For some reason this technique is considerably less effective when the man does it to himself.) Both partners should know this does not need to be painful; it should bring only a sense of pressure. She should repeat this technique every few minutes, making sure to use only the pads of her fingers. (If she used her fingernails, it would certainly remove his desire to ejaculate, but probably for a longer time than she had in mind.)

They should do this three to six times before attempting insertion. Couples who practice this technique for several weeks typically increase to approximately ten to fifteen minutes of vaginal containment with active thrusting. They usually need to continue this exercise for four to six months for permanent reconditioning.

Helping Women Heighten Their Sense of Pleasure (PC Exercises)

Sexual stimulation within the woman's vagina relates much more to *pressure* than to *frictional* sensitivity. This makes sense because the related muscle group (the PC muscles) contains an abundant supply of pressure-sensitive nerve endings.

The wife needs to apply a firm, muscular squeezing pressure upon the penis within the vagina to give herself greater sexual stimulation. A larger object introduced into the vagina does not help increase sexual sensitivity because sensitivity depends on contraction of the muscles rather than expansion. Therefore, penis size has no direct effect on sensitivity for the wife. She can experience more satisfying stimulation, though, when she tightens her PC muscles during thrusting of the penis. More stimulation results in reflex contraction of the vagina, which is part of the pattern that leads to orgasm for her.

Women can do these exercises easily, and some report *finally* being able to achieve orgasm after strengthening these muscles and then using them during lovemaking. (After childbirth, these exercises can more quickly help restore the tone of the vaginal muscles.)

The simplest way to find the PC muscles is to stop urine flow with the knees about two feet apart. Sit on the commode and let the urine flow, but then stop it without moving the knees. In nearly every woman, this procedure will exercise the PC muscles. Once you know which muscles you must contract, you can do this exercise while standing in line at the grocery store or sitting at your desk.

How often should you do them? Start with five to ten contractions in the morning plus the same number each time you use the bathroom. Hold each contraction for several seconds. You should work up to having enough control that you can release as little as a teaspoon of urine at a time. It gets easier.

After four days, increase the number to ten contractions, six times a day. Gradually, after four to six weeks, work up to about three hundred contractions per day. It will take a total of about ten minutes. By then you should begin noticing a difference.

After a total of about ten weeks you should have quite strong muscles, and you can stop doing the exercises. Occasionally check to see if you can still tightly squeeze one finger in the vagina. (If you can't, resume doing the exercises.)

Sexual activity itself also helps strengthen these muscles. If you do some of these voluntary contractions during foreplay, you can heighten sexual tension. Your voluntary contractions help condition the PC muscles for the involuntary contractions of orgasm. *Not only can you experience more intense pleasure, you can shorten your response time by consciously contracting these muscles.*

Sharing How You Feel About Your Own Body

Now that you've articulated what you feel about your spouse's body, talk openly with your spouse about your own body. Dim the lights or wear sunglasses if this is too difficult for you to do in broad daylight.

> Going from the top of your head to the bottom of your toes, talk about how you feel about each part. How do you wish it were different? What do you like about it?

Time and circumstances change our physical appearance (accidents, surgery, and gravitational pull all contribute to this). As Gypsy Rose Lee said, "I still have everything I had ten years ago—except now it's all lower." Wisdom suggests that kindness and grace are always appropriate and that the beloved can always find something to appreciate.

While your husband or wife is talking, listen without interrupting. Then summarize what you hear being said. Clarify or expand on what your spouse has heard.

In Song of Solomon 8:5, after the lovers are married we read that the women of the city ask this:

> Who is this coming up from the wilderness,
> Leaning on her beloved?

The king and his wife are returning from a weekend away. Now she is so beautiful as to be hardly recognizable to them. Earlier they criticized her appearance. Now they ask, "Wow! Who's that?"

Think of the old movie *Rocky*, starring Sylvester Stallone. If you've seen it, you'll remember his girlfriend, Adrian. She started out looking homely. But by the end of the movie, as she responded to his love, she had become beautiful.

- If people who knew you years ago saw you now, what would they say?
- Interact with this statement: "Now that I've got him (or her), I can 'let myself go.'"
- True or false: I make my physical appearance, my attractiveness to my spouse, a priority.
- True or false: People judge the ability and success of a man in terms of his wife's appearance.
- True or false: People judge the ability and success of a woman in terms of her husband's appearance.
- On a scale of one to ten, how important is it to you that your spouse find you attractive?
- List things you can do to make yourself more appealing to your spouse, both in private and in public.
- Read this quote from marriage counselor/sex therapist Marty Klein, and state whether you agree or disagree in terms of your own experience:

> Although you might wish it weren't so, if you're like millions of women, your body isn't supermodel slim and probably never will be. In a perfect world, this is no big deal. Yet in my experience . . . I've discovered that an extra ten, twenty, or thirty pounds can have a troublesome effect on a woman's

sex life. Interestingly, it's generally not the woman's partner who finds the weight gain a turnoff—it's the woman herself who allows her erotic pleasure to be held hostage by the number on the scale or a pair of too-tight jeans. This isn't to say that some husbands aren't put off by weight gain, particularly if it's substantial—say thirty pounds or more. But fortunately, very few men cite a gain or loss of ten to twenty pounds as the key to their partner's attractiveness. Instead, most men talk far more about how their wives feel about their weight.[3]

Now interact with this statement:

> Many a woman says "gross" when she sees a man wearing a Speedo bathing suit. Yet a woman does have *some* visual orientation. And her man's hygiene and weight still factor into her ability to fully enjoy his body.

End by expressing love and admiration for your spouse's body.

Sharing How You Feel About Your Lovemaking

Work toward getting more and more comfortable talking about details of your love life. The following topics are listed for you to discuss outside of the context of lovemaking. If you think of others, add them.

- The time of day we are usually together sexually is _____.
- Is that time optimal for both of us?
- The place where our lovemaking usually takes place is _____.
- Place(s) where we would like it to happen are _____.
- We usually have _____ amount of light in the room when we make love. Could this be improved in any way?

- Some variety in lighting we would like to try is _____.
- Do hygiene issues ever inhibit our desire? (Four hours at the gym with the guys may have elevated his testosterone level but, like three-day-old fish, he stinketh.)
- Does one of us usually initiate more than the other? Is this the way we both want it?
- What are our unspoken signals that say, "I'm interested"?
- Are there other ways either of us would like to communicate interest or have interest communicated?
- What do we usually wear? (One wife in the Pacific Northwest shared, "There's a movement afoot in some local Christian subcultures. Some now suggest that women should not dress sexy for their husbands because this is the 'world's' way of viewing sex. Flannel is the fabric of choice." But there is nothing spiritual about being dowdy.)
- How long does it usually take her to reach climax, from beginning to end? (This is where the husbands at workshops sometimes jokingly yell, "Hours!")
- How long does it usually take him to reach climax, from beginning to end? (This is where wives at workshops sometimes yell, "Seconds!")
- How do we want to be pursued? Hint and then back off? Hint and then try again in a different way? Hint and go for it? No hints—use the direct approach. Other?
- How do we want to be directed? Discussion outside of sex? Gentle redirecting of hands? Verbally?
- How do we generally redirect? How does each of us feel about that?
- What kinds of caresses do each of us prefer? On what parts of the body? *With* what parts of the body?
- What positions increase excitement for each of us? What sustains desire? What decreases interest?
- Do we have any uncommunicated fantasies? Strip Monopoly? Showering together? Digital photos?
- What degree of dress or undress does each of us like?

- What are our preferred kinds and colors of apparel? (Some men actually don't like black nightgowns, but their wives have been buying them for years, operating with the mistaken notion that all hubbies find black exciting.)
- Are we each courageous enough to walk into an intimate apparel department and buy something we would enjoy seeing him or her wear?
- How can we draw the five senses into our lovemaking?
- Interact with this statement: "We're totally comfortable being naked together, but the surprise and delight of seeing each other nude no longer brings the erotic rush it did when we were first married." Is this true for you? What are the pros and cons of love "settling down and becoming more secure"?
- What sets the mood for him? For her?
- How much do you want left to the imagination?
- What elements enhance the whole experience for you?
- List an assortment of ideal atmospheres you'd like to try.

Preferred Sexual Practices

At a marriage conference, we handed out the following survey. Each partner was asked to state his or her desires (there's one for each—first wives, then husbands). The husbands and wives then discussed their answers. Please use this opportunity to do the same—respond to the survey separately, then talk together about your answers. We've included some "off the wall" possibilities to help relax the mood. Remember to keep a sense of humor.

Sex practices—her preferred practices: gross or great?

Scale					
No way Gross I'd rather die		Okay, if you like but it does not sound "special"			Oh, yeah Gotta have it Gonna be great!
1	2	3	4	5	6

"Missionary position" only—limited to one position for life

| 1 | 2 | 3 | 4 | 5 | 6 |

No one set position—more changes than a man with a TV remote

| 1 | 2 | 3 | 4 | 5 | 6 |

Oral/genital foreplay—to do

| 1 | 2 | 3 | 4 | 5 | 6 |

Oral/genital foreplay—to be "done unto"

| 1 | 2 | 3 | 4 | 5 | 6 |

Oral/genital orgasm—to do

| 1 | 2 | 3 | 4 | 5 | 6 |

Oral/genital orgasm—to be "done unto"

| 1 | 2 | 3 | 4 | 5 | 6 |

Anal intercourse

| 1 | 2 | 3 | 4 | 5 | 6 |

Man on top

| 1 | 2 | 3 | 4 | 5 | 6 |

Woman on top

| 1 | 2 | 3 | 4 | 5 | 6 |

Whipped cream on top

| 1 | 2 | 3 | 4 | 5 | 6 |

Side to side

| 1 | 2 | 3 | 4 | 5 | 6 |

Front to back

    1   2   3   4   5   6

Watching partner undress

    1   2   3   4   5   6

Being watched as I undress

    1   2   3   4   5   6

Cuddling only

    1   2   3   4   5   6

Mood lighting

    1   2   3   4   5   6

Black lights (with body paint)

    1   2   3   4   5   6

Only during solar eclipses

    1   2   3   4   5   6

See-through lingerie

    1   2   3   4   5   6

Industrial-grade opaque flannel lingerie ("But it's *comfortable*")

    1   2   3   4   5   6

Foreplay

    1   2   3   4   5   6

Floor play

    1   2   3   4   5   6

Assisted by sexual devices (vibrator)

    1   2   3   4   5   6

Costumes—Braveheart, Warrior Princess

    1   2   3   4   5   6

Early morning (mouthwash on the nightstand)

    1   2   3   4   5   6

Late night (No Doz on the nightstand)

    1   2   3   4   5   6

Nooners (Who works?)

    1   2   3   4   5   6

Before 10:00 PM (Some partners do want to go to sleep early!)

    1   2   3   4   5   6

Anytime, anyplace

    1   2   3   4   5   6

Desired frequency (circle one):

Tri-weekly   Try weekly   Try weakly   Other:

Actual frequency (circle one):

Tri-weekly   Try weekly   Try weakly   Other:

Usual order in which I would like these "done unto me" (rank in order of preference):

___ Mouth to mouth kissing
___ Fondling breasts
___ Fondling vagina
___ Oral foreplay/sex

___ Intercourse
___ Orgasm
___ Other:

Interact with this statement (there are no right or wrong answers): A woman's responsiveness does not appear to be connected to any special lovemaking technique. Instead, responsiveness and satisfaction are significantly affected by the relational context in which lovemaking takes place.

Sex practices—his preferred practices: gross or great?

Scale					
No way Gross I'd rather die		Okay, if you like but it does not sound "special"			Oh, yeah Gotta have it Gonna be great!
1	2	3	4	5	6

"Missionary position" only—limited to one position for life

    1   2   3   4   5   6

No one set position—more changes than a man with a TV remote

    1   2   3   4   5   6

Oral/genital foreplay—to do

    1   2   3   4   5   6

Oral/genital foreplay—to be "done unto"

    1   2   3   4   5   6

Oral/genital orgasm—to do

    1   2   3   4   5   6

Oral/genital orgasm—to be "done unto"

1	2	3	4	5	6

Anal intercourse

1	2	3	4	5	6

Man on top

1	2	3	4	5	6

Woman on top

1	2	3	4	5	6

Whipped cream on top

1	2	3	4	5	6

Side to side

1	2	3	4	5	6

Front to back

1	2	3	4	5	6

Watching partner undress

1	2	3	4	5	6

Being watched as I undress

1	2	3	4	5	6

Cuddling only

1	2	3	4	5	6

Mood lighting

1	2	3	4	5	6

Black lights (with body paint)

    1   2   3   4   5   6

Only during solar eclipses

    1   2   3   4   5   6

See-through lingerie

    1   2   3   4   5   6

Industrial-grade opaque flannel long johns ("But it's *comfortable*")

    1   2   3   4   5   6

Foreplay

    1   2   3   4   5   6

Floor play

    1   2   3   4   5   6

Assisted by sexual devices (vibrator)

    1   2   3   4   5   6

Costumes—Brave Heart, Warrior Princess

    1   2   3   4   5   6

Early morning (mouthwash on the nightstand)

    1   2   3   4   5   6

Late night (No Doz on the nightstand)

    1   2   3   4   5   6

Nooners (Who works?)

    1   2   3   4   5   6

Before 10:00 PM (Some partners do want to go to sleep early!)

| 1 | 2 | 3 | 4 | 5 | 6 |

Anytime, anyplace

| 1 | 2 | 3 | 4 | 5 | 6 |

Desired frequency (circle one):
Tri-weekly   Try weekly   Try weakly   Other:

Actual frequency (circle one):
Tri-weekly   Try weekly   Try weakly   Other:

Usual order in which I would like these "done unto me" (rank in order of preference):

___ Mouth to mouth kissing
___ Fondling penis
___ Oral foreplay/sex
___ Intercourse
___ Orgasm
___ Other:

Interact with this statement (again, no right or wrong answers): A woman's greater responsiveness does not appear to be connected to any special lovemaking technique. Instead, responsiveness and satisfaction are significantly affected by the relational context in which lovemaking takes place.

Understanding Your Attitudes About Sex

Individually answer the following questions. Later, you may wish to discuss some or all of your responses with your partner.

If you're having a sexual problem, would you prefer that it have a physical, emotional, or interactional cause? Why?

What are the prerequisites for your becoming sexually aroused? What factors are physical? Do they seem to have changed in the last few years? If so, how? Why?

Do you feel comfortable keeping your eyes open during lovemaking? Why or why not?

Do you think of men and women as more alike or more different? Why?

What do you see as the greatest barriers to attaining satisfying intimate relationships?

Have you learned any lessons about yourself and the opposite sex the hard way?

If you had to lose one of your senses *for sex only*, what would it be and why?

Should contraceptive responsibilities be assigned or shared between men and women?

Do you remember trying to get answers about your body, sex, or similar topics as a young child? How did the person you asked respond? How did you feel?

Are you embarrassed by your lacking any information?

How do you view sex and sexuality during this season of your life? In what ways is it different from five or ten years ago? Are there things you feel you have missed? If so, what?

Close your eyes and imagine a couple having a pleasurable sexual interlude. When you are finished, open your eyes. How old were they? How does this reflect on your perception of sex?

What did you learn from your mother about gender roles? Your father? Do you hold their views today? Have their views changed any? How do your views differ from theirs?

Preventing Moral Failure

Your sexuality is a precious gift to be protected. You can prevent many future sexual difficulties by following God's guidelines for sexual purity.

Read 2 Samuel 11–13, then answer the following questions.

- Is there a member of the opposite sex in your life about whom your spouse has expressed discomfort? Is his or her "radar" accurate?

- Spend a few moments dealing with any unconfessed sin in your thoughts. What time can you set aside for regular confession?

- If you were to develop deep affection for the wrong person, in whom will you confide?

- List some of the consequences of committing sexual sin:

- How might such sin affect your relationship with God?

Consider these words from a wife about her husband's philandering:

I am trying very hard to understand. That doesn't mean I don't feel any pain or anger. I'm not happy about what he did, and sometimes I think about dismembering him, and good friends have offered to help me dig up the back yard and bury him. I'm not saying I'm standing by this man no matter what. I'm taking it day by day. I know one thing: I'm not going to leave someone who's been my best friend for twenty years. I was numb. I still am. I think any decision I make is highly personal, and there's no one formula that's right. This is a really horrible trauma for everyone who has been touched by it, and answers don't come—at least for me—immediately.[4]

- List ways unfaithfulness could affect your marriage and extended family.

- How could unfaithfulness affect your relationships at church?

- How could unfaithfulness affect your relationships at work?

- List those whom you would be ashamed to face if you were ever unfaithful.

- List how unfaithfulness would affect your thoughts about yourself and your future love life.

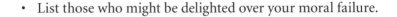

- List those who might be delighted over your moral failure.

- List how the other person involved might be affected by an affair.

- List medical risks.

- How can you strengthen the "glue" binding your marriage?

- What action can you take to keep or bring your thoughts in line with God's?

- Pray that God will cleanse your thoughts, bring your affections in line with His desires, and keep you from stumbling.

Although we included the following questions in chapter 15, they're important enough to add here for review: *Are you being tempted?*

- Do you make special trips past her desk or his house?
- Do you manipulate situations so you can be alone in secluded, private settings?
- Have you started taking special care of your dress, your

physique, and overall appearance? Are you wearing an alluring scent?

- When you are around him or her, do you feel like you're sixteen again?
- Do you find yourself thinking of this person frequently outside of the usual context of your contact?
- Do you purposely withhold some conversations, letters, or events from your spouse?
- Do you dread accountability times? Do you not even *have* a person to whom you are accountable for your thoughts and actions?
- Do you find yourself thinking of this person instead of your spouse when you watch romantic movies?
- Do you think of this person during romantic activities with your spouse?
- Do you talk about him or her more than about your spouse?
- Is the love you feel for this person infatuation that wants to possess, or is it true love? Real love wants the other to be all he or she can be in Christ—a love that would never lead the loved one down a treacherous path away from God. Are you acting with his or her best interest at heart?

Let an application of the Golden Rule help determine the state of your relationship. Ask yourself, *Would I want someone else to treat me as I am treating his or her spouse, even if only in my heart?*

Like a beautifully wrapped package under a Christmas tree, the gift of sexuality, that mysterious, exclusive gift you reserve for each other, becomes, remains, or can become again a celebratory expression of the love you share together.

> Hurry, my beloved,
> And be like a gazelle or a young stag
> On the mountains of spices.
> > —Song of Solomon 8:14

For Further Consideration

- What is your strategy to maintain personal sexual purity?
- How do you deal with loneliness?
- What are your usual means of avoiding emotional pain?
- Do you resent it when your spouse questions your wrong behavior?
- In the last twenty years, more and more sexually explicit material has appeared on TV. One survey reported that seven of eight intimate relationships on prime time TV were between non-married individuals. What impact will this have on the coming generation? What impact does it have on you?
- To whom are you personally accountable?
- Many movies, magazines, and TV shows portray homo-sexual relationships as an "alternate lifestyle." What is your response?
- What risk factors for sexual addiction do you have?
- Does your church have a ministry to sex addicts? Who will help the spouses of the addicts?
- How might understanding the "fear of the LORD" (Prov. 2:5) and knowing you've been "bought with a price" (1 Cor. 6:20) affect your thought life?

Relational Intimacy Exercises

Guidelines for Communication

1. Listen. Try to understand your partner before explaining your own point of view.
2. Recognize that you do not need to agree.
3. Do not criticize, defend yourself, or apologize.
4. If you disagree but can understand how he or she sees it another way, say so.
5. When your spouse is finished speaking, summarize what you heard, and say, "Here's what it sounds like to me; I think you're

saying . . ." (Just be careful you don't do this so much that you sound like an echo canyon or a wannabe psychiatrist.)

Exploring Background Influences

Start talking about sex by answering the following questions:

- Think through your sexual attitudes from childhood through adolescence and adulthood. How did they form and change?
- From whom did you learn about sex? Was the information accurate?
- Do you tend to gravitate more toward the "Sex is a terrible, horrible sin" or the "Do it often, do it right, use a condom every night" mentality?
- What attitudes did your family communicate about sex? Was affection demonstrated openly in your home?
- Are you comfortable using the actual names for body parts or do you use euphemisms?

Read Psalm 139:1–18 together.

Dealing with Past Sexual Sin

Consider Solomon's background. His father, King David, initiated an adulterous relationship with Bathsheba, Solomon's mother. The end result was the murder of Bathsheba's first husband and the death of the child produced from David and Bathsheba's first union. Then Bathsheba and David married and had Solomon. Solomon was a prime candidate for having "baggage" about sex from his family background. And while Solomon had an imperfect view of sex (as seen by his having many wives) he wrote many of the proverbs about marital fidelity that we've included in this book (particularly Prov. 5–7).

Perhaps an important part of Solomon's background is the fact that his father openly acknowledged and repented of his wrong.

History tells us that David wrote Psalm 51 after the prophet Nathan confronted him about committing adultery and murder. You, too, can break destructive family cycles that may have introduced wrong thinking or actions related to sex. The following suggestions may help:

- Mentally review your sexual history before the Lord; take inventory.
- Read Psalm 51—David's confession after committing adultery with Bathsheba. Pray through this Psalm, and confess your sin to the Lord.
- Assume your past choices will continue to have a lasting effect on you. If you've asked God to forgive you, know that you're forgiven; but realize that you may yet struggle with the consequences of your poor choices.
- Forgive any other person(s) involved.
- Determine if going back to ask forgiveness would cause more damage than healing. If it would help, make that contact.
- If you and your fiancé(e) have engaged in sexual sin before marriage, confess this to God individually and together if you have not done so before now. Take measures to stop. If you're married and the two of you were engaged in sexual activity before marriage, confess this individually and together if you have never done so.
- Determine how much to disclose. Before marriage, share about the past in general terms. (Avoid confiding details such as where and how you had sex, how often, frequency of orgasms, etc.) This conversation ideally should precede a commitment to marry. Your wife- or husband-to-be *does* have the right to know if you've been a practicing homosexual, if you've had previous marriages, and whether you're a virgin, for example.
- Determine what steps you can take to strengthen your moral purity.
- Recognize that guilt will probably recur, and remind yourself of God's forgiveness when it does.

- If your sexual sin includes adultery, the decision of what and how much to disclose to your spouse and how to rebuild your relationship goes beyond the scope of this book. However, we recommend *Torn Asunder: Recovering from Extramarital Affairs* by Dave Carder with Duncan Jaenicke.[5]

Recognize, too, that no book or conference can fully address your specific needs. You may need qualified professional counsel.

- Determine how your background and past experiences have made you view sexual issues differently than God views them.
- Pray, thanking God for His grace and forgiveness. Ask Him to help you retrain your mind to think as He would have you think. (See Romans 12:1–2.)

For Wives: How Can I Improve Our Relationship?

- How do I make my marriage a priority?
- Can he trust me? Do I hold personal information in confidence? (For example, do I tell my closest friends his private thoughts if he wants me to keep them confidential?)
- How can I make meeting his sexual needs a priority?
- How can I make myself more attractive to him? Get rid of the nightly face cream? Change out of my pajamas or sweats before he arrives home from work? Do my hair and makeup on weekends?
- Are the two of us unified in how we view spending habits? Domestic responsibilities?
- How can I develop my potential for God's glory, fully using my gifts and talents so that my husband is married to a godly, interesting woman? (According to one survey, the greatest cause of stress is undeveloped potential; certainly, a significant cause of depression in women is undeveloped potential.)

- Do I speak well of him or do I refer to him in public as "The Pig"?
- Do I withhold trust from him even in areas where he's proved himself trustworthy (such as interacting with other women or spending habits)?
- Am I warm and supportive of him? Do I affirm his strengths and gifts?
- How can I be more fun to be with?
- Does my attitude of submission toward my husband reflect the relationship of the church to Christ?
- Do I demonstrate a gentle, quiet spirit?
- If someone were to ask my husband, would he be able to say honestly, "Being with this woman strengthens my relationship with the Lord"? Could he say, "I have seen the heart of Christ in her"?

List three of your husband's most admirable traits:

For Husbands: How Can I Improve Our Relationship?

Take a minute to write down three of your wife's favorite things.

List three admirable traits.

Next, write three times when you felt strong feelings of love for her.

Now answer the following questions.

- Am I doing a great job of "bringing home the bacon" but sitting on the sofa like Porky Pig when I get home? When the kids get in the way, do I throw something or yell, "Honey, move the kids; they're blocking my view of ESPN!"?
- How can my actions demonstrate that I love my wife?
- Do I withhold trust from my wife even in areas where she's proved herself trustworthy (such as interacting with other men or spending habits)?
- How do I make my marriage a priority?
- Can she trust me?
- Do I love her sexually in a sensitive, understanding way?
- Am I doing all I can to make myself attractive to her?
- Are the two of us unified in how we view spending habits? Domestic responsibilities?
- Am I developing my potential for God's glory, fully using my gifts and talents?
- Do I help make it possible for her (by my financial and time commitments) to develop her potential and use her gifts and talents? Do I relegate her to household domestic duties?
- Do I speak well of her?

- Am I warm and supportive of her? Do I affirm her strengths and gifts?
- Am I fun to be with?
- How can I do a better job of conversing with her?
- Does my sacrificial love for my wife demonstrate the love of Christ for His church?
- Could someone point to how I treat her and say, "That's how Christ treats the church"?
- Is my love for my wife helping her grow in grace? In holiness? Do I pray for her? Do I tell her so?
- If someone were to ask my wife, would she say, "Being with this man has strengthened my relationship with the Lord"? Could she say, "I have seen the love of Christ in him; I've seen the dedication and his servant heart"?

Questions for Couples About Leaving and Cleaving

What are some ways we have observed other couples do a good/ bad job of leaving their parents?

In what ways have we left our own parents?

Are there any ways in which we have *not* left our parents? (List them.)

Are there ways in which we are not cleaving to each other?

What pressures do we feel that hinder us from leaving? From cleaving?

Strengthening Your Communication

Answer these questions together:

- Most of what I know about relationships, I learned from . . .
- When it comes to interacting with people, I'm pretty good at . . .
- I feel closest to you when . . .

On a scale of one to ten, rate yourself, then your partner, in these areas:

- *Listening.* I pay attention when you speak, staying graciously attentive. I "stay with you" rather than "tune out." I refrain from interrupting or thinking of a quick answer while you're speaking.
- *Respect.* I look up to you. I see you as a unique human being with legitimate viewpoints. I defend your right to be in charge of your own life. You can count on me to be on your team. I consider and often accept your suggestions. Your words have weight with me. I speak to you in a courteous tone.

- *Acceptance.* I accept the way you are. I do not try to change your personality. I allow you to disagree without trying to force you to see things my way, getting defensive, or arguing. I give you freedom in friendships with others.
- *Being self-revealing.* I am vulnerable with you about my feelings and fears, desires, dreams, and fantasies. I confide in you about my weaknesses as well as my strengths. I tell you when I feel embarrassed about something you have said or done. I let you in on what is going on with me.

Complete the following thoughts and discuss your responses.

When it comes to conversational intimacy, I see *myself* . . .

a. as being closed as a mall on Christmas Day. (I keep things well hidden.)
b. as open twenty-four hours a day. (I hold nothing back.)
c. as closed but beginning to open up more.
d. sometimes open, sometimes closed.
e. as open, but regretting it and finding the risk too great.
f. other:

When it comes to conversational intimacy, I see *you* . . .

a. as being closed as a mall on Christmas. (You keep everything well hidden.)
b. as open twenty-four hours a day. (You hold nothing back.)
c. as closed but beginning to open up more.
d. as sometimes open, sometimes closed.
e. as open, but regretting it and finding the risk too great.
f. other:

Some ways I avoid intimacy when we're getting uncomfortably close, are . . .

a. to laugh or crack a joke.
b. to shrug it off as though I don't care.
c. to get huffy or angry.
d. to analyze everything under a microscope, hiding behind a wall of intellectualizing.

Some ways it seems like you avoid intimacy when we're getting uncomfortably close, are . . .

a. to laugh or crack a joke.
b. to shrug it off as though you don't care.
c. to get huffy or angry.
d. to analyze everything under a microscope, hiding behind a wall of intellectualizing.

Communicating About Anger

Thomas Jefferson said, "If very angry, count to a hundred." Mark Twain said, "When very angry, swear." Most of us gravitate toward extremes. We either hold it all in or we blow up. Which is more characteristic of you? Your spouse?

Circle each statement that accurately reflects your attitude about anger:

- It's a sin.
- Only weak people get angry.
- It's a negative emotion.
- It destroys relationships.
- It indicates something is seriously wrong in the relationship.
- It clouds our ability to think straight.
- It's helpful for identifying problems and trying to solve them.
- It motivates us to good actions.
- It's inevitable in any relationship.
- It's not compatible with loving and caring.

- It's immature. If the other is angry, it's a character flaw.
- Other:

Anger often interrupts intimacy. How do you deal with it? How does your spouse deal with it? By . . .

a. external politeness but inner rage.
b. yelling at the dog, the kids, and other safer targets.
c. pretending it's not there. ("I'm *not* angry!")
d. bottling it up—Old Faithful ready to erupt.
e. filing it for future ammunition.
f. withdrawing to your cave.
g. stonewalling.
h. playing sports or doing aerobics to work it off.
i. translating it into other feelings (hurt, disappointment).
j. crying.
k. praying.
l. striking something.
m. striking someone.
n. screaming and yelling insults.
o. yelling and arguing for hours at a time.
p. other:

Rage destroys relationships, and Proverbs is full of references that speak against it. Yet, while it's more socially acceptable, holding in anger is also destructive because your spouse has to guess what's upsetting you. In addition, anger turned inward leads to depression.

The Bible includes nearly four hundred specific references to anger and most of them refer to the anger of God. Thus, we can conclude that anger by itself is not an evil emotion. It's what we do with it that can be sinful.

Anger includes a spectrum of emotions, ranging from frustration to rage. It can actually be positive if it moves us to right action. Picture Jesus driving the moneychangers out of the temple. These men were making a house of prayer into an unethical marketing venture. If you get upset about the plight of the poor, your anger may make you do something about it. If a child being abused makes you feel outraged, your feelings are righteous.

Everyone experiences anger. So the goal is not to keep from disagreeing, but to learn to "fight fair." Discuss these as possible guidelines for your times of disagreement before they arise:

- No lying. (If your spouse asks, "What's wrong?" you shut down communication by answering, "Nothing" if something is bothering you.)
- No slamming doors.
- No yelling or profanity.
- If you're extremely upset, you may leave the room, but you must say, "I need time to cool down, so I'm going to leave now. But I'll be back soon so we can discuss this."
- Don't let the sun go down on your anger. Agree that you'll never go to sleep with anger still churning. This does not necessarily mean the entire problem with solutions must be hashed out between midnight and 4:00 AM; it means you've worked through it to the point where the intense anger has subsided and you've agreed on a time when you *will* work it out.
- Ask for forgiveness. Even if you're only 2 percent wrong, say you're sorry for the part which is your responsibility. It will start the process of reconciliation. (Say, "I'm sorry *that I . . . ,*" not "I'm sorry, but . . ." or "I'm sorry, if . . ." or "I'm sorry you . . ." Ask without strings, "Will you forgive me?")
- If someone asks for your forgiveness, never bring it up again unless he or she asks you to cite examples to help identify a specific pattern in his or her behavior.
- After you "make up," recognize that your emotions may need time to catch up with your mind. You may need some transition time before you feel you can snuggle or have sex. More women report having difficulty with this than do men.

Dealing with Resentment

Complete the following together.

Sometimes it's hard to let go of old hurts because it entitles me to . . .

a. feel angry.
b. create a situation in which *you* can "see how it feels."
c. withhold sex.
d. justify an occasional binge.
e. get my "martyr card" punched. I get sympathy from others.
f. experience depression that I can blame on you.
g. flirt or have an affair, if I ever want one.
h. other:

Sometimes it feels like you hold on to resentment because it entitles you to . . .

a. feel angry.
b. create a situation in which *I* can "see how it feels."
c. withhold sex.
d. justify an occasional binge.
e. get your "martyr card" punched. You get sympathy from others.
f. experience depression that you can blame on me.
g. flirt or have an affair, if you ever want one.
h. other:

Now take turns answering the following to determine the extent to which the two of you agree or disagree.

• One of the nicest things you ever did for me was . . .
• Something you did that hurt me and I've never forgiven is . . .
• Something you did that hurt me and I've forgiven but I keep getting reminded about is . . .

- Something you said that meant a lot to me was . . .
- Something you've done recently that hurt me was . . .
- Something you've done recently that I really liked was . . .
- Sometimes it seems you have never forgiven me for . . .

Do you need to ask for, give, and receive forgiveness for specific offenses? Remember that "forgive and forget" does not mean the memory no longer registers it. It means you make a conscious decision not to dwell on it or bring it up.

Now determine ways in which letting go of resentment might benefit you.

Releasing my resentment might benefit me by . . .

a. making me feel freer to relate to you as friend and lover.
b. allowing me to feel more open to improving our relationship.
c. providing a sense of release from the negative emotions that have a grip on me.
d. freeing my emotions, which are currently destroying me.
e. letting me discover that enjoying a relationship with you is better than resenting you.
f. other:

Commit together to break away from destructive patterns:

> "This day we leave our resentments behind and make a new start."

Date: _____

Signatures: _____

_____

Now join hands and pray together:

Dear Lord, thank you for your grace and forgiveness. Help us to extend that same grace and forgiveness to each other. We now release our past resentments, asking you to give us a new start and help us leave behind those hurts that could destroy our future together. Help us learn to relate as friends and lovers. In Jesus' name, Amen.

In the future, other past unresolved conflicts may arise. While it's important to let go of the past, it's also helpful to sit down and go through the process of giving and receiving forgiveness for the specific offenses as they come to mind. You could start a conversation with something like, "Honey, I know we put the past behind us, yet it's hard to keep from continuing to feel hurt because I keep feeling upset that we never resolved [the specific issue of concern]. Neither of us said we were sorry; we just left it up in the air. Can we deal with that now?"

Improving the Process of Sex

The Song of Solomon (SOS) is one of God's answers to our "SOS" about sexual difficulties. In this book of the Bible we see a couple expressing their love verbally and explicitly. In studies done on failed marriages, sexual incompatibility was the third most common marital problem. This goes hand in hand with poor communication; if a husband and wife can't talk to each other, the intimacy in their marriage is stunted as well.[6]

Now that you've been working on your relational skills, begin moving toward a discussion of more intimate aspects of your lives. Each couple has their own love language. Consider the words Solomon says to his bride in 4:1–4:

> How beautiful you are, my darling,
> How beautiful you are!
> Your eyes are like doves behind your veil;

Your hair is like a flock of goats
That have descended from Mount Gilead.
Your teeth are like a flock of newly shorn ewes
Which have come up from their washing,
All of which bear twins,
And not one among them has lost her young.
Your lips are like scarlet thread,
And your mouth is lovely.
Your temples are like a slice of a pomegranate
Behind your veil.
Your neck is like the tower of David
Built with rows of stones,
On which are hung a thousand shields,
All the round shields of the mighty men.

This poetry was written about three thousand years ago. Had its author spoken these words to a gentile North American girl today, she might have run from the room crying. Terms occur that we do not generally consider positive (hair like a flock of goats?), but knowing the writer intended his lovely bride to interpret his metaphors as supremely complimentary, we get the gist of what he was saying to her.

A friend drew the following picture to show what Solomon's bride would look like if we took literally everything he said about her.

The Bible is filled with Hebrew poetry, yet Solomon's small, beautiful wisdom book provides a graphic, poetic, descriptive demonstration of what it sounds like to be totally romantically, erotically head-over-heels in love with your spouse.

Read Song of Solomon to each other, trying to imagine how the writer intends his imagery to compliment his beloved. (Study Bibles and commentaries can aid here if you want further help in deciphering the language.)

Write Love Letters

Solomon and his bride verbalized their feelings about each other's body. Do as they did, using your own terms. Write a love letter to your spouse, each of you describing your sweetheart's body. If you are at a total loss about how to begin, simply follow Solomon's outline:

Him for her:

How _____ you are my darling,

How _____ you are!

Your eyes are like _____.

Your hair is like _____.

Your teeth are like _____.

Your lips are like _____.

Your temples are like _____.

Your neck is like _____.

Your _____ [add your own favorite part(s)] is like _____.

And you are wholly desirable.

This is my beloved and this is my friend.

Her for him:

Your head is like _____.

Your eyes are like _____.

Your lips are like _____.

Your hands are like _____.

Your abdomen is like _____.
Your legs are like _____.
Your appearance is like _____.
Your mouth is like _____.
Your _____ [add your own favorite part(s)] is like _____.
And you are wholly desirable.
This is my beloved and this is my friend.

Now read them to each other.

Warning Signs in Communication

A number of researchers studying marriage have identified several key negative responses in communication that are predictors of marital failure. If you recognize these in yourself and/or your spouse, seek help immediately.

Clam up

Do either you or your spouse frequently "shut down" conversation with a perfunctory, "Yes, honey" or by getting up to make a sandwich rather than giving an answer. (Men tend to do this more than women without realizing that this approach damages intimacy.)

Blow up

In the heat of conflict, do you try to outdo each other with caustic remarks? Do you have escalating conflicts? They start something like this: "Honey, you didn't take out the trash." Then they progress to, "Honey, you never take out the trash," to "Honey, you're too stupid to take out the trash," to ". . . and so is your mother!"

Shoot down

Do you feel as though your spouse often negatively interprets an innocent remark? For example, he says, "I see you got your hair cut." She assumes, "He hates my hair cut. Otherwise he would have said he liked it." If she makes his favorite dinner, does he automatically assume she must be feeling guilty because she spent too much at the mall?

Put down

Does your spouse sometimes make you feel that your opinions, preferences, and even you as a person are of no value and unworthy of respect? (This might present itself in vicious looks or caustic remarks.) If one says something as simple as "It's cold in here," does the other respond with, "It's not cold. You'd be cold in an oven"?

Spiritual Intimacy Exercises

1. Describe your early faith experiences. Remember together how each of you came to know the Lord. Recall the people who directed your spiritual progress and share how.
2. What spiritual qualities and gifts attracted you to your spouse?
3. Describe your current spiritual walk.
4. What spiritual practices are important to you as part of daily life in marriage? Do you envision these being done as a couple or individual or both?
5. Did you grow up in denominational setting? If so, how important is it to you?
6. What characteristics (core beliefs, values, music styles, sermon approach, drama) are important to you in the church where you worship together?
7. What values do you consider very important as part of your married life?
8. Describe what your daily relationship with God is like and what practices you engage in as part of your spiritual walk.

9. What spiritual exercises would you like to better understand and perhaps employ (e.g., fasting, silence and solitude, memorizing scripture together, Bible reading, etc.)?
10. When you envision yourselves as a married couple and also as parents, what does the spiritual climate look like in your home? What practices are essential?
11. Join hands and pray together, either aloud or silently, asking God to bless your marriage and help you to honor Him together.

To Help Me Feel
Close to You: His and Hers

At our marriage seminars we've surveyed women, asking what helps put them "in the mood." Here's what they said:

- Do all these things during the day, not just at night.
- Be attentive when I talk.
- Show interest in what's going on with me through conversation and thoughtfulness.
- Provide me with lots of emotional/verbal communication.
- Don't focus constantly on "downer" circumstances at work.
- Compliment me during the day on both inner and outer beauty.
- Say affectionate things.
- Avoid barbed comments.
- Give or mail me a love note—personal romantic thoughts from the heart.
- Take me out to dinner.
- Hire a babysitter.
- Brush my hair.
- Give me a massage.
- Take me out once a week.
- Hold hands with me.

- Take a walk with me.
- Pray with me—more than just the dinner blessing.
- Slow dance with me. You don't need lessons; just hug me to music.
- Watch romantic movies. Yes, these are chick flicks. You married a "chick."
- Have candlelight dinners at home—no waiter to interrupt.
- Share personal romantic thoughts from the heart.
- Take weekend getaways at least once a year.
- Make a big deal of our anniversary.
- Tell me what you find romantic. Beach? Mountains? Dirt biking?
- Kiss me for real, not just little pecks, puckers, or air kisses.
- Hug for real. Go for the full face-to-face deal.
- Take your time at foreplay. God did not give us all this skin for nothing.
- Talk to me about what you want during sex.

When surveyed about how they want their wives to help them feel close, here's how some men answered:

- Speak words of affirmation.
- Respect me.
- Support my dreams.
- Affirm me.
- Let me know you're with me when I win.
- More than that, let me know you're with me when I lose.
- Just show up.
    Naked.
    With food.
    And a subscription to satellite TV with the full sports
      package.

Contraception?
Oh, Baby . . . Maybe

A garden locked is my sister, my bride,
A rock garden locked, a spring sealed up.
—SONG OF SOLOMON 4:12

Part of preparing for marriage is to discuss your views about contraception and decide what you want to do, if anything. The subject is surrounded by controversy and strong opinion. Contraception involves periodic abstinence or the use of a medication, device, or method to prevent sperm from fertilizing a woman's egg. (We reject methods of birth control that allow fertilization but prevent implantation.) Couples should seek God's wisdom about such issues as the spacing of children and the number of children you wish to have. Contraceptives can be to lovemaking what NutraSweet and "salt-free" are to food. These substitutes may not taste as good in cheesecake or potato chips as the real thing, yet for some the health and lifestyle benefits of using them may outweigh the advantages of caution-free living. And at least people using them are eating.

When I (Dr. Bill) sit down with couples during premarital counseling sessions, I ask them to sit with their backs touching each other. Then I tell them, "Without looking at how your partner is answering, hold up the number of fingers for how many children you want to have." It's always interesting to find out whether couples have discussed this, if they agree, and how they plan to reach their goal without "going over." Couples frequently run into conflict in this important area, so it's best to resolve differences as early as possible. A mutual friend of ours remains single today because the young man with whom she was in love told her when he proposed that he did not want children.

In Christian circles, two primary schools of thought exist. The first school believes that because Psalm 127 says "children are a gift of the LORD" (v. 3), avoiding this "gift" hinders God's blessing. Thus they consider it inappropriate to use any predetermined method to avoid conception. Many of these patients do, in fact, maintain a rigorous schedule of cycle monitoring to "abstain electively" during the fertile period. This strikes us as being a contraceptive method (in fact, it is called the "rhythm" or "sympto-thermal" method of contraception). It requires charting a woman's temperature to determine the time of ovulation; it also includes observing bodily indicators, such as changes in vaginal discharge and the cervical opening. Generally, the "safe zone" is considered the time from one week before menses through five days after menses. This method may violate the spirit of these people's convictions. It should also be done in light of biblical guidelines for abstinence given in 1 Corinthians 7, where Paul writes that abstaining within marriage should be . . .

1. by agreement.
2. for a short time.
3. for the purpose of devotion to prayer.

The Old Testament includes additional times of abstinence: seven days during menses, seven days after menses, the evening before worship, and forty to eighty days after the birth of a child. Reverting to these dietary and ceremonial laws, however, violates the new covenant (see Acts 10:1–16; 1 Cor. 8:8; 1 Tim. 4:3–4). Peter says that taking people who are under the new covenant and subjecting them to old covenant rules adds encumbrances that weigh them down. Some have followed Levitical requirements to abstain during menses and seven days following. Shall we observe all ceremonial and dietary laws of the old covenant?

Note that the times of abstinence in the old covenant were during *infertile*, not *fertile*, times.

Some believe the primary purpose of sex is reproduction. We would argue that the primary purpose of sex is oneness, but that secondary purposes are reproduction and pleasure. A look at Song of Solomon, God's poetry book on marital sexual love, shows us that God intended sex not only for reproduction. The book is filled with images that focus on pleasure, and in its eight chapters, it never mentions children or reproduction even once.

The second school consists of those who consider choosing contraception and family planning appropriate as long as they respect the sanctity of human life. This entails avoiding methods that may permit conception but that cause spontaneous abortion. Intrauterine devices (IUDs) may fall in this category (the evidence is still sketchy). Some suggest that oral contraceptives likewise put a baby at risk—both combination and progesterone-only approaches (see discussion on pp. 242–44).

Couples deciding they will use contraception should acquaint themselves with what is available and then prepare to discuss their options during a premarital appointment with their physician. It's asking a lot to expect a doctor to explain each method in detail—how it works, and its pros and cons. By studying the options, however, and "narrowing the field" before the appointment, couples should be able to find a suitable method of contraception that fits their needs.

Yet discussing methods of contraception might be premature. Deciding if they should even *use* contraception remains one often-overlooked yet critical issue for engaged couples to talk through. A patient named Shelly made a medical appointment to talk about contraception two weeks before her wedding. Up to that point, she and her fiancé had given it little thought. Their limited education came from high school health class and medical reports on morning talk shows. Because they had left almost no time for any of the hormone-related methods to take effect, their immediate options were greatly limited. A good rule of thumb is for couples to have their premarital medical visit three months before marriage if they plan to use hormone-based contraceptives. This allows enough time for the medication to take effect, to correct any breakthrough bleeding, or "spotting," and to move the time of menses away from the wedding date.

Generally the woman visits her family practice doctor or ob-gyn. We strongly suggest that the future husband attend the consultation portion of the appointment so he can hear the medical explanations and ask any questions that might help the couple arrive at a suitable solution.

Sometimes doctors prescribe Nitrofurantoin or a similar antibiotic during this visit, for the bride to take with her on the honeymoon. A woman having intercourse for the first time may experience pain and blood in the urine from a bladder infection related to sexual activity (the so-called "honeymoon cystitis"). Antibiotics can help clear up this infection. The medication can be especially useful for couples planning to honeymoon far away from medical facilities—it's better to have it and not need it than to need the antibiotic and not have it.

Methods

Abstinence

Some say abstinence is the only 100 percent effective method of birth control. Actually, this is technically untrue. As in the case of the couple whose story we shared in the first chapter, along with similar cases, some couples conceive via "outercourse," without ever having vaginal intercourse. Nevertheless, abstinence is certainly the most effective method of avoiding pregnancy.

Marrying a partner who has a sexually transmitted disease may require periodic or protracted periods of abstinence, and it's possible for affected couples to have mutually satisfying sexual experiences without sexual intercourse. Nevertheless, continued abstinence appears to fall outside of God's original design for the "one-flesh" marriage relationship.

Withdrawal

Withdrawal involves having vaginal intercourse but then withdrawing the penis right before ejaculation. We do not recommend this method for a number of reasons. First, the psychological one. It's sort of like sitting down to a nice dinner in a restaurant, eating your salad, cutting your steak, but then having the steak pulled away just as you're about to take a bite.

From a contraceptive standpoint, sperm is in the seminal fluid that a male releases before ejaculation. So sperm often enter the vagina even if ejaculation does not take place there. In addition, a man cannot always control the time of ejaculation. Thus, the husband may find that, although he had good intentions, it's "too late"—his timing is off a little—and ejaculation takes place prior to withdrawal.

Some claim the Bible condemns this method based on the Onan story in Genesis 38. As discussed earlier, God did not condemn Onan merely because he interrupted the act of sex. (Others base their condemnation of masturbation on this passage.) Rather, the text indicates that Onan invoked God's wrath because he enjoyed the pleasures of sex with his sister-in-law, but then disobeyed the biblical command to give his brother an heir.

Douching

Douching involves trying to flush the seminal fluid out of the vagina immediately following intercourse, using one of a number of liquid substances. Not only does such douching occasionally upset the sensitive chemical balance of the vagina, it also is an ineffective means of preventing conception. Sperm begin swimming toward their destination long before a woman has a chance to stop them by douching, and many sperm have safely reached the "sanctuary of the cervical mucus" before any liquid could "hose" them out, drown them, or destroy them.

Chemical barriers

Chemical barriers include foams and jellies. They contain spermicides—chemicals that kill sperm. Chemical barriers work only fairly well by themselves; doctors usually recommend their use in conjunction with barrier contraceptives such as condoms or diaphragms. Chemical barriers cause minimal side effects. Some men and women have allergic reactions that cause burning or swelling, but such difficulties can often be alleviated by changing brands. Foams and jellies are relatively inexpensive and can be purchased without prescriptions. Some chemical barriers require insertion up to fifteen minutes before intercourse; others work instantly. Foams have a slightly higher success rate, but without a barrier, such as a condom or diaphragm, the foams do not reduce the likelihood of transmitting sexually transmitted diseases, nor do they provide sufficient protection against pregnancy.

Sponge

Approximately two inches in diameter, the sponge comes filled with a spermicidal. When the wife inserts it before intercourse, it provides protection for up to twenty-four hours, even with multiple encounters. She must leave it in place, however, for at least six hours after intercourse for effective prevention of conception. It has a 75 to 88 percent effectiveness rate per year. (It seems to be less effective for women who have been pregnant.) Insertion instructions come with the packaging. The sponge differs from the diaphragm in several ways: its over-the-counter availability, its one-size-fits-all sizing, and its disposability.

Barrier Contraceptives

Male condom

Available over the counter, condoms (or "rubbers") prevent sperm from reaching the egg by placing a latex rubber "boot" (which looks like the finger of a glove) over the erect penis before it enters the vagina. The condom is currently the best barrier for preventing some sexually transmitted diseases (STDs), although the media has greatly overstated its effectiveness in this regard. Statistics vary from a 3 to 12 percent failure rate with typical use. Many men complain of decreased sensitivity from wearing a condom. Also, condoms can break, leaving the woman without any protection. Thus condoms are more effective when used in conjunction with chemical barriers and are not *completely* reliable protection against STDs.

The condom is currently the only temporary contraceptive available for male use (as opposed to vasectomy, which—although reversible in about 75 percent of cases—is considered "permanent"). Scientists are always trying to develop injections and medications that inhibit sperm production (including a male contraceptive pill that's currently being tested[1]), but to date nothing effective enough to recommend is available.

Female condom

Picture a plastic pouch shaped like a cylinder that's open at one end. The female condom is such a pouch with rings at both ends. The sealed end with the ring holding it open is inserted into the vagina forming a barrel-shaped bag with the open ring at the outside of the vagina, permitting penile entry. Intercourse takes place inside the pouch and the seminal fluid is captured within the pouch so it never reaches the cervical mucus. The female condom is more resilient and thicker than most male condoms so that it rarely, if ever, ruptures during correct usage. Cost runs at less than two dollars per condom.

Female condoms do provide some protection against STDs if one partner has acquired a herpes infection or HPV (venereal wart) infection prior to marriage. The odds are high, though, that the uninfected spouse will eventually contract the STD.

Forty to sixty percent of female condom users discontinue its use, which may be why it has never caught on in the United States. Besides being bulky and messy, it's been described as being "like having a romantic encounter with a zip-lock bag." Some research suggests that it's also slightly less effective than the male condom. When surveyed, those who continued said they found it more pleasurable than the male condom. The female device is less constricting and can be inserted up to eight hours prior to intercourse, so insertion doesn't spoil the mood.[2]

Diaphragm

Approximately the size of the palm of the hand, the diaphragm is a round latex "hat" that a woman places over her cervix. Diaphragms come in several sizes, so a woman planning to use one must see her doctor for fitting. The cost of the diaphragm is the expense of the medical office visit plus that of the diaphragm itself (which is usually twenty to thirty dollars, including its case and a tube of spermicidal gel). Clever sperm, however, can find their way around the edges of the diaphragm, making "chemical warfare" necessary in conjunction with this approach. In other words, it necessitates putting some spermicidal foam or jelly made for diaphragm use inside and around the edges of the diaphragm. The diaphragm should remain in place for eight to ten hours after use. Once removed, it should be washed in soap and water, dusted with a fine coating of talc, and stored in its case. (I had one patient who did not use her case, and her dog gnawed on her diaphragm.)

Diaphragms with holes should be discarded. To find holes, rips, or tears, hold the diaphragm up to a light source to see if any pinpoints of light shine through. Next, fill the diaphragm with water to make sure it doesn't leak. Because some researchers suspect a possible talc/ovarian cancer link, wisdom would suggest rinsing the diaphragm before applying cream and inserting.

A woman using the diaphragm has about a 5 to 10 percent chance of conceiving in a year. A lot depends on how vigilant she is about using it regularly and correctly. Many diaphragm users simply insert theirs every evening, and if romance happens they are "prepared." They must reapply the diaphragm gel if more than two hours have elapsed since insertion. Likewise, more gel is recommended for each additional "romantic interlude" that evening. This does not mean the diaphragm should be removed. The diaphragm should be left in place and more cream added to the vagina.

Cervical cap

The cervical cap is more popular in Europe than in the United States. In fact, doctors here must order it from a single source in California. As with the diaphragm, a physician must fit the cervical cap to the patient, yet it is more difficult to insert and can irritate the cervix. The cervical cap is approximately as effective as the diaphragm, although it is slightly less likely to dislodge.

Major drawbacks of both physical and chemical barriers include messiness, clumsiness, and elimination of "spontaneity." Most couples get around the lack of spontaneity and the awkwardness of stopping to apply cream or use a condom by keeping a sense of humor. Making contraception a team effort can also ease some of the tension.

Oral contraceptives

The most commonly prescribed contraceptives are combination oral contraceptive pills. The word *combination* means the pill contains both estrogen and progesterone in various dosages. It is designed to inhibit ovulation (prevent egg release) and artificially control the menstrual cycle (that is, generate a light flow). Different women require different combinations to avoid breakthrough bleeding—"spotting"—which is a common side effect that normally can be expected to disappear after several cycles. Some women may also experience the complete absence of menstrual flow. Although having no flow is generally not considered a serious complication if the woman has taken her pills regularly, there often is some concern that she may be pregnant, so she should at least contact her physician's office. The newer low-dose pill works effectively, but it may cause some side effects also. Your physician will explain the possibilities, as will the package insert that accompanies each new package of pills (although this lengthy fine-print document defies careful reading by most patients).

The pills cost about twenty to thirty dollars per cycle, and most health insurance companies deny coverage for them. A woman must take her pills daily as prescribed to effectively prevent conception. One of my patients, a teenager, borrowed her friend's pills thinking, *If I take one just before having sex, I won't get pregnant.* She got pregnant.

It's important to note the effect that oral contraceptives may have on a woman's interest in sexual activity. Because the pills artificially regulate the female menstrual cycle by overriding the woman's own hormone production, low-dose pills cause a low estrogen state and also block the ovaries' production of testosterone. Testosterone, as we said earlier, is the male hormone that stirs the libido (or sex drive). A definite percentage of otherwise normal women find that while taking birth control pills they have virtually *no* sex drive. As one pill user said, "Being on the pill certainly prevents pregnancy for us. But not so much because it's effective. It's because it has decreased my interest so much that I desire sex only about once a month." Often, switching to a pill with a slightly different combination of hormones will solve this problem.

Another side effect derived from the pill's decreasing estrogen level is a decrease in vaginal elasticity and ability to lubricate. This simply means that intercourse while taking the pill may be uncomfortable without the addition of a vaginal lubricant. Anyone can buy lubricants without a prescription, and they are a wise investment, especially for newlyweds. When women stop taking the pill, they often stop needing/requiring lubricants.

It is important to know whether the pills are "combination" or "progesterone only." The progesterone-only pills have a higher level of break-through ovulation. After giving birth, when mom is nursing, estrogen should not be prescribed, so these pills are a popular choice. Break-through ovulation is rare with combination pills taken correctly, but it may factor into a couple's decision about which type of contraception works best for them.

Some medications, such as certain antibiotics, reduce the effectiveness of oral contraceptive pills. Check with your physician whenever additional medication is required. Certain patients experience side effects such as bloating, nausea, and headaches. If these cause significant distress or concern, consult your physician or, at minimum, read the FDA insert that comes with the packaging. Note that the effectiveness of this and the hormonal approaches discussed below is lessened in women weighing more than 150 pounds.

The intrauterine device (IUD)

The IUD is quite effective, but I don't currently recommend it. The IUD is merely a formed piece of plastic placed within the uterus. It apparently works this way: conception occurs in the fallopian tube, just as if one were using no contraception. Yet when the so-called pre-embryo—the tiny developing baby—reaches the uterus, it is unable to implant (attach to the wall of the uterus). Thus, it aborts without the woman ever knowing it. The abortion risk, coupled with a risk of infection within the uterus that can lead to infertility, renders this method unacceptable, in my view. Some research has suggested that the IUD may work in some other way than I have described and that it actually prevents pregnancy rather than terminating it. Until we have more data, however, I recommend using other techniques.

Progesterone implant (Implanon)

A single-rod implant placed under the arm, Implanon provides contraceptive protection for up to three years. Insertion requires a simple procedure performed by a medical professional, and the implant can be removed at any time. After removal, fertility is rapidly restored to preimplant status. Like other progesterone-only contraceptives, Implanon is associated with irregular menstrual bleeding and sometimes the complete absence of monthly bleeding. Yet for women who do not tolerate estrogen well, it's certainly worth considering.[3]

Progesterone injection

A similar strategy involves receiving a slow-release progesterone injection. Protection is usually reliable for three months. Once injected, it cannot be removed. Afterward, the return to normal cycling and fertility is rather unpredictable (and may take up to six months). Side effects with progesterone include possible spotting, bloating, and moodiness in some women. The progesterone injection is effective, but not quite as effective as the combination pill.

The NuvaRing

The NuvaRing is a soft, flexible vaginal ring about two inches in diameter. It looks like a small rubber bracelet, is inserted like the diaphragm, and contains the same hormones commonly found in combination oral contraceptives (more about that below).

A patient using the NuvaRing flattens it and inserts it, as she would a tampon, into her vagina at the beginning of her menstrual cycle. She leaves it in the vagina for twenty-one days and then removes it. After a seven-day menstrual week, she inserts a new ring.

The hormones in the ring penetrate directly through the vaginal wall, providing a slow, steady delivery. Because of this, manufacturers can include the least hormone of all the combination approaches with a protection rate that compares with that of combination oral contraceptives. And less hormone means fewer side-effects. The NuvaRing is about as effective as the oral contraceptive pill.

The contraceptive patch

The contraceptive patch is a square that adheres to the skin like a piece of tape. The patient wears it in a discreet place (abdomen, buttocks, chest but not breast), and changes it weekly for three weeks. The fourth week she removes it, allowing for menstrual flow.

The patch delivers the same types of hormones found in combination oral contraceptives. Hormones pass through the skin and into the bloodstream. It has about a 97 percent effectiveness rate, and the cost currently runs between $25 and $40 per month.

There is some concern about clotting complications with the patch. It appears that the hormones absorb through the skin too well in certain women, so until the manufacturers figure out proper dosages, some patients would do better to use an alternate technique.

Sterilization

When a couple feels certain they want no children or no *more* children, they may wish to consider surgical sterilization. While surgeons can sometimes reverse sterilization procedures, individuals should refrain from sterilization unless they feel certain by decision and conviction that they desire no future children, even considering the unlikely scenarios of death, divorce, or other catastrophe. A couple must prayerfully come to the place of mutual, settled conviction concerning biblical principles of childbearing and family planning.

For women

Sterilization generally involves interrupting the fallopian tubes to prevent sperm from reaching the egg. While oophorectomy (removal of the ovaries) or hysterectomy (removal of the uterus) also result in permanent sterility, most doctors steer away from recommending these more extensive procedures for contraception because of risk and side effects, not to mention a high expense that few insurance companies cover. Since the tubes are located in the abdomen, tying or blocking them requires making an incision to do a surgical procedure, allowing access to the abdominal cavity.

A variety of techniques are available: tying the fallopian tubes, cauterizing them with electricity, and blocking them with plastic clips or rubber bands. Individual doctors and circumstances dictate the procedure of choice. Such a procedure may include use of the laparoscope (so-called Band-aid surgery) that the surgeon inserts through a small incision at the navel, as well as other instruments that are inserted at the pubic-hair line. Patients generally tolerate these procedures well and can undergo them on an outpatient basis. These procedures bring moderate abdominal discomfort and occasional significant shoulder pain, which are normal responses to the carbon dioxide used to inflate the belly for visual exposure and to provide room to operate.

Often patients elect to have tubal sterilization immediately following childbirth. This is accomplished with a small incision below the umbilicus, taking advantage of the anesthesia used during childbirth. The laparoscope is not used in these cases because the increased uterine size brings the tubes near the navel. Tubal sterilization procedures have low failure rates—approximately one (or fewer) in four hundred. Following recovery from surgery, few side effects remain. However, occasionally during the procedure on the tube, some of the blood vessels that supply the ovaries are disrupted. This may account for menstrual disturbances in some patients.

If the patient has carefully weighed the pros and cons of permanent sterilization and decides on a tubal procedure, the freedom from fear of conception can be liberating. Many couples have reported a dramatic rise in frequency of intercourse and satisfaction following female sterilization. On the other hand, several of my patients have regretted sterilization decisions they made at a young age. For many, though, a tubal reversal using microscopic techniques can often restore fertility. It is costly, however, and it will not always work. Thus, couples should be certain before choosing sterilization options.

For men

Vasectomy, the sterilization procedure in the male, involves surgical interruption of the vas deferens. The vas deferens is the tube that carries sperm from the testicle to the storage gland, the seminal vesicles. Because of the external location of the testes within the scrotal sac, a patient can have a vasectomy in the doctor's office under local anesthesia. It costs less than tubal sterilization in the female and usually has few side effects after the surgical incision has healed. Patients should bear in mind that vasectomy is performed in a location on the male anatomy that is before the "storage gland." In other words, fertility remains after the vasectomy until the storage tanks are empty. Thus, couples need to use alternate protection for several ejaculations following vasectomy. Safety demands a zero sperm count before a couple can rely on the vasectomy for prevention of pregnancy. This takes usually a month or two. After that time, the failure rate is quite low—less than 1 percent. Medical investigation linking vasectomy with prostate cancer will require clarification in the years to come. At this writing, no research has established a *clear* hazard. Patients should, however, consult with the urologist or family-practice doctor who performs the procedure to explore the current status of this research.

Beyond Contraception

Finally, after trying to prevent conception for years, one in six couples find themselves faced with a fertility problem once they start trying to build their family. Others find that once they have a child or two and want more, they have difficulty conceiving. Couples considering the use of contraceptive methods must realize that increasing age can play a contributing role in infertility. "I never dreamed during all those 'how to prevent pregnancy' lectures in health class that I might someday be unable to get pregnant," says the president of an infertility support group. "I wish I hadn't taken my fertility for granted."

At the opposite end of the fertility spectrum, it may interest you to know that, according to the *Guinness Book of World Records*, the "Fertile Myrtle Award" goes to a peasant woman from Moscow who gave birth to sixty-nine children (sixteen sets of twins, seven sets of triplets, and four sets of quadruplets). A more typical couple has about an 85 percent chance of conceiving per year if they pay no attention to the monthly cycle and enjoy a vigorous, contraceptive-free love life.

Recommended Resources

Contraception

Cutrer, William, and Sandra Glahn. *The Contraception Guidebook: Options, Risks, and Answers for Christian Couples.* Grand Rapids: Zondervan, 2005.

General

Glahn, Sandra. *Solomon Latte.* Chattanooga, TN: AMG Publishers, 2006.

Rosenau, Douglas E. *A Celebration of Sex: A Guide to Enjoying God's Gift of Sexual Intimacy.* Revised and updated. Nashville: Nelson, 2002.

Sex addiction

Burkett, Lori A., and Mark A. Yarhouse. *Sexual Identity: A Guide to Living in the Time Between the Times.* Lanham, MD: University Press of America, 2003.

Laaser, Mark. *Healing the Wounds of Sexual Addiction.* Grand Rapids: Zondervan, 2004.

Sex and aging

Rosenau, Douglas E., James K. Childerston, and Carolyn Childerston. *A Celebration of Sex After 50.* Nashville: Nelson, 2004.

Sexual abuse

Langberg, Diane Mandt. *Counseling Survivors of Sexual Abuse.*
  Longwood, FL: Xulon Press, 2003.
Tracy, Steven R. *Mending the Soul: Understanding and Healing
  Abuse.* Grand Rapids: Zondervan, 2005.

Notes

Chapter 2: What Is Sex?

1. "Sex on TV4," Kaiser Family Foundation, November 9, 2005, http://www.kff.org/entmedia/entmedia110905pkg.cfm (accessed April 6, 2006).
2. Glen Gabbard and Roy Menninger, eds., *Medical Marriages* (Washington, DC: American Psychiatric Press, 1988), 101.

Chapter 3: The Male Anatomy

1. Lisa Bannon, "Growth Industry: How a Risky Surgery Became a Profit Center for Some L.A. Doctors," *Wall Street Journal*, June 6, 1996, 1.
2. Clifford Penner and Joyce Penner, *The Gift of Sex* (Waco, TX: Word, 1981), 70.

Chapter 4: The Female Anatomy

1. Herbert Miles, *Sexual Happiness in Marriage* (Grand Rapids: Zondervan, 1976), 70.

Chapter 5: The Sexual Response Cycle

1. Archibald D. Hart, Catherine Hart Weber, and Debra Taylor, *Secrets of Eve* (Nashville: Nelson, 2004).
2. Clifford Penner and Joyce Penner, *Restoring Intimacy*, 106, as

quoted in Marjorie Hansen Shaevitz, *Super Woman Syndrome* (New York: Warner Books, 1984), 57.

3. Peter Wish, PhD, a Florida sex therapist.

4. Stephen Perrine, "Secrets of the Male," *Glamour*, February 1996, 172–75.

5. David Strovny, "The Importance of Foreplay," askmen.com, http://www.askmen.com/love/love_tip/sextip18.html (accessed May 4, 2006).

6. Mark Clements, "Sex in America Today," *Parade*, August 7, 1994, 4–5.

7. From Chi Chi Sileo, "Studies Put Genetic Twist on Theories About Sex and Love," *Insight*, July 3–10, 1995, 36–37.

8. Mark Wingfield, "Survey: Wives Value Romance," *Baptist Standard*, October 7, 1998, http://www.baptiststandard .com/1998/10_7/romance.html.

9. Vickie Kraft, *The Influential Woman* (Dallas: Word, 1992), 72–73.

10. Harold Wahking and Gene Zimmerman, *Fulfilled Sexuality* (Grand Rapids: Baker, 1994), 38.

11. Katherine Burnett-Watson, "Low Sex Drive—Says Who?" *Aphrodite: Women's Health*, March 27, 2006, http://www .aphroditewomenshealth.com/news/low_libido.shtml.

12. Shankar Vedantam, "Desire and DNA: Is Promiscuity Innate? New Study Sharpens Debate on Men, Sex and Gender Roles," *Washington Post*, August 1, 2003, A01.

13. Eric S. Raymond, "Sex Tips for Geeks: On Being Good in Bed," http://catb.org/~esr/writings/sextips/bedplay.html.

14. Richard Foster, *The Challenge of the Disciplined Life: Christian Reflections on Money, Sex, and Power* (San Francisco: HarperCollins, 1991), 154.

15. Chris Vognar, "Culture Crash," *Dallas Morning News*, March 29, 1997, 7C.

Chapter 6: The Wedding Night and Beyond

1. "Porn in the USA," CBS Worldwide, September 5, 2004.

2. L. Koutsky, "Epidemiology of Genital Human Papillomavirus Infection," *American Journal of Medicine* 102.5A (1997): 3–8.

3. W. Cates Jr. and the American Social Health Association Panel, "Estimates of the Incidence and Prevalence of Sexually Transmitted Diseases in the United States," *Sexually Transmitted Diseases* 26, supp. 4 (1999): S2–7.

4. Kathy Peel, "Great Sex!?" *Today's Christian Woman* [online], 1995, at http://www.christianity.net/tcw/.

5. Henri Troyat, *Tolstoy* (New York: Dell Publishing, 1967), 568.

6. National Campaign to Prevent Teen Pregnancy, "20 Percent of Young Teens Have Had Sex" [press release], May 20, 2003.

7. Laura Sessions Stepp, "Study: Half of All Teens Have Had Oral Sex," *Washington Post*, September 16, 2005, A07.

8. "Teens Delaying Sexual Activity; Using Contraception More Effectively," CDC press release, December 10, 2004, http://www.cdc.gov/od/oc/media/pressrel/r041210.htm (accessed May 5, 2006).

9. "Teens Break No-sex Vows, Study Suggests; Some Say Oral Sex Not Sex," *Christian Century*, December 27, 2003. Accessed online at http://www.findarticles.com.

10. Sandra Glahn's verse-by-verse Bible study of Song of Songs, *Solomon Latte* (Chattanooga, TN: AMG, 2006), explores this passage in detail.

11. S. Craig Glickman, *A Song for Lovers* (Downers Grove, IL: InterVarsity Press, 1980), 106.

12. Jody Dillow, *Solomon on Sex* (Nashville: Nelson, 1977), 153.

13. As cited by Mary and Patrick DeMuth, "Opening the Door to Healing When Childhood Sexual Abuse Affects a Marriage's Intimacy," *Marriage Partnership*, Fall 2005, 38.

14. Robert T. Michael, John H. Gagnon, Edward O. Laumann, and Gina Kolata, *Sex in America: A Definitive Survey* (Boston: Little Brown, 1994). This book was based on interviews with 3,432 Americans between the ages of 18 and 59. It is the popular report of the most authoritative study ever of sexual behavior in the U.S. A companion report, *The Social Organization of*

Sexuality: Sexual Practices in the United States, by Edward O. Laumann, John H. Gagnon, Robert T. Michael, and Stuart Michaels (Chicago: University of Chicago, 1994), is addressed to social scientists, counselors, and health professionals.

15. Douglas E. Rosenau, *A Celebration of Sex* (Nashville: Nelson, 1994), 3.
16. Gary Inrig, *Whole Marriages in a Broken World* (Grand Rapids: Discovery House, 1997), 185.
17. Quoted in ibid.

Chapter 7: Questions About Varying Levels of Interest

1. *TV Guide*, untitled sidebar, February 8, 1997.
2. Edward O. Laumann, Anthony Paik, and Raymond C. Rosen, "Sexual Dysfunction in the United States: Prevalence and Predictors," *Journal of the American Medical Association* 281 (February 10, 1999): 537–44.
3. Edward O. Laumann, John H. Gagnon, Robert T. Michael, and Stuart Michaels, *The Social Organization of Sexuality: Sexual Practices in the United States* (Chicago: University of Chicago, 1994). Also reported in the companion volume, Robert T. Michael, John H. Gagnon, Edward O. Laumann, and Gina Kolata, *Sex in America: A Definitive Survey* (Boston: Little Brown, 1994).
4. Ibid.
5. Jody Dillow, *Solomon on Sex* (Nashville: Nelson, 1977), 120.
6. Social Issues Research Center, "The Smell Report," 1999–2003, http://www.sirc.org/publik/smell_diffs.html (accessed May 19, 2006).
7. Dr. Alan Hirsch, a neurologist and psychiatrist at Chicago's Smell and Taste Treatment and Research Foundation, as reported by Carolyn Abraham, *The Globe and Mail*, March 11, 1998.
8. Karen Scalf Linamen, *Pillow Talk: The Intimate Marriage from A to Z* (Grand Rapids: Revell, 1996), 190–91.

9. According to Ethel Person, MD, author of *By Force of Fantasy* (New York: Basic Books, 1995).

10. See Stephanie von Hirschberg, "It's All in Your Head," *New Woman*, September 1995, 114, 118–19, 140–41.

11. E. L. Zurbriggen and M. R. Yost, "Power, Desire, and Pleasure in Sexual Fantasies," *Journal of Sex Research* 41.3 (2004): 288–300.

Chapter 8: Questions About Orgasm

1. "Orgasm." Dictionary.com. *The American Heritage Dictionary of the English Language*, 4th ed., Houghton Mifflin Co., 2004. http://dictionary.reference.com/browse/orgasm (accessed November 16, 2006).

2. Archibald D. Hart, Catherine Hart Weber, and Debra Taylor, *Secrets of Eve* (Nashville, Nelson, 2004).

3. Jack and Carole Mayhall, *Marriage Takes More Than Love* (Colorado Springs: NavPress, 1978), 208.

4. Herbert J. Miles, *Sexual Happiness in Marriage* (1976; reprint, Grand Rapids: Zondervan, 1996), 67.

5. Clifford Penner and Joyce Penner, *Restoring the Pleasure* (Waco, TX: Word, 1993), 117.

6. Ibid., 97.

7. It may interest you to know that the most orgasms reported in an hour by a male was sixteen; the most prolific female subject reported 134.

8. Harold Wahking and Gene Zimmerman, *Fulfilled Sexuality* (Grand Rapids: Baker, 1994), 60.

9. Ibid.

Chapter 9: Other Questions Couples Ask

1. Rachel and Leah scrapped over mandrakes. See Genesis 30:14–16.

2. Joseph Adelson, "Sex Among the Americans," *Commentary*, July 1995, 26–30.

3. Gary Chapman, *The Five Love Languages* (Chicago: Moody, 1995), 116.

4. Robert Bruce and Debra Bruce, *Reclaiming Intimacy in Your Marriage* (Minneapolis: Bethany House, 1996), 112.

5. James K. Childerston, PhD, Carolyn Sue Childerston, MA, and Douglas R. Rosenau, EdD, "Maturing into Intimacy," American Association of Christian Counselors Conference, Nashville, TN, October 2005 (lecture notes).

6. David Schnarch, "Joy: With Your Underwear Down," *Psychology Today*, July–August 1994, 38–43, 70, 74, 76, 78.

7. Carin Rubenstein, "What Turns YOU On? (Hint: It's Not Work)," *My Generation*, July–August 2002, 54–58.

8. Mark Clements, "Sex After 65," *Parade*, March 17, 1996, 4–7.

Chapter 10: What Is Marriage?

1. Gary Bauer, "All You Need Is Love, Almost," *LA Times*, June 5, 2006, http://www.latimes.com/news/printedition/opinion/la-oe-bauer5jun05,1,6099.story?coll=la-news-comment (accessed July 21, 2006).

2. John Gottman and Nan Silver, *The Seven Principles for Making Marriage Work* (New York: Random House, 1999), as quoted at http://canadianparents.com, "Happy Marriages: Can They Be Predicted?" (accessed July 21, 2006).

Chapter 12: A Word to Wives

1. Gordon Fee, "The Cultural Context of Ephesians 5:18–6:9," *Priscilla Papers* 16 (Winter 2002): 1.

2. Vickie Kraft, *The Influential Woman* (Dallas: Word, 1992), 22.

Chapter 13: A Call to Purity

1. See Matthew 19:9; 1 Corinthians 5:1; 6:13; 2 Corinthians 12:21; Galatians 5:19; Ephesians 5:3; Revelation 19:2.

2. Henri Troyat, *Tolstoy* (New York: Dell Publishing, 1967), 578.

3. David Hoffeditz, *They Were Single Too: Eight Biblical Role Models* (Grand Rapids: Kregel, 2006), 10.

4. Ibid.
5. Paul Buckley, "Movie Aside, Virginity at 40 Is Worthwhile," *Dallas Morning News*, September 17, 2005, 5G.
6. Frank Hobbs, "Examining American Household Composition: 1990 and 2000," U.S. Census Bureau, 2005.
7. Leigh McLeroy, *Moments for Singles* (Colorado Springs: NavPress, 2004), 148.
8. Lauren Winner, *Real Sex: The Naked Truth About Chastity* (Grand Rapids: Brazos Press, 2005), 154.
9. Stephen Perrine, "Secrets of the Male," *Glamour*, February 1996, 175.
10. Philip Yancey, *Rumors of Another World* (Grand Rapids: Zondervan, 2003), 82.

Chapter 14: Protect Your Sexuality

1. Dave Carder with Duncan Jaenicke, *Torn Asunder: Recovering from Extramarital Affairs* (Chicago: Moody, 1992), 54–55.
2. "Adultery: The New Furor over an Old Sin," *Newsweek*, September 30, 1996, 58.
3. Ibid.
4. Pew Research Center Web site, "A Barometer of Modern Morals: Sex, Drugs, and the 1040," March 28, 2006, http://pewresearch.org/social/pack.php?PackID=7.
5. In the University of Chicago National Opinion Research Center's survey (1996), respondents were asked, "Have you ever had extramarital sex?" The positive responses were significantly less than previously reported results from Kinsey, which were one-third of men and one-fifth of women. See Michael W. Wiederman, "Extramarital Sex: Prevalence and Correlates in a National Survey," *The Journal of Sex Research* 34:2 (1997), 167.
6. Ibid.
7. Carder with Jaenicke, *Torn Asunder*, 55.
8. Ibid.
9. Philip Yancey, *The Jesus I Never Knew* (Grand Rapids: Zondervan, 1995), 118–19.

10. Gordon MacDonald, *Rebuilding Your Broken World* (Nashville: Nelson, 1990), xvii.

11. Ibid., 53.

12. Ibid., 47.

13. Book review of *The Myth of Monogamy: Fidelity and Infidelity in Animals and People* by David P. Barash and Judith Eve Lipton (New York: W. H. Freeman, 2001), at about.com Web site (accessed July 27, 2006). While the book is written from a completely secular perspective, the goal of the research was actually to help those in monogamous relationships to remain faithful.

Chapter 15: Developing a Loyal Heart

1. Elisabeth Elliot, *Quest for Love: True Stories of Passion and Purity* (Grand Rapids: Baker, 1996).

2. Quoted in "Adultery: The New Furor over an Old Sin," *Newsweek*, September 30, 1996, 58.

3. Willard Harley, *His Needs, Her Needs: Building an Affair-Proof Marriage* (Grand Rapids: Revell, 1994), 12–13.

4. Richard Foster, *The Challenge of the Disciplined Life: Christian Reflections on Money, Sex, and Power* (San Francisco: HarperCollins, 1991), 161.

5. Eugene Peterson, interview with Sandra Glahn, October 25, 1996.

6. Foster, *Disciplined Life*, 162.

7. "Adultery: The New Furor over an Old Sin," 58.

8. Quoted in ibid.

Chapter 16: When Delight Becomes Obsession: Sexual Addiction

1. *Elle* magazine, May 1999, 170ff.

2. Russell Willingham, *Breaking Free: Understanding Sexual Addiction and the Healing Power of Jesus* (Downer's Grove, IL: InterVarsity Press, 1999).

3. Mark Laaser, *Faithful and True: Sexual Integrity in a Fallen World* (Grand Rapids: Zondervan, 1996), 101.

4. Patrick Carnes, *Out of the Shadows: Understanding Sexual Addiction* (Center City, MN: Hazelden Information Education, 2001).

5. Timothy Egan, "Wall Street Meets Pornography," *New York Times*, October 23, 2000, http://www.nytimes.com /2000/10/23/technology/23PORN.html.

6. *Los Angeles Times Magazine*, 2002.

7. Steve Kroft, "Porn in the USA," CBSNews.com, September 5, 2004.

8. Stephen Arterburn and Fred Stoeker, with Mike Yorkey, *Every Man's Battle: Winning the War on Sexual Temptation One Victory at a Time* (Colorado Springs: WaterBrook Press, 2000).

Chapter 17: Sexuality and Aging

1. "Oldest Woman to Give Birth (67) Has Twin Girls," *The Mercury*, January 17, 2005. http://www.themercury.com .co.za/index.php?fsectionId=2848fArticleID=2375535.

2. Discovery Health Channel Web site, "Sex and Aging," http:// health.discovery.com/centers/sex/sexpedia/ageingandsex .html (accessed July 28, 2006).

3. Daniel P. Jones and Leslie Barnes Fluharty, "Information on Sexuality and Aging," College of Wooster Web site, http:// www.wooster.edu/psychology/moreinfo.html (accessed July 28, 2006).

4. Jill Neimark, "The Beefcaking of America," *Psychology Today*, November–December 1994, 32ff.

5. Sex101 Web site, "Sex and Aging," http://www.sexinfo101 .com/sh_aging.shtml (accessed July 28, 2006).

6. Leonard Sweet, *Soul Tsunami* (Grand Rapids: Zondervan, 2001), 246, 249, 280.

7. Edwina Caito, "When He's Not in the Mood: Tips for Dealing with Your Partner's Waning Libido," Clubmom Web site,

http://www.clubmom.com/display/233452 (accessed February 20, 2006).

8. From a *Redbook* magazine survey of more than one hundred thousand married women, cited in Janet Wolfe, *What to Do When He Has a Headache: Creating Renewed Desire in Your Man* (New York: Hyperion, 1992).

9. Gail Salz, "Bring Back That Lovin' Feeling," *Good Housekeeping Online*, http://magazines.ivillage.com/goodhousekeeping/hb/health/articles/0,,284595_686993-4,00.html (accessed July 27, 2006).

10. Irwin Goldstein, "Male Sexual Circuitry," *Scientific American*, August 2000, 70.

11. Mary Lawless, "When He's Not in the Mood," LHJ.com (accessed July 27, 2006).

12. Ronald Rolheiser, *The Holy Longing: The Search for a Christian Spirituality* (New York: Doubleday, 1999), 210–11.

13. Robert Butler and Myrna Lewis, *Love and Sex After Forty: A Guide for Men and Women for Their Mid and Later Years* (New York: Harper and Row, 1986), 132.

Chapter 18: Questions from Our Readers

1. Jack Hitt, "The Second Sexual Revolution," *New York Times Magazine*, February 20, 2000, 34ff.

2. Joel Goodnough, "Redux: Is the Oral Contraceptive Pill an Abortifacient?" *Ethics and Medicine*, Spring 2001, 48.

3. John Leland, "The Science of Women and Sex," *Newsweek*, May 29, 2000, 48–52.

4. Archibald D. Hart, Catherine Hart Weber, and Debra L. Taylor, *Secrets of Eve: Understanding the Mystery of Female Sexuality* (Nashville: Word, 1998).

5. Centers for Disease Control and Prevention, "Cohabitation, Marriage, Divorce, and Remarriage in the United States," *Vital Health and Statistics Series* 23.22 (2002), 29.

6. Cited in *Christian Single*, September 1999.

7. *U.S. News and World Report,* May 19, 1997, 56–60, 62, 64.

8. As quoted by Rebecca Chalker, *Ms* magazine, November–December 1995, 49–52.

9. Gracie Hsu, "America: Awash in STDs," *The World and I,* June 1998, 56ff.

Chapter 19: Relational Intimacy in Marriage

1. John Gottman and Nan Silver, *The Seven Principles for Making Marriage Work* (New York: Three Rivers Press, 2000).

Workbook: Exercises for Developing Intimacy

1. Philip Elmer-Dewitt, "Now for the Truth About Americans and Sex: The First Comprehensive Survey Since Kinsey Smashes Some of Our Most Intimate Myths," *Time,* October 17, 1994, 62–66, 70.

2. One Health/Gallop Poll found that those who talk explicitly with their partners about their desires were more than twice as likely to enjoy satisfying love lives. From "Are the Sexes Out of Synch? A Health/Gallop Poll," *Health,* July–August 1994, 52–58, 60.

3. Marty Klein, "The Naked Truth: Is Weight Wrecking Your Sex Life?" *McCalls,* January 1996, 95–96.

4. "Adultery: The New Furor over an Old Sin," *Newsweek,* September 30, 1996, 58.

5. Dave Carder with Duncan Jaenicke, *Torn Asunder: Recovering from Extramarital Affairs* (Chicago: Moody, 1999).

6. Robert Bruce and Debra Bruce, *Reclaiming Intimacy in Your Marriage* (Minneapolis: Bethany House, 1996), 102.

Appendix: Contraception? Oh, Baby . . . Maybe

1. "Male Contraceptive Pill in the Works," CBS Broadcasting, November 28, 2006. http://www.cbsnews.com/stories/2006/11/28/earlyshow/contributors/emilysenay/main2211410.shtml?source=RSSattr=Health_2211410.

2. William Cutrer and Sandra Glahn, *The Contraception Guidebook* (Grand Rapids: Zondervan, 2005), 77.
3. Ibid, 121–22.

Index

99249

Overton Memorial Library
Sexual intimacy in marriage /
RWC 306.7 C989s 2007

99249